Iron-Age Societies

B

Social Archaeology

General Editor
Ian Hodder, University of Cambridge

Advisory Editors
Margaret Conkey, University of California at Berkeley
Mark Leone, University of Maryland
Alain Schnapp, U.E.R. d'Art et d'Archéologie, Paris
Stephen Shennan, University of Southampton
Bruce Trigger, McGill University, Montreal

Published

In preparation

Iron-Age Societies

From Tribe to State in Northern Europe, 500 BC to AD 700

LOTTE HEDEAGER

Translated by John Hines

BLACKWELL
Oxford UK & Cambridge USA

First published 1992

Blackwell Publishers
108 Cowley Road
Oxford OX4 1JF
UK

Three Cambridge Center
Cambridge, Massachusetts 02142
USA

British Library Cataloguing in Publication Data

A CIP catalogue record for this book is available from the British Library.

Library of Congress Cataloging-in-Publication Data

Hedeager, Lotte.
    Iron-age societies: from tribe to state in northern Europe, 500 BC to AD 700 / Lotte Hedeager: translated by John Hines.
        p. cm. —— (Social archaeology)
    Includes bibliographical references (p.) and index.
    ISBN 0-631-17106-1 (acid-free paper)
    1. Iron age—Scandinavia. 2. Social archaeology—Scandinavia. 3. Scandinavia—Antiquities. I. Title. II. Series.
GN780.22.S34R43 1992
936.3—dc20   91-41746
                                                                      CIP

Typeset in 11 on 12½ pt Garamond
by Photo·graphics, Honiton, East Devon
Printed in Great Britain by TJ Press (Padstow), Ltd., Padstow, Cornwall

This book is printed on acid-free paper

Contents

Preface

The archaeological material from the Scandinavian Iron Age faces
the researcher with a methodological dilemma that for more than a
hundred years has stood in the way of a comprehensive understanding of the period. On the one hand, the material is very rich in both
qualitative and quantitative terms, and cries out for analysis and
interpretation. On the other hand, it is more diverse than the remains
of any other period of prehistory, even though the timespan, from
500 BC to AD 700/800, is no longer than, for instance, the Scandinavian Bronze Age. For this reason, the establishment of an historical
overview of this part of Danish prehistory has been both more
difficult and less convincing. The major periods into which the Iron
Age is traditionally divided – the pre-Roman (Celtic) Iron Age, the
Roman Iron Age and the Germanic Iron Age – are usually treated
as separate entities, each of which has required its own specialization.
As a result, cultural-historical interpretations have frequently, with
the support of written sources, sought to reconstruct concrete historical events or sequences of events. My aim, in this book, is to
demonstrate that an analysis of all the archaeological evidence of
the Iron Age provides hitherto missed opportunities for forming a
comprehensive perspective on the development of society through
the whole Iron-Age period of more than one thousand years, a
perspective which more narrowly based studies cannot achieve. It
is, moreover, precisely in Denmark that the evidence is sufficiently
rich and representative for such a project to be possible, provided
that the correct theoretical and methodological tools are used.

In order to lay the foundations for such an analysis it was necessary to undertake the making of a complete record of all the archaeological remains of the Iron Age, which means about 10,000 grave finds, hoard finds and loose finds (Bornholm, however, has been omitted, since the culture of this island is more closely linked with that of Öland and Gotland than with eastern Denmark). I have, however, included settlement sites only as far as they were accessible in published form, together with the addition of some personal observations from archaeologists who have been responsible for extensive settlement-history investigations in recent years in various parts of the country.

Taking this material as my starting-point, I have sought to reveal the economic growth and political centralization which manifests itself in the course of the Iron Age in the form of the earliest kingdoms, and which is the essential preliminary to the emergence of a state structure in northern Europe. It has been my intention to show the formation of states as a cumulative historical process that cannot be reduced to a simple theoretical formula. In this way this book is also a concrete contribution to the discussion, not of the origins of the state, but of the process of state formation.

In my work on this book, I have chosen to keep reliance on the European historical sources to an absolute minimum, because I wanted the evidence of the archaeological sources to form the basis for my interpretations to the greatest permissible extent. I hope, therefore, that the results may stand as a starting-point for future dialogue with historically based interpretations.

This study was originally inspired by the anthropological evolutionary theories of the 1970s and the early 1980s, particularly those theories concerning state formation. A first draft of the book was ready by 1985. Although my interests since then have tended more in the direction of an ideological-historical understanding of both written and archaeological sources, not least the supra-regional political and economic connections in Iron-Age Europe, I have retained the original shape of the study because it reflects a consistent theoretical and methodological approach. This shows how far it is possible to go by way of long-term regional analysis of the internal development of a society on the strength of archaeological evidence and with the consistent application of a well-defined set of methods and theories.

A number of people and institutions have assisted me in various ways: Bent Aaby, the National Museum, Copenhagen; Steen Andersen, Haderslev Museum; Jens-Henrik Bech, Museet for Thy og Vester Han Herred; Eliza Fonnesbech-Sandberg, Københavns Amtsmuseumsråd; Forhistorisk Museum, Moesgaard; Mogens Hansen, Vesthimmerlands Museum; Steen Hvass, Vejle Kulturhistoriske Museum; Jørgen A. Jacobsen, Fyns Stiftsmuseum; Kirsten Lindhardt, the National Museum; Per Lysdahl, Vendsyssel Historiske Museum; Helge Nielsen, Køge Museum; Poul-Otto Nielsen, the National Museum; Bjørn Poulsen, byarkivet i Åbenrå; Bjørn Stürup, Kulturhistorisk Museum Randers; Svend Åge Tornbjerg, Køge Museum; Stine Wiell, Haderslev Museum. Unless otherwise indicated, the drawings are by Catherine Oksen.

Greatest thanks are due to those who have helped and inspired me through the years to work in archaeology from a social-historical perspective, namely Jonathan Friedman, University of Copenhagen; Mike Rowlands, University College London; Peder Mortensen, Moesgaard; Mogens Trolle Larsen, University of Copenhagen, and last but not least Kristian Kristiansen, Ministry of the Environment, the National Forest and Nature Agency.

Thanks are also due to Ian Hodder for his active contributions to the translation and publication of the book in English.

Statens humanistiske Forskningsråd (the National Research Council for the Humanities) financed the work with a three-year grant and also financed the translation.

Lotte Hedeager
University of Copenhagen
February 1991

This book is dedicated
To Kristian, who made the work possible
To our son Niels, who did not make it impossible!

1

Archaeological and Theoretical Frameworks

Background to the Research

The Origin of the State in Scandinavia

My principal aim in this study is to use archaeology to shed some light upon the economic growth and political centralization which in the course of the first millennium AD were the bases of the earliest state formation in Denmark. In addition, my main thesis is that this state formation took place in the period between the Earlier and Later Iron Age (which in the terms used here means the Later Roman Period, AD 180/200–350/400), but that it had its necessary preconditions in the Earlier Roman Period and was subsequently consolidated in the Earlier Germanic Period (the Migration Period), before a period of expansion in the Later Germanic Period and Viking Period (for the chronology, see figure 1.5). This shifts the discussion of the origins of the state in Scandinavia to a context several centuries earlier than that which is the focus of traditional views. I shall give a brief account of the reasons for this, and of the relationship with previous discussion of the origins of the state in Denmark and Norway.

For many years a largely unquestioned equation has been made between Harold Bluetooth's creation of a unified kingdom and the first formation of a state in Denmark. This has effectively blocked discussion of the origins of the state as an historical process, since it overlooks the fact that unification of a kingdom in itself depends upon the pre-existence of the basic components of a state organization, and that these do not emerge without historical reasons.

Randsborg, for example, accepted this historical paradox without hesitation in his study of the origins of the Viking state (Randsborg 1980). The excavations and dating of Dannevirke however have reposed the question with renewed force, and in recent years Hellmuth Andersen (in particular) has made critical re-interpretations of the earliest history of royal power, and has drawn attention to its even earlier origins (Andersen 1985a, b).

On the other hand, for most of the 1970s and much of the 1980s archaeologists were attempting to use simple evolutionary models to interpret the Iron Age, models which coped with the very substantial changes and variations to only a limited degree (Särlvik 1982; review Hedeager 1984). The Iron Age was identified as a chiefdom society in several studies (Odner 1973; J. Jensen 1982; Myhre 1978, 1987a), even though these scholars noted a series of organizational features which could be evidence of more complex social and political organization. In 1978 I published a first interpretation of the transition between the Earlier and Later Roman Periods as being the reflection of incipient state formation, in accord with Kristiansen, whose study of the transition from the Bronze to the Iron Age had indicated that one could no longer speak of a tribal society in the Iron Age (Kristiansen 1978c, 1980). From the beginning of the 1980s, the evolutionary models were increasingly regarded with scepticism, and the question of early state formation began to impinge on debate. In Norway, Bjørn Myhre and others pursued research which led to similar conclusions concerning earlier state formation (Myhre 1987b, c), and I myself published more comprehensive arguments in favour of a process of state formation in the Iron Age (Hedeager and Kristiansen 1981; Hedeager 1978c, 1987). Renewed interest in the problem of state formation has also led to the inclusion of historical sources (Resi 1986; Näsman 1988) which had hitherto been cultivated in German and English research in particular (notably Wenskus 1961; Thompson 1965, 1966). The results of major settlement-site excavations have undoubtedly contributed to a changed perception of the organization of Iron-Age society (Lund 1988), as have the excavations around Gudme and Lundeborg in south-eastern Fyn which are now associated without qualification with a *villa regalis* of the Migration Period (Hauck 1987, p. 153).

A second point of entry into the investigation of the origins of the state has been retrospective, attempting to follow some of the elements of the administration of the later medieval state back in time. This method has concentrated particularly on the history of the parish and of place names. One could justifiably claim that in Denmark these questions dropped out of the archaeologist's portfolio after a number of productive studies earlier in the century, for instance from Clausen (1916) and Aksel E. Christensen (1938) on the age of the parish system, although elements of the debate have been carried on by historians. The source-critical tradition, however, pretty well squeezed the life out of the formation of theory and proscribed even the notion of bringing forward interpretative studies which reached beyond the sources themselves. But outside Denmark, in Sweden and Norway, these methods have inspired productive co-operation between archaeologists, place-name specialists and historians. Björn Ambrosiani's studies of Iron-Age settlement in the Mälar region (e.g. Ambrosiani 1964, 1982), followed by Hyenstrand's work on the origins of the hundredal system (Hyenstrand 1974), led to a discussion of the origins of administrative structure and consequently of the state. Thus in Sweden the way was opened up for a debate on the emergence of the state in the Later Iron Age which was nourished by the excavations on Helgö (most recently Lundström 1988) and of early fortifications, not least Eketorp (e.g. Borg, Näsman and Wegraeus 1976) and Torsborg (e.g. Engström 1984). In Norway too, the question of the origins of the state has been treated both historically-retrospectively and on a more archaeological-anthropological basis (especially Myhre 1987b, c). I shall take up the place names again in this investigation, as I regard them as a form of archaeological evidence in the context of settlement study.

The interpretations which are presented here can now hardly be regarded as shocking, although to attribute the inception of state formation to the Later Roman Period may still provoke argument. What is essentially new in this work, however, is the treatment of state formation as an historical process that can only be explained and understood if it is studied in a long-term perspective.

The Meaning of a Long-term Perspective

One of the dilemmas of archaeology, one that it shares with historical research, is the incompatibility of period studies with any prospect of establishing more comprehensive historical explanations. The thorough plotting and investigation of archaeological material usually requires the archaeologist to restrict himself or herself to a limited area in time and space simply because of the volume of the evidence.

The chances of understanding and explaining the period or the area under study are concomitantly restricted, as each historical epoch is the result of an historical process. The Roman Iron Age did not begin in the Roman Iron Age; an essential set of its preconditions are the changes which had already taken place in the previous period. A further series of problems harden this ageless dilemma. The basic data of archaeology frequently change character at the transition from one period to the next, especially if major social changes are involved. It is consequently often difficult to undertake comparative studies following single methodological principles. At the same time, questions arise concerning the representativity of the evidence. In order to cross these data-orientated and methodological barriers it is necessary to construct an integrated historical and theoretical perspective upon the epoch being studied.

Several developments in Iron Age research during the last fifteen to twenty years have further crystallized the need to construct a long-term perspective. In the first place, the major settlement-site excavations of recent years have provided a plot of the development of the village through most of the Iron Age, and, although many pieces have yet to be found before the extent of variation of settlement will be known, the main features are quite clear. These studies have raised the question of continuity of settlement with renewed force, and have spotlighted the problem of how to interpret the reorganization of the settlements and the homesteads that took place. Thus a change from period studies to continuity studies is already under way in settlement research, and a series of new questions on the subject of social and economic organization has arisen.

If these essentially new results are to be perceived and interpreted in relation to the rich archaeological material from graves and hoards, there is a need for a formula that will make that possible. Grave finds especially have provided a basis for social analysis, but often just within individual periods; this applies, for example, to my own earlier studies (Hedeager 1978b, 1978c, 1980). It is still customary to treat the various major periods of the Iron Age as separate entities, although there have been exceptions (Myhre 1978). A perceptible need has therefore arisen for a more comprehensive interpretation of the Iron Age which could in due course direct future specialist research and continuing discussion. We are arguably right at the beginning of a truly historical understanding of this epoch.

An integrated analysis and interpretation of the grave and hoard finds has never been attempted. The analysis of this material, which forms the core of this book, should therefore be regarded as a pioneering foray aimed at finding a methodologically and source-critically viable path; it must, on the one hand, take account of the extent of variation in the material and, on the other, be sufficiently loose-knit for it to be possible to locate the material within a single formula. A long-term perspective however also requires a theoretic frame of reference which can contain and compare the major social and economic differences that manifest themselves from the egalitarian village communities of the Early Iron Age to the Viking-Period kingdoms. I shall therefore give a short account of the attempts that have been made to solve these problems in the composition of this study.

In order to follow the changes in a *long-term perspective* it has been necessary, first, to lay the foundations for analyses with the recording of all of the 10,000 or so grave, hoard and loose finds of the Iron Age. The settlement sites are included as far as is practicable on the basis of published literature.

With the same end in view, I have elected to analyse the three main archaeological categories – hoards, graves and settlements – individually (chapters 2, 3 and 4). This makes it theoretically and methodologically possible to delimit and follow one particular category of finds, with its intrinsic problems, through the whole of the Iron Age. It also brings a sequential consistency in analysis and interpretation into the process which is otherwise easily lost in the traditional comparative description of the find categories period by period. In this way we can obtain 'self-standing and at least partially independent sectional results that respect the specific archaeological and cultural contexts which in their different ways characterize religious, social and economic life' (see chapter 8, p. 225). But such an approach demands a holistic perspective as well, so that the interpretation of the three main categories does not drown in specialist archaeological problematics, just as it also ultimately demands some joint interpretation. For this reason importance is attached to giving an account not simply of the general theoretical bases but also of the theoretical problems which are germane to the understanding and interpretation of the three find categories. In order for there to be no doubt how these are associated with analyses and interpretations, each chapter is constructed as an independent or autonomous unit, with an introduction comprising a theoretical assessment of the problems, followed by archaeological application, analyses and – in the case of all three chapters – comprehensive interpretations. At the same time this chapter structure is also an expression of the relative autonomy that can be attributed to ideology, social organization and the means of production.

This further means that the summarizing chapters (5 and 6) are not, indeed cannot be, a traditional summary. On the contrary, drawing on the basis of the earlier chapters, they attempt to provide a new level in the interpretation of Iron-Age society. There may consequently appear to be a surplus of unused data in the individual chapters which are only indirectly involved in the general interpretations. These data do however give the reader a fair chance of testing these interpretations, and so, possibly, of arriving at different conclusions.

Chronology

We have noted that the extensive and very varied archaeological data must be manipulated into an operational form in order to be used in analyses of long-term change (figures 1.1–4). An operational chronology[1] in this case is a phasing which is sufficiently broad to allow as much as possible of the archaeological material to be located within its segments and which at the same time is sufficiently sharply focused for chronological variations in material culture to be detected. What this actually resolves itself into is the major periods which were established at the end of the last century, of which a brief account is given here.

Archaeological material – and thus the basis for chronological classification – varies greatly across the Iron Age. In 1874 Sophus Müller published *En Tidsadskillelse mellem Fundene fra den ældre Jernalder i Danmark [A Relative Dating of Finds of the Earlier Iron Age in Denmark]*, which became the basis of the Iron-Age chronology used by all later researchers. Twenty years later Müller was able to publish a phasing of the whole Iron Age which in essence is the same as the broad phasing within which we still work today (Müller 1897; cf. also Gräslund 1974; Ørsnes 1969a). Müller's work, in conjunction with Montelius's *Den nordiska Jernålderns Kronologi 1–3 [The Chronology of the Scandinavian Iron Age 1–3]* (Montelius 1895–7), established the chronological framework for the phasing of the Iron Age on the basis of typological (style-development) studies and studies of combinations of types in closed finds. Through contact finds and agreement of types between the Germanic and provincial

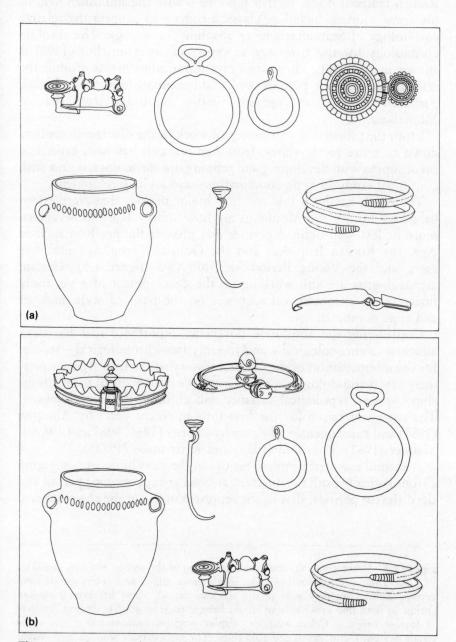

Figure 1.1 Grave goods (a) and votive goods (b) of the Earlier pre-Roman Iron Age. (drawn by Eva Koch)

Roman material it was further possible – with the additional help of historical sources, including classical coins – to connect the relative chronology of Scandinavia to an absolute chronology. The absolute chronology for the Iron Age as expressed by Montelius (1895) is shown in table 1.1. There are only minor adjustments around the transitions between periods which differentiate the chronological partition of the Iron Age we usually use today from that of Montelius.

From the pioneering chronological work of the nineteenth century down to more recent times, Iron Age research has been especially preoccupied with developing and refining the chronological grid with continued study of type combinations and style development.

The result has been that the four major periods that were established by Müller and Montelius are now subdivided into seventeen more or less well-defined periods and phases: the pre-Roman Iron Age, the Roman Iron Age and the Germanic Iron Age into five each, and the Viking Period/Age into two (figure 1.5). Certain archaeologists are still working on the development of a yet more finely tuned chronological sequence on the basis of style analyses and type combinations.

Considering the absolutely dominant importance that has been attached to chronological – and recently fine-chronological – studies for the interpretation of the cultural history of the Iron Age, surprisingly few methodological assessments have been made of the relationship between typological variance and chronological development. The issue was raised for the first time in recent years by Almgren (1955) and subsequently taken up by Ørsnes (1966, 1967 and 1969b), Malmer (1963), Gräslund (1974) and Kristiansen (1978a).

A second essential problem resides in the possibility of comparing chronologically both the different artefact groups *within* a period and the different periods, that is, the representativity of the chronological

---

Figure 1.2   Grave goods (a) and votive goods (b) of the second and first centuries BC, the Later pre-Roman Iron Age. Both grave goods and votive goods have become richer than they were in the previous period. There has been a marked change in both find groups: from simple bronze rings to unique, de luxe artefacts of foreign origin – Celtic weapons, display wagons, cauldrons (e.g. the silver cauldron from Gundestrup) and gold rings. The earliest-built wooden boat (dated to the third century BC) comes from Hjortspring in southern Jutland. (drawn by Eva Koch, after Hedeager 1988a, p. 74)

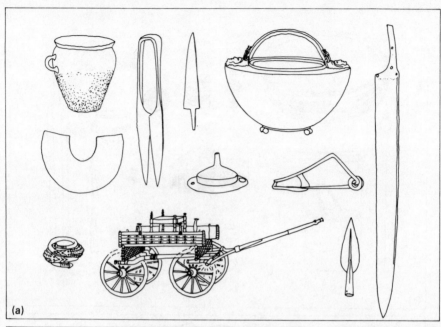

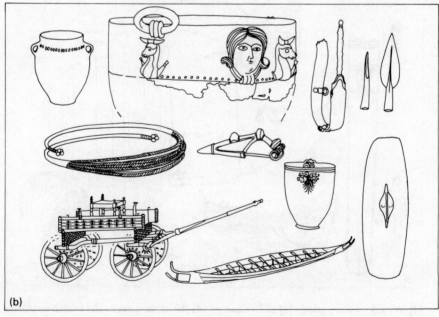

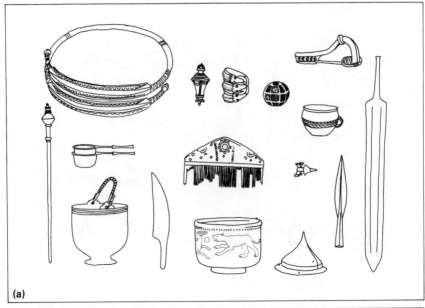

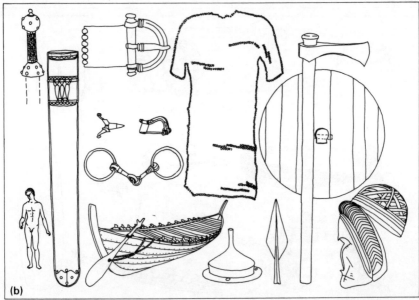

Figure 1.3   Grave goods (a) and votive goods (b) of the first to the fourth centuries AD, the Earlier and Later Roman Iron Age. In this part of the Iron Age there is a marked division between what is sacrificed to the gods and what is deposited in graves. The grave goods are dominated by personal dress accessories and adornments, often made in precious metal, and, not least, pieces of Roman table service: glass, tankards, jugs, ladles, strainers and so on. The votive finds, however, exclusively comprise weapons and other military gear (including tools, boats, horse gear) and small Roman statuettes. (drawn by Eva Koch, after Hedeager 1988a, p. 16)

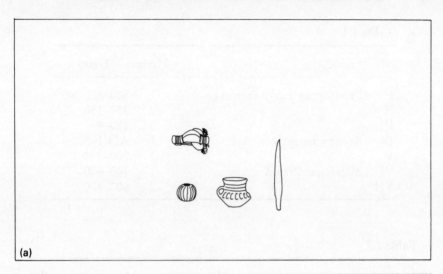

(a)

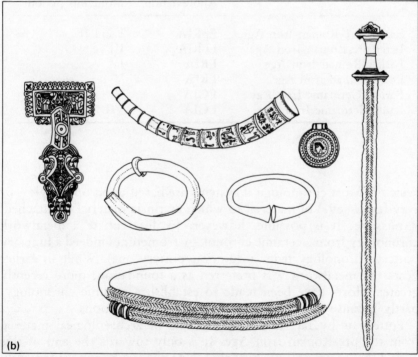

(b)

Figure 1.4 Grave goods (a) and votive goods (b) from the fifth to seventh centuries, the Germanic Iron Age. Grave goods have almost completely disappeared now; conversely, colossal amounts of valuables are sacrificed to the gods: arm-, neck- and finger rings, bracteates, brooches and so on, often of high artistic value and great beauty, as well as simpler payment rings, whose value lies solely in their weight. The majority of the votive finds from this part of the Iron Age are of gold. (drawn by Eva Koch, after Hedeager 1988a, p. 18)

Table 1.1

	Period	Phase	Dates
I	Pre-Roman Early Iron Age	1	500–300 BC
II		2	300–150
III		3	150–1
IV	Roman Early Iron Age	1	AD 1–200
V		2	200–400
VI	Migration Period	1	400–600
VII		2	600–800

Table 1.2

	Abbreviation	Montelius period
Earlier pre-Roman Iron Age	EpRIA	I and II
Later pre-Roman Iron Age	LpRIA	III
Earlier Roman Iron Age	ERIA	IV
Later Roman Iron Age	LRIA	V
Earlier Germanic Iron Age	EGIA	VI
Later Germanic Iron Age	LGIA	VII

systems. Most chronological systems are based upon one single – or very few – set(s) of material to which extrinsic material is 'attached' if possible. It is possible, however, to differentiate a metalwork chronology from a ceramic chronology (sometimes indeed a funerary pottery chronology from a domestic pottery one). While in earlier years the metalwork was preferred as a foundation, more recently greater efforts have been made to establish a ceramic chronology, partly because of the many settlement-site excavations.

Pottery is by far the dominant class of archaeological material from the pre-Roman Iron Age. It is only towards the end of this period that metal objects, brooches in particular, become sufficiently common to support a free-standing metalwork chronology (Klindt-Jensen 1953, based on the metalwork chronology; Becker 1961, based upon the pottery).

The grave finds of the Roman Iron Age – and the major bog deposits – have provided a basis for a comprehensive chronological classification anchored by the typological sequence of brooches and the absolute dates of Roman imports. Funerary pottery, however, has also been introduced in recent years (S. Jensen 1976, 1978; Lund Hansen 1977; Liversage 1980).

Stylistic studies of fine metalwork have been absolutely dominant in the context of the Germanic Iron Age, and they are the basis for the chronological phasing. Pottery chronology, however, is still quite unclear as far as most of the Germanic Iron Age is concerned. Precious-metal hoards are the largest producers of archaeological material from this period. Since some artefact classes are never found in combination with others, stylistic analyses become the only factor which can synchronize the individual classes (cf. Johansen 1979). In the Later Germanic Iron Age it is possible to assign secure chronological points to the stylistic studies through a limited number of closed grave finds (Ørsnes 1966). Only at the beginning of the Earlier Germanic Iron Age can the same be done with the finds.

The chronologies for the Iron Age are based upon different groups of material and to a very great extent are not methodologically compatible. It is also the case that major categories within the archaeological data cannot be dated more closely than to within very wide chronological phases. If the precise chronological divisions are to be determinative in the definition of the problems which it is desired to solve, the involvement of great sections of the archaeolog-

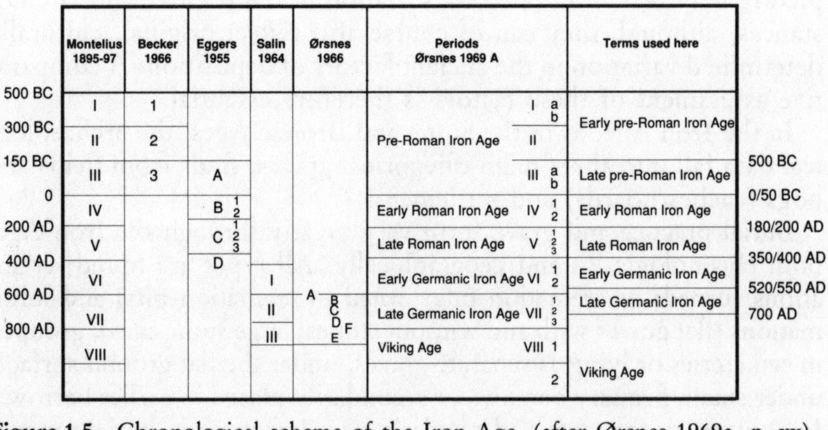

	Montelius 1895-97	Becker 1966	Eggers 1955	Salin 1964	Ørsnes 1966	Periods Ørsnes 1969 A	Terms used here	
500 BC	I	1				Periods: I a / b	Early pre-Roman Iron Age	
300 BC	II	2				Pre-Roman Iron Age II		
150 BC	III	3	A			III a/b	Late pre-Roman Iron Age	500 BC
0	IV		B 1/2			Early Roman Iron Age IV 1/2	Early Roman Iron Age	0/50 BC
200 AD	V		C 2/3			Late Roman Iron Age V 2/3	Late Roman Iron Age	180/200 AD
400 AD			D	I		Early Germanic Iron Age VI 1/2	Early Germanic Iron Age	350/400 AD
600 AD	VI			II	A B C D E F	Late Germanic Iron Age VII 2/3	Late Germanic Iron Age	520/550 AD
800 AD	VII			III		Viking Age VIII 1		700 AD
	VIII					2	Viking Age	

Figure 1.5   Chronological scheme of the Iron Age. (after Ørsnes 1969a, p. xx)

ical material must necessarily fall into justified doubt (Hedeager 1990).

In consequence, it is Müller's (1888–95) and Montelius's (1896) broad chronological phasings with the addition of more recent adjustments which I regard as a functional chronological tool⁻ in this study. The simple fact is that it is possible to date the majority of archaeological finds within this system.² Table 1.2 sets out the periods and abbreviations used.

Representativity

It is an essential prerequisite for the study of cultural variance that one has some perception of, and a degree of control over, those factors which may have exercised significant influence on the representativity of the data (Schiffer 1976; Kristiansen 1974a, 1978c, 1980, 1985; Hedeager 1978a, 1980, 1985).³ The circumstances under which flat graves and graves in barrows are found, for instance, are not the same. The former category is most commonly found as a result of ploughing or various forms of construction work; the latter is principally linked to the numerous barrow clearances of the last century. Bog finds, however, are first and foremost the products of peat cutting or drainage work. Local amateurs and active local museums have also, through the years, influenced the recovery of no insignificant part of the material that forms the present collections of the National Museum.

Consequently, regional and chronological variation in the find picture may be conditioned by variation in the present find circumstances, although they can of course also reflect original, culturally determined variation in the ancient factors of deposition. A comparative assessment of these factors is therefore essential.

In the Iron Age, as in the Stone and Bronze Ages, the archaeological data fall into three main categories: graves, finds from fields and bogs (caches/hoards) and settlements.

Burial practice and grave form vary greatly through the Iron Age, both chronologically and geographically. All types are found: cremations (urned; in cremation pits; urned in cremation pits) and inhumations (flat graves with and without stones; large stone cists), grouped in cemeteries or lying as separate graves, under the flat ground surface, under small, primary barrows or secondarily placed in earlier barrows. In contrast to the even and regularly paced changes in burial practice of earlier epochs, burial practice and grave form in the Iron Age are a mixture of virtually every conceivable variety.

Hoards and sacrificial deposits include a wide range of different artefact classes from the humble (e.g. the 'bog pots') to the unique (e.g. the silver cauldron from Gundestrup or the wagons from Dejbjerg). Most striking in this category are the many gold hoards of the Germanic Period and the great weapon deposits of the Roman Period.

The category of finds labelled 'settlements' includes a large group of recorded settlement-site layers and features such as pits as well as a number of properly excavated buildings and settlements.

The factors which have been effective in the production of these many find classes are quite diverse. Comprehensive studies of representativity have been carried out on the Roman Iron-Age graves (Hedeager 1985), on Iron-Age settlements (Hvass 1985a) and on the gold hoards of the Germanic Period (Geisslinger 1967; Fonnesbech-Sandberg 1985). These studies show that the distribution of the graves of the Roman Period and the hoards of the Germanic Period can, in the large view, be regarded as representative for Denmark as a whole, while the settlements reflect nothing like an authentic prehistoric settlement pattern (cf. below, where the individual studies are specifically involved). Other find classes are certainly under-represented: grave finds of the Germanic Period in the whole country, and graves of the pre-Roman Iron Age in eastern Denmark (Sjælland, Lolland and Falster). Let us now take a closer look at the problems which are linked to representativity.

Besides the assessment of the situation regarding the circumstances of discovery, one must also attempt to evaluate the geographical representativity of the data: how large must the data set be in order to form a representative sample of the original prehistoric material? Will areas that are weakly represented in the find picture continue to be so in the future? It is extremely important to ask this question of the archaeological data, which are never – and never will be – complete.

Inevitably, we do not know the result of future find accessions, but we can, alternatively, reconstruct the find picture for any particular find category or type at fifty, seventy-five or 100 years ago and compare this with the present distribution. This simple test was first used by Malmer, who could show that the internal relationship between six different bracteate types in Sweden had been constant from 1850 (with forty-five examples) to 1950 (with 190 examples), checked at a series of twenty-five-year intervals (Malmer 1963, pp. 182ff., figure 12). This means, in other words, that the find picture as it appeared in 1850 on the strength of forty-five bracteates was representative for the data 100 years later. The same also holds true for bracteate types in the remainder of Scandinavia.

Most recently, a similar procedure has been applied to the grave and settlement-site finds of the Late pre-Roman Iron Age and the Earlier Roman Period in Sjælland. On the basis of the geographical distribution of 1900 (with thirty sites), of 1940 (with fifty-seven sites) and of 1970 (with seventy-nine sites), it has been possible to conclude that the distribution map of 1900 is representative for the distribution seventy years later (Liversage 1980, p. 10 and figure 2).

As far as most find categories are concerned, the accession of new finds has diminished considerably in the last thirty to forty years; compare the find frequencies for pre-Roman Iron-Age graves (cremations) (figure 1.6); Roman-Period graves (inhumation and cremation) (figure 1.7), metal finds from fields and bogs (figure 1.8) and gold finds from fields and bogs (figure 1.9). The find frequency for field and bog finds (figures 1.8 and 1.9) is virtually the same; gold finds however begin earlier and are brought in more frequently to the National Museum than other finds from fields and bogs. This of course is a reflection of the unique character of gold, but does not alter the fact that the find circumstances, and thus the geographical representativity of this category, is linked to that of the other finds from fields and bogs. Only the settlement-site finds show a very different picture, as the frequency of finds in this category is increasing strongly (figure 1.10).

All in all, we can assume that the graves and hoard finds (i.e. finds

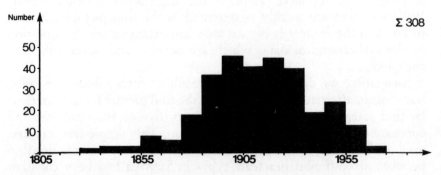

Figure 1.6 The year of registration for grave finds of the pRIA.

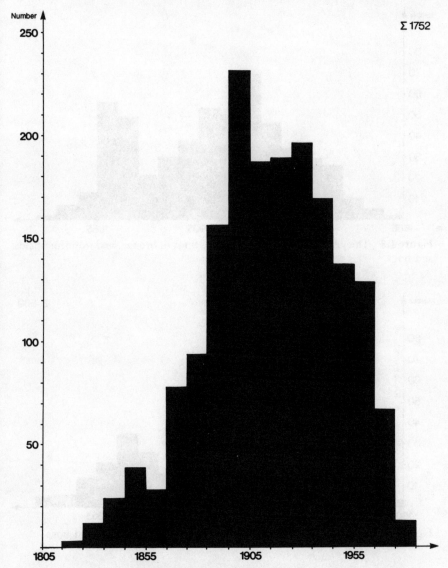

Figure 1.7 The year of registration for grave finds of the ERIA and LRIA.

from fields and bogs) are generally geographically representative, at least at the regional level, but that this is not true for the settlements. But it must be emphasized that representativity is not a constant factor, for it varies according to the problems that are under investi-

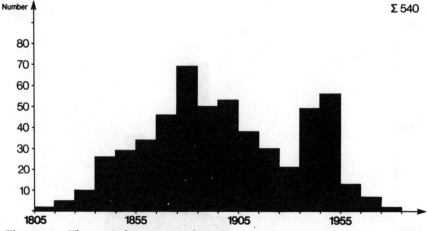

Figure 1.8   The year of registration for grave finds of bronze, and iron from fields and bogs.

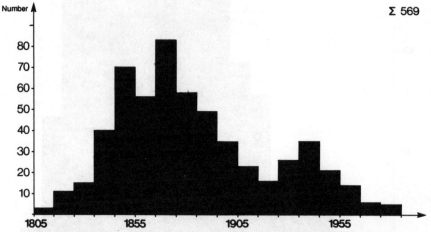

Figure 1.9   The year of registration for finds of gold from fields and bogs.

gation and according to the area that is selected for analysis. The need for data is the greater the smaller the units within which one wishes to work and the more specific the problem one wishes to solve. A particular category, for example, may be geographically representative at the *amt* (= county) or *herred* (= district) level, but not at the parish level.

The question, therefore, is not *whether* the archaeological data

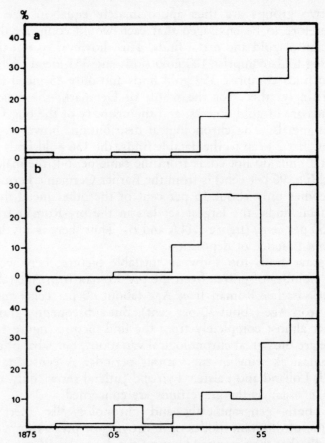

Figure 1.10 The year of registration for settlement finds: (a) Sjælland, Møn, Lolland, Falster and Bornholm; (b) Fyn and the surrounding islands; (c) Jutland. (Hvass 1985a, figure 24)

can be used in numerical, statistical, combinatorial (etc.) analyses; what is crucial, rather, in every single case is *how* they are used. These specific questions will be taken up individually in due course, in connection with the subsequent analyses. I now turn to some general variations in the relationship between graves and hoards through the Iron Age.

In this, attention will be given to two groups of finds: those that come from bogs/meadows and those from fields. The former group contains 454 finds, the latter 444 (omitted here are 23 finds from the shore/coast, 49 from barrows and 149 without reliable find details).

These two groups are thus approximately equal in size, and it was therefore to be envisaged that each would comprise the same proportion of gold and metal finds. This, however, is not the case, as the bog finds comprise 100 gold finds and 353 metal finds, while the field finds comprise 359 gold finds and only 85 metal finds.

Surprisingly, then, for the whole of Denmark, the majority of field finds are of gold objects, and the majority of the bog finds are of other metals. The chronological distribution, however, is very different. If we keep to the datable finds, the 136 gold finds and the 357 metal finds do not come from the same period; the majority of the gold (i.e. 90 per cent) is from the Earlier Germanic Period, from which comes only about 15 per cent of the other metal finds. Of these metal finds, the largest set lies in the pre-Roman Iron Age (about 50 per cent) (figure 1.11A and B). Thus there is anything but a constant practice of deposition.

The grave finds too show an unstable picture; here we find a massive number of graves from the pre-Roman Iron Age (about 30 per cent), Earlier Roman Iron Age (about 40 per cent) and Later Roman Iron Age (about 30 per cent). But subsequently grave finds disappear almost completely from the find picture (figure 1.11C).

There are thus great chronological variations; but what of possible geographical skewing in the various periods? A census taken for Sjælland, Lolland and Falster, Fyn and Jutland shows only a certain imbalance as far as the grave finds are concerned.

Thus both geographically and chronologically there is an expression of different modes of destroying or preserving wealth; it was hardly that they stopped burying the dead in the Germanic Iron Age – or in Jutland in the later Roman Period – but without proper

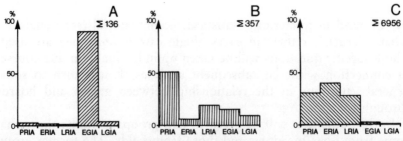

Figure 1.11   The percentile distribution of the individual artefact classes by period: A gold (136 finds); B bog and loose finds (357 finds); C graves (6,956 finds). (Finds which actually lie on the cusp between two periods are placed in the earlier one.)

grave goods these graves are virtually impossible for the archaeologist to find.

I have attempted to evaluate the geographical and chronological representativity of the major find categories from fields, bogs and graves, but the final major category, the settlement sites, cannot be subjected to the same procedure at present; the find circumstances are different and the data set is still full of lacunae. The settlement sites as a find category are *neither* geographically *nor* chronologically representative (Hvass 1985a).

Theoretical Context

A range of different theoretical directions has developed in archaeology in recent years that simultaneously exhibits shared features and substantive differences. It is generally important to make clear that these developments derive from different historical and intellectual contexts which produce different criteria by which 'meaningful' interpretations and explanations are identified (Kristiansen 1991). For this reason some of the theoretical debate of recent years is meaningless at a certain level. One can of course discuss various priorities with regard to interpretation: this applies, for instance, to Hodder's (1982a) and Kristiansen's (1984a) proposition that traditional 'new archaeology' neglected symbolical and ideological aspects of social life. But when subsequently the discussion becomes a question of principle, concerning criteria for interpretation and explanation, different directions limit the scope for real dialogue (cf. the debate between Hodder (1982b) and Binford (1987)).

Hodder has revitalized and modernized the historical-normative tradition and given it the name of 'post-processual' or 'contextual' archaeology. The conception of culture and explanation involved here is historically particular and idealistic to a degree, in contrast with Binford's conceptions which belong to generalizing anthropology and are relatively materialistic. Thus the criteria for *knowing* are subjective hermeneutical interpretation against objective deductive explanation respectively. Friedman has shown how the dominance of these two intellectual directions is linked to global changes in economy and politics (Friedman 1989). This is to say that the selection of a direction is not a purely academic choice but that it has political and ideological preconditions and consequences at a more general level.

The present study has as its theoretical starting-point the general new orientation within archaeology which has been called 'processual archaeology' or 'new archaeology', and more particularly the direction which has been developed on the foundations of a theoretical synthesis of Marxist anthropology and history which some call structural Marxism. I distance myself therefore from the more extreme positivistic ideas in processual archaeology that aim to establish so-called testable rules, divorced from historical context. In this I am in agreement with the critique of Hodder (1982a, b), Rowlands (1982) and others of recent years. However, I also distance myself from the tendency to explain everything on the basis of symbolical structures, which includes contextual archaeology's elevation of history as unique and not rule-bound (Hodder 1982a, b, 1986a). I do not deny that symbolical structures play a part in the establishment of social identity and social order in the form of rituals, and that every interpretation must respect the relevant cultural and historical context. But this does not automatically imply the absence of rule-bound historical processes. On the contrary, these are the precondition for the construction, by way of generalization, of theories of how societies function and change themselves, theories which can give us a basis for new, concrete interpretations and (perhaps) modifications to theory. In this connection, the theoretical conceptual framework represents a tool with which one can think, while the methodological analyses of the data are aimed at bringing the data into a scientific form which makes thinking possible.

The reader will not find, therefore, large deductive hypotheses constructed and linked with criteria for their testing, although some such do appear occasionally in connection with particular and defined problems. My understanding is, on the contrary, that a work of so complex a character as the present one can only be carried out by proceeding inductively – from analysis to interpretation, applying the general conceptual framework of theory in combination with specific theoretical formulations of problems. Since the theoretical concepts are tools with which to think, the reader is likewise not to expect a direct connection between general theory and empirical data.

Anthropologists and archaeologists whose subject area is non- or pre-capitalist society have found it difficult to apply Marxist theory, which was developed on the foundation of nineteenth-century capitalism. For Marx, the accumulation of capital was at the heart of capitalism, and profit was defined as the difference between the costs of production and the value of the workers' products, as the costs must always be lower. Profit is measured as profit produced in monetary form, and thus in principle not translatable to non-capitalist societies.

This was the problem which particularly occupied Maurice Godelier in the 1960s (see Godelier 1971, 1973, 1978). Consequently, at the centre of his works is the analysis of the economic systems to which he sought to give a more general significance by extending his area of research to include so-called primitive or traditional societies – under the inspiration, among other things, of the debate between substantivists and formalists. He collected and analysed data concerning the development and function of the economic systems, and subsequently formed his economic theory on the basis of his observation that kinship-determined, political and religious relationships functioned just like economic relationships.

Godelier's greatest importance thus lies in his demonstration that kinship relationships and religious institutions in many societies function as relations of production, and that these phenomena therefore belong to both the infrastructure and the superstructure (to use Marx's terminology). The precondition for such a view is that the infrastructure and the superstructure are not conceived of as separate institutions but as functions, which in principle can include all social relationships. So Godelier writes:

> To my mind, a society does not have a top and a bottom, or even levels. This is because the distinction between infrastructure and superstructure is not a distinction between institutions. Its principle, rather, is one of a distinction between functions. (Godelier 1978, p. 763)

The limitations of structural Marxism, however, lay in its lack of historical and geographical perspective, which was the result of its linkage to anthropological studies of small societies. In a critique of the conception, in both Marxism and anthropology, of society as a closed entity, Friedman, Ekholm, Rowlands et al. have shown in a series of works that there is a need to open and relativize the conception of society (Friedman 1976, 1982; Friedman and Rowlands 1977; Frankenstein and Rowlands 1978; Ekholm 1981). Under the influence of Wallerstein and Braudel, among others, they spoke instead of an interaction between structures from local to global systems. Friedman re-interpreted, *inter alia*, a series of classical ethnographical studies of social variation on the basis of a historically cyclical model of transformation (Friedman 1975a, 1976, 1979, 1982,

1983), while Kristiansen (1978b, 1982), Frankenstein and Rowlands (1978), Pearson (1984), Nash (1977) and myself (Hedeager 1978a, b) employed this theoretical starting-point in a new analysis and interpretation of sequences in the prehistory of Europe (further Rowlands, Larsen and Kristiansen 1987).

According to structural-Marxist theory and the models mentioned, the truly central factors in the study of societal change ('culture change') may be summarized as follows:

that no society is transformed in a vacuum, but is some part of a larger system;

that transformations can only be explained on the basis of their historical background in an earlier system;

that structural changes in a local society must necessarily affect other local societies (e.g. centre-periphery relationships), and must take place within a larger system;

that the social reproduction of the society is conditioned by a larger, supra-social system which is beyond its control;

that the social structures which are both subject and object in this social reproduction likewise do not control this process, but that they are a dominant force.

This means, put another way, that it is the sum of the dominant relations of production within the larger geographical units which determines historical development. In consequence, changes are dependent upon the interplay between local, regional and possibly supra-regional/international structures.

This general model can be employed in two ways. In the first of these it can be used for the analysis of the spatial distribution of social forms. In the second it can be used for the construction of historical models of particular social forms. These two areas of investigation are complementary, and neither of them is adequate on its own. An historical model requires a special combination of ecological factors, and infra- and superstructures. In a spatial model the variance on each of these levels and the interplay of internal limitations is investigated. A combination of these may produce a third model, an historical one, which covers variance in all levels of organization through time.

It is natural therefore that this theoretical framework has particular appeal to historical anthropology and thus also to archaeology; archaeological data in their own way form a basis for analysis which is much better, at least for the revelation of long-term change, than anything anthropologists can obtain. The results which can be achieved through an analysis of archaeological data consequently are of significance in the further development of the theoretical framework. However, as general theory, it is basically a tool with which to think, an aid to organization and interpretation. A more specific definition of particular social institutions (religion, social organization) and social formations (tribe, state) has to be undertaken separately. Since these are defined by the substantive analyses and interpretations of the historical context in which they are to be used, an account of them is given in due course in the following chapters.

NOTES

1 The archaeological material of the Iron Age is much more complicated and heterogeneous than that of earlier periods. At the end of the last century, Müller was able to write in conclusion to his *Danske Oldsager* [*Danish Antiquities*] that 'the material of the Iron Age comprises 672 forms, to which, however, many could be added that are either of minor significance or only exist in single or very few examples. Compared with the 269 forms of the Stone Age and the 422 forms of the Bronze Age, this large number shows how much more complicated and varied the culture was in the last epoch of Antiquity' (Müller 1888–95, II, p. 1).

Since Müller's day, the material of the Iron Age has been subjected to extensive typologizing, and, concurrently, the material has increased substantially. Types, subtypes, intermediary types, transitional types etc., are operational terms in extensive use. This wealth of detail undoubtedly gives scope for a wide range of cultural-historical analyses, but it is inapplicable as the basis for a broad cultural-historical analysis for which *similarities* in the archaeological material are more important than *differences*, and *functions* are more important than *types/subtypes*.

2 The following supplement may, however, be supplied for the individual periods: for the pre-Roman Iron Age: Becker 1961; for the Roman Iron Age: Eggers 1951, 1955, Almgren 1897, Beckmann 1966, 1969, Hansen 1987; for the Earlier Germanic Iron Age: Salin 1904 on Style I, Eggers 1955; for the Later Germanic Iron Age: Ørsnes 1966. The great majority of archaeological finds can be located within these chronological phases. Some of course belong to transitional phases, so that they could with equal justification be assigned to either period, according to the criteria chosen. I have attributed such finds to the phase where they naturally fit the cultural milieu, so that, for example, grave finds from the cusp of the Later Roman Iron Age and the Earlier Germanic Iron Age (Norling-Christensen 1956: the Haraldsted phase, Albrectsen 1968: Period III, Hansen 1969, 1971: Period C3, Jensen 1978: the Nydam Brooch horizon) are counted in the Later Roman Iron Age and the gold find from Brangstrup (for instance) (Herbst 1866) is attributed to the Earlier Germanic Iron Age.

3 The basis of the present studies is a virtually complete record of the following find categories: grave finds, bog and loose finds, and gold finds. The recording

occupied the years 1973–80, and no subsequent updating of the find lists has been undertaken. The collection of the National Museum was fully recorded for all find categories and periods. All the graves of the Roman Iron Age were recorded from the following museums: Vendsyssel Historiske Museum, Kulturhistorisk Museum Randers, Forhistorisk Museum Moesgaard and Haderslev Museum. The analyses of the material from Fyn are based upon Albrectsen's comprehensive publications, *Fynske Jernaldergrave* [*The Iron-Age Graves of Fyn*] I–V (1954–73). The loose finds are given in the find lists with their museum numbers and register numbers, as they were arranged according to place numbers. The lists of place numbers used are printed in *Archaeological Formation Processes*, ed. K. Kristiansen, Copenhagen 1985, fig. 37. No primary recording of settlement-site material has been undertaken.

2

Ideology and Ritual Communication

Power and Ideology

Archaeological works of recent years reflect a steadily growing understanding of the difference between 'modern' and 'primitive' economies. Where the modern (capitalist) economy can be described and analysed in economic terms, the primitive (or pre-capitalist) economy has to be defined much more in social terms (e.g. Polanyi 1968).

But there is, as was noted, less cognizance of the social and economic function of ideology/religion in so-called primitive societies, for this is usually supposed to take the form of an ideological superstructure after the pattern of religion in our own society. For anthropologists such as Fried, Harris and Service, all of whom have been influential in archaeology in recent years, society is divided into a series of layers: from the technological stratum at the bottom to the ideological superstructure. In such work the religious/ideological stratum is treated as a passive reflex of the social universe, not as an active factor which can be invested with decisive significance in understanding the process of social reproduction (e.g. Fried 1967). In the course of the last few years a more profound understanding of the role of ideology has gained ever greater influence in archaeology (e.g. Hodder 1982a, b; Miller and Tilley, eds, 1984; Spriggs, ed., 1984).

The source of this development is contact with the Marxist – especially structural-Marxist – tendency in anthropology (represented by, for instance, Althusser, Balibar, Terray, Ray, Meillassoux, Godelier, Friedman, Bloch and Augé). In consequence, an analysis of ritual communication and ideology, as it can be found reflected by the archaeological evidence, is taken to be of fundamental importance in the present work.

Ideology is regarded as an active participant in social reproduction, not simply as a passive and abstract reflection of the more 'real' society. The function of ideology is first and foremost to legitimize the political power of the dominant groups. This power is not a given thing, but must be continually re-created. Power has to be institutionalized and legitimized through rituals which are a special form of formalized communication involving, for example, songs, dances and material symbols.

In contrast with linguistic communication, ritual communication, as Bloch shows, is poor in semantic potential and in its capacity for logical argumentation. In natural language it is always possible to say new things, and to argue; in this formalized language (song, dance etc.) this possibility is sharply limited or totally lacking.

> Communication is not easily or at all adjustable to the reality of a particular place or time because of its arthritic nature. Reasoned contradiction or argument, which implies a supple form of link-up with previous utterances, is equally reduced or ruled out. (Bloch 1977, p. 329)

Ritual communication is thus exempted and protected from rapid change. Its individual elements can be understood as manifestations of a cyclically recurrent event. Of course rituals can be changed from generation to generation. What is crucial is that nevertheless they are all, in their moment, *regarded* as unchanged.

A second essential element in ideology is its complex relationship to social reality. At the same time as it helps to legitimize power and influence, it obscures reality by ritual mystification that makes the social world appear in an organized and unchallengeable form – as part of nature. One could even say that the substance of the ideas – their truth or falsity – is irrelevant. Any idea can become a point of ideology at that moment when it serves the interests of the dominant groups and can thus be presented as part of nature (Godelier 1978, p. 766). The individual members of primitive societies cannot choose between being 'believers' or 'non-believers'. Although the ideological universe may differ in character and function in different social systems, *belief* is a non-existent concept.

I shall now give a few examples of how these general traits of ideology can emerge during the development of hierarchical (pre-state) societal forms. In tribal societies, where the vertical relationships of kinship link the living and the dead, ideology/religion and society are inseparable. The unifying element is mythology, through which the individual is linked to the group and its ancestors. Gods, ancestors and people are inseparable (e.g. Friedman 1975b). In hierarchical societies, however, religion and society are not fully identical. The monopolization of power and religion belongs to an elite. Gods and people are regarded as separate, and ritual communication is focused upon the establishment of a good relationship with the gods, who for their part do not necessarily wish mankind well. The gods have to be propitiated, and this job can only be performed by specialists. The world of the ancestors is no longer part of the kindred's world but a land of the dead, which is a mirror-image of this world with all social relations intact. Within this interplay of power, dominance and ideology, Godelier picks out two factors whose interrelationship is decisive for the legitimization of the system: violence and consent. This raises the question of what the conditions might be for dominant groups to come to share that explanation of the world which appears to be self-evident in their eyes (Godelier 1978, p. 767).

The relationship between the individual and society, between violence and conformity, has been the central issue for the group of French philosophers and anthropologists which includes Clastres and Lefort. For them, the internal process of development in primitive societies, the formation of classes and a state, is internally incompatible, and is dependent upon certain individuals' reprehensible urge to dominate and the remainder of society's reprehensible willingness to be subjected (e.g. Clastres 1977). This view is an extension of a new general tendency to see primitive societies as primitivistic, culturalistic and individualistic. Symbols, significance, understanding, insight and so on are the key concepts, and the individual society has to be seen as a totality which is something unique, distinct and separate. In archaeology, Hodder, among others, has become a spokesman for this new departure.

For Godelier, the individual too has significance, but in a quite different way. For him, classes can only develop out of the classless society in legitimate ways. The process of transformation must have been slow, and social legitimacy must for long periods carry greater weight than violence and subjection etc. (Godelier 1978). Ideological legitimacy thus becomes the most important instrument in this process, and in this a prominent place is taken by ritual.

Ritual communication, simply, makes the social world appear

both fixed in its organization and universal, without beginning or end. Bloch emphasized two characteristic elements in ritual communication. First, time is annulled (there is no beginning and no end); second, the individual is depersonalized.

The annulment of time means in reality that the connection with ancient time is close and unbroken, and is used to legitimize the present. Genealogies, for instance, are an expression of this position. When Fried explains the development of a stratified society as 'unequal access to basic resources' (Fried 1967, chapter 5) he considers that the stratified society emerges *on the basis* of inequalities in property relationships and thus not *as a result* of inequalities whose foundation and legitimacy is located in the ideological and thus the genealogical. That genealogies are subject to continual revision and manipulation simply underlines their significance (e.g. Goody 1973).

Depersonalization of the individual, according to Bloch, is at the same time both the strength and the weakness of the process of ritualization. Through a steadily more ritualistic communication with the environment a political leader will have the chance of creating an office of which he himself is the only legitimate possessor. Thus power is transmitted from him as a person to the office – he himself is depersonalized. But with ritualized power he simultaneously loses the chance of influencing events to his own advantage. Authority is linked to the office, not to the person, and he is therefore not irreplaceable but can be removed from office in certain circumstances.

Weber, and subsequently Bloch, among others, have worked on the dualism of power: the relationship between power and status, and between symbolic power and real power. Ritualized power means that *power exercised* is transformed into *ritual status* through rituals, but means at the same time that status in this process is separated from its source: the function of power. In other words, power creates status through rituals but at the same time separates status from the real world: status and rituals are located *outside society*. They become part of nature. Power can be changed, but the status it has created will remain (Bloch 1977, p. 331).

The ritual representation of status can therefore remain unchanged under different forms of power. This also means that eventually so great an opposition between ritual status and real power can emerge that the ritual representation of status has to be modified, abandoned or given an entirely new function in a new system. One must also be careful to note that a society in transition can still maintain ideological and ritual functions which in their origins are in conflict with the new order of society and so eventually have the character of ritual relicts.

The leader who can unite ritual and political power in his office will be strong. Bloch emphasizes the strength of a common sacral and political function for a leader (Bloch 1977, p. 331). But at the same time, as we have seen, important limitations may reside in the restrictive and stabilizing character of the ideological system. Advantage may then be limited to the phase in which the monopoly of power and the hierarchy is established. The problem may however be solved by separating the two functions. This separation involves the simultaneous establishment of a distinct 'priesthood' to concern itself with the vertical relationships of society and a political leadership with horizontal functions, primarily military leadership. A division of political and religious leadership thus contains decisive evolutionary potential, as we shall see demonstrated in due course.

In what follows, an attempt will be made to apply these general insights in order to understand and explain ritual investment and its changes in the course of the Iron Age. First, however, I shall look briefly at some earlier studies and their significance for the topic.

The Distinction of Wealth: Ritual Hoarding and Grave Goods

Ideology and Ritual Consumption

Ritual communication is constructed out of a series of symbolic elements, of which some are in material form and therefore of interest to archaeologists. One result has been that the study of social structure on the basis of grave finds took a leading role in newer archaeological research of the 1970s. The starting-point for this was a supposition that there is normally a relatively simple connection between variations in grave rite/grave furnishing and social variation (Ucko 1969; Binford 1972; Chapman 1977; Chapman et al., eds, 1981). A series of quantitative analyses of grave goods has been undertaken on the strength of this, by which various grades of social differentiation in prehistoric societies have been revealed (e.g. Randsborg 1974; Hedeager 1978a, 1980; Hedeager and Kristiansen 1981; Frankenstein and Rowlands 1978; Hodson 1979). If one tries to probe further behind these general variations the picture becomes more complicated, and a number of kinship-, age- and gender-determined variations appear (Shennan 1975; Gebühr and Kunow 1976).

Other factors too can be operative, producing variation in grave furnishing and grave rites without necessarily reflecting major changes in social structure. Indeed the relationship between ideology and social reality can be so complex and contradictory that rather than reflecting the actual situations ideology may distort or directly contradict them. A powerful person of high status might, for instance, be buried humbly with only a few symbols of his wealth and position, while rising and rival social groups may be buried with great symbolic display. It is frequently just one particular group within a society that expresses its status through burial practice. In other periods, however, burial practices appear to extend to include a substantial proportion of the population, with an emphasis on playing down differences rather than stressing them.

There has usually been a general tendency to regard burial practices as a direct, passive and objective reflex of the social structure of the community and not as an active factor in social reproduction. Today we know very little about what sort of factors were present in the community to condition variations in the symbolic substance of grave rites, nor can we tell whether it may eventually be possible to draw up general rules concerning this topic. But in a series of recent studies the attempt has been made to approach the question through analyses of the role of ideology, including the role of material symbols, in the reproduction of the community (Højlund, ed., 1979; Blackmore et al. 1979; Ingold 1980; Hedeager and Kristiansen 1981; Hodder, ed., 1982b).

Clarification of the relationship between social reality and ideological legitimization is therefore fundamental to the study of ritual variation in grave rites. This can only be achieved by the investigation of ritual communication in its entirety within the wider framework of material production and reproduction. According to Kristiansen,

> studies of mortuary practice shall never contribute significantly to the explanation of social evolution if we do not try to analyse and explain their full range of variation in time and space and consider them against the larger framework of social reproduction. And we further have to accept that there exist no single methodological parameters that cover all such variations, not even within a single region. The only unifying framework is theory. (Kristiansen 1984a, p. 77)

Unlike grave finds, the ritual deposits of valuable objects (votive finds) have only rarely been the subject of analysis and interpretation within the new archaeology. There are several reasons for this. In the first place there are difficult problems of interpretation involved with this group of finds, since, in contrast to the grave finds, we are faced with rituals that are alien to our own religious cognition. One might add to this that the ethnographic literature is lacking in information (see, however, Levy 1982, pp. 17ff.), and the concept seems not to have played any particularly prominent role in American archaeology either. In the prehistory of Europe, however, the caches (votive and safe-deposit hoards) form, alongside the grave finds, the most important group of finds in both quantitative and qualitative terms. It is crucial, then, for an understanding of the development of prehistoric society, first that this group of finds should be located in theory, and second that it should be analysed and interpreted (most recently Stjernquist 1962–3 with a proposed systematics).

As a starting-point, the votive deposits may be taken as an expression of ritual investment/deposition on a par with the grave finds and may therefore be looked at in connection with these. Such a perspective has led to a number of important studies of Bronze-Age ritual consumption, particularly in recent years (Kristiansen 1978b, 1984a; Bradley 1981, 1982, 1987a, 1987b; Levy 1982). In these studies, fundamental importance is attached to an investigation of ritual consumption and the interplay between this and the process of social and economic reproduction.

It is crucial to come to a deeper understanding of the conditions which underlie ritual investments in the form that they actually take. Only through this is it possible to discover the connection between the cultural representation of the hoards and their material function. What is needed meanwhile is a more accurate analysis of the whole group of hoard finds in order to clarify what variations are hidden behind this general and imprecise term; that is, a methodological and analytical identification which makes it possible to bring this group of finds into the interpretation of the process of social reproduction on a par with the grave finds.

The Context of Iron Age Hoarding

Ritual investment did not stay the same throughout prehistory either in volume or in the material symbols selected; at some times graves

are richly furnished and at others votive hoards are the more conspicuous category. It is necessary, then, to start by giving a clear
statement of the course followed by various ritual investments
through the Iron Age; whether they are mutually exclusive, as one
may predict a priori as their purpose was different, or coincident.
First, however, we should clarify the form of destruction of which
the caches are an expression. Finds from bogs are traditionally
regarded as religious and finds from dry land as secular. There are
problems in this interpretation which I will note briefly here.

An interpretation of the caches based upon a distinction of bog
finds from dry-land finds reflects present *find circumstances* but not
the *circumstances of deposition* of prehistory. What were bogs, what
was meadow and what was dry land in the Iron Age, as opposed to
the present day? Bogs and higher-level dry areas producing finds
can be regarded as reasonably secure indicators of the original circumstances of deposition, but finds from modern meadowland or
wetland may in certain cases have been deposited originally in what
were boglands. While the bog finds have mostly emerged as a result
of peat-cutting and the dry-land finds as a result of ploughing, finds
from meadowland and wetland are frequently accompanied with
reports of first ploughings (sometimes following the preliminary
clearance of alder scrub) or drainage work. It is unclear whether in
the Iron Age these areas were meadow or truly bog.

A separation of religious from secular deposits on the basis of
find circumstances thus has a degree of implicit uncertainty, an
uncertainty further emphasized by the frequently common contents
of the two groups. Objects which are interpreted as sacral because
of their find circumstances are also found in contexts that would
allow their interpretation as secular and vice versa; the gold hoards,
for instance, represent the first group: found on dry land but interpreted as sacrificial items.

In place of or in addition to find circumstances as the most
important key to the interpretation of these deposits, it is possible
to investigate *what* in fact has been deposited: which artefact classes
and in what combinations. Definite bog finds will be brought into
the picture subsequently, as a supplementary consideration. This
procedure is only applicable to hoards of the EGIA, the varied
composition of which contrasts with the single deposits of earlier
times (e.g. the neckrings of the EpRIA and the vessels of the LpRIA).
In this context the major weapon deposits, which will be discussed
later, are excluded.

Hoards of the EGIA contain artefacts of gold, silver and bronze. If all the deposits were secular, i.e. deposited with the aim of bringing the artefacts back into circulation, one should expect them sometimes to be mixed. It is important to discover, then, whether that is indeed the situation or whether by contrast definite groups can be observed. If that is the case, further investigation has to be made as to whether particular groups are universally linked to bogs and thus support the interpretation which find circumstances suggest.

There is another way too in which the hoard-find category is less clear and reliable a group to work with than are the grave finds. We know that the deposition of grave goods in a single grave is a single action, while a hoard, theoretically at least, may be put together through several actions over a considerable period of time. If a certain systematic form can be observed within the contents of a hoard, this strengthens the view that, in some cases at least, a series of deposits is involved.

Ritual deposition is also, as noted, found in graves. What objects are used in this communication? Do some artefact classes appear both in grave and hoard finds, which can thus be linked both ritually and ideologically? Or are they in mutually exclusive distribution in such a way that particular types of object which are deposited as sacrifices to the gods cannot be used in the same period to confirm human status in the form of grave goods? Does this form of ritual destruction differ in substance in different parts of the country, or can distinct chronological variations be seen?

The analyses that follow will concentrate on two points. It is essential first to show the changing trajectory which ritual depositions take through the Iron Age, that is, the contents of the hoards must be compared with that of the graves both chronologically and geographically. In the second place the hoards are investigated with a view to classification as religious or secular. Only through these means is it possible to reach the necessary insight into the use of the rituals as an active instrument in the establishment of positions of political and economic power during the Iron Age, as the alternative to the exercise of force. This is the basis for the interpretations in chapters 3 and 4 below.[1]

An attempt, then, will be made to answer the following questions in the analyses below.

1 *Find circumstances*: What is involved here is whether a particular artefact type is found in graves and/or hoards; for hoard finds

the find circumstances are also of significance, whether in a bog or on dry land.

2 *The artefact set*: What is involved here is an analysis of the context in which the artefacts studied appear. What form does the context for a particular artefact type take in graves and in hoards? For hoards the supplementary question has to be asked of whether definite systematic variations in this context can be recognized.

3 *Geographical variation*: The question here is whether a particular artefact group is evenly distributed over the whole land or whether, for instance, in one area it is deposited in graves, in another in hoards, or even whether it is found in different ritual contexts in the same areas.

4 *Chronological variation*: The question here is whether possible variation in geographical and contextual circumstances may be explicable through chronological considerations. In other words, can chronologically determined variations in the ritual consumption of the community be recognized within the chronological framework selected (see pp. 6 ff.).

5 *Treasure hoards – votive hoards*: After this the question of the interpretation of the hoards can be attempted. This is of relevance to EpRIA and EGIA, the two major periods with many finds of rings.

6 *Ideology and ritual communication*: This first investigation, directed towards understanding ritual communication/destruction in the Iron Age, concludes with an interpretation that is to be regarded as a *sectional result*. This is applied in the following chapter on political and social systems, and subsequently in connection with the concluding arguments and the final model of society.

The set of problems delineated here requires all the finds from graves and hoards from the whole Iron Age to be available for analysis. Not only is this a very large body of data – more than 10,000 finds, of which the majority comprise more than one object – but it is also, as already noted, a very varied one. This further means that the methods which are applied have to be very general, and the categories in which the objects are placed have to be very broad. I have already given an account of the chronological framework (chapter 1, pp. 6ff.), and have summarized geographical representativity (chapter 1, pp. 13ff.).

The material is analysed within the framework of the major chronological periods: the Earlier and Later pre-Roman Iron Age, the Roman Iron Age and the Germanic Iron Age. For each of these, the first step is to investigate the presence of each individual artefact class in graves and hoards respectively, so that the find circumstances can be revealed. A distribution map of the individual artefact classes follows, and this is further supplemented with information relevant in this context, that is, whether the find context is a grave, bog or dry land. In this way an overview of the geographical and possible geographical-ritual variations is created.

The question of the context of artefacts which are found in hoards follows this: i.e. whether certain types are found in systematic correlation with others in particular combinations, or conversely whether there are objects which always exclude one another in spite of being contemporary. This can be seen in combination diagrams that are presented in association with the distribution maps.

With this done, the foundation should have been laid for the interpretation of the hoard finds as either religious or secular deposits and thus also for a provisional interpretation of ritual investments in the Iron Age.

An Analysis of Ritual Consumption

Earlier pre-Roman Iron Age (EpRIA)

Large bronze neckrings   The large bronze neckrings are a character-istic element of the set of finds of the pRIA, especially the so-called crown neckrings (figure 2.1; Müller 1895, nos. 59–61) and the individual rings with transverse moulded bands (figure 2.1; Müller 1895, nos. 56–8). Altogether there are forty-seven rings with definite provenances. There are also three Celtic rings (torques) (figure 2.2).

Find circumstances: The majority of the bronze neckrings are bog finds; a few are dry-land finds, but none are grave finds.

Artefact set: All these neckrings are individual finds, that is, they are found without any sort of associated finds.

Geographical variation: Crown neckrings and knobbed neckrings show a complementary distribution in Denmark, with the latter found on Sjælland and the former from the rest of the country. The simpler neckrings (figure 2.1; Müller 1895, nos. 56–8) have a largely western distribution, that is, in south and central Jutland and western Fyn.

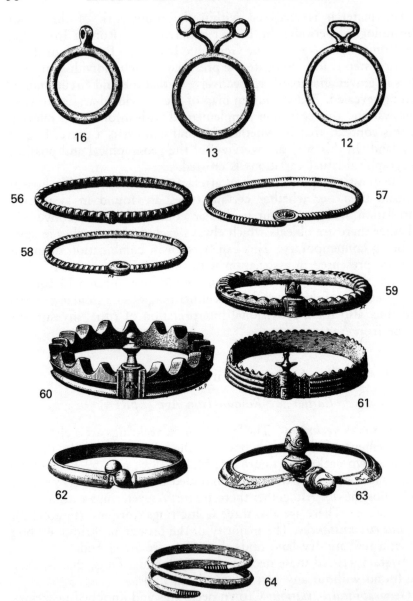

Figure 2.1 Selected artefacts of the Earlier pre-Roman Iron Age. (after Müller 1895)

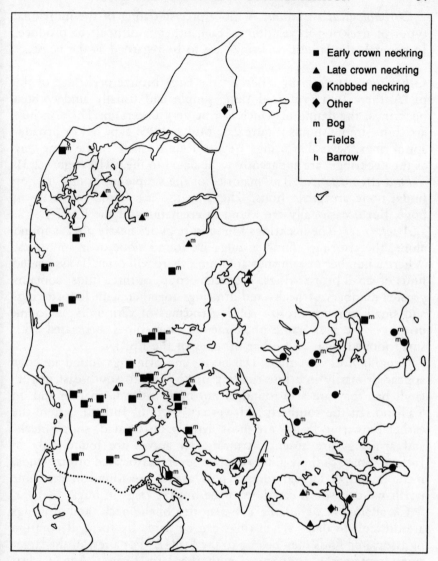

Figure 2.2 The distribution of classified bronze neckrings of the pRIA. Early crown neckrings = Müller's types 56–8; late crown neckrings = Müller's types 59–61; knobbed neckrings = Müller's types 62–3. (Cf. figure 2.1)

Chronological variation: A more precise dating of the individual types of neckring in relation to each other is difficult to produce. In general, the largest neckrings are to be regarded as the latest.

Other types of neckring   Besides the large bronze neckrings of the pRIA there is a group of thin, simple and usually undecorated neckrings, the dating of which can be very uncertain. The armrings are thin, simple spirals (figure 2.1; Müller 1895, type 64) or broader spiral rings. Several armrings are also found which, in the same way as the neckrings, are apparently to be dated to the pRIA (figure 2.3).

Find circumstances: The majority of the simple neckrings are bog finds; none are grave finds. The armrings are found primarily in bogs, but occasionally are found in cremations of the EpRIA.

Artefact set: The neckrings found in bogs are nearly always found alone; the armrings found in bogs are found alone or in multiples. Where a number of armrings are found there will often be associated finds of small bronze rings. A special group, of three finds, contains greater numbers of neck- and armrings together with looped rings and small, smooth bronze rings. Armrings of various types found in graves are a sporadic phenomenon, sometimes associated with small looped rings and other bronzes of the EpRIA.

Geographical variation: The neck- and armrings found in bogs appear primarily in a line running north-west to south-east in Jutland, but they are also found in northern Jutland, on Fyn and on Sjælland. In the southern and western parts of Jutland, where the earlier crown neckrings are most densely distributed, simple neck- and armrings are absent. Armrings in graves are found only in Jutland. Some of these graves contain several associated bronze finds, including small looped rings. These graves are found in the same north-west to south-east line as the bronze rings in bogs.

Chronological variation: The majority of the neck- and armrings are difficult to date. When rings can be dated by form, decoration or associated finds they belong to the EpRIA. For a few of the larger spiral armrings a connection with the Late Bronze Age is clear (Müller 1933, p. 14; Becker 1956, p. 63). Only one armring has been found in a context datable to the LpRIA.

Looped rings   An artefact type characteristic of the EpRIA is the looped ring, either small with a transverse loop (some with a loop at 90 degrees) (figure 2.1; Müller 1895, type 16), or larger with a loop at a right angle (figure 2.1, Müller 1895, types 12–13). Looped

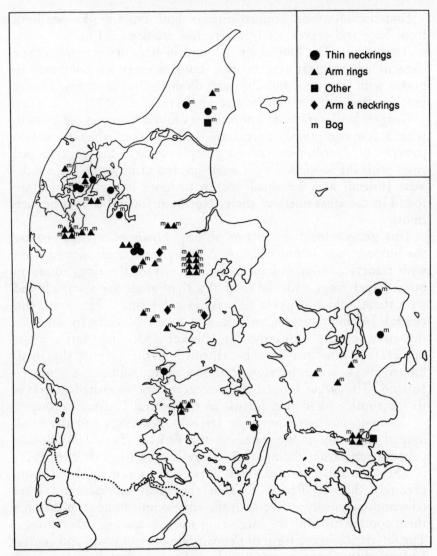

Figure 2.3 The distribution of armrings and thin neckrings of bronze in the EpRIA.

rings may be made either of bronze or of iron. The majority of these rings may have been iron. They are found in bogs and in graves, more frequently in the latter. Large iron looped rings are only known as grave finds; such rings in bogs would presumably have rusted away.

Find circumstances: Looped rings of both types are known both from bogs and graves. Only a very few are dry-land finds.

Artefact set: The looped rings found in bogs are a characteristic element in the great ring hoards. Looped rings are combined in graves with iron pins, but also with double-spiral brooches, bronze bracelets and other minor bronze artefacts.

Geographical variation: Looped rings found in graves are known, with a few exceptions, only from Jutland. Here they form two patterns of distribution, almost complementary: the large looped rings with the loop at a right angle are found in south and south-west Jutland, and the small ones with loops at a right angle are found in the areas north of there. Northern Jutland is void of such finds.

This geographical distinction is not, however, maintained by the looped rings found in bogs. Although the small looped rings with transverse loop comprise the majority of the rings found in bogs, larger rings with the loop at a right angle are always found with them, which is never the case in grave finds. The south and central Jutlandic group, which was formerly differentiated on the basis of grave inventories (Becker 1956, pp. 58ff.; 1961, pp. 248ff.), can thus only be affirmed in the case of the small looped rings, which never – or almost never – appear in southern Jutland. The larger looped rings however are deposited in graves to the south and in ring hoards in the central Jutlandic group.

Chronological variation: The large looped rings and the small looped rings are to be dated to the EpRIA (Period I). Becker proposes an earlier dating of the large looped rings (Becker 1961, p. 251); the small looped rings, however, cannot be dated more precisely than to Period I. That the small looped rings were contemporaneously in use with the large ones can be seen through their combination in the large ring hoards, among other things. The difference in the form of deposition between south and central Jutland cannot then be attributed to chronological difference, just as variations in distribution cannot simply be explained as the reflection of local groups. The small looped rings are often accompanied by several bronze artefacts, including bracelets, in graves in the central Jutlandic group; however, this is never the case in the south Jutlandic group.

Later pre-Roman Iron Age (LpRIA)

Cauldrons   A total of between nineteen and twenty-one cauldrons which have been found in bogs or in graves are attributed to the LpRIA (figure 2.4; cf. Müller 1895, type 185). Four of them are definite bog finds and between ten and twelve are definite grave finds, but the remaining five were found on dry land without any context suggesting a grave.

Find circumstances: The cauldrons appear in bogs, graves and on dry land without any context suggesting a grave.

Artefact set: The cauldrons found in bogs and cauldrons from dry land are all individual finds. Cauldrons from graves frequently contain a rich set of associated finds with a full weapon set (sword, shield and javelin/lance) and gold finger rings.

Geographical variation: The cauldrons are found in all of Denmark, but are most poorly represented in south and central Jutland. It is not possible to detect marked differences in the form of deposition from region to region.

Chronological variation: These cauldrons cover a period of about 400 years. Where a date of deposition can be ascertained it can be seen to have taken place in the LpRIA (for the most part, in fact, towards the end of this period). No chronological difference between bog-deposited cauldrons and those placed in graves can be detected.

Other de luxe items   The find material of the LpRIA becomes markedly variegated, and various imported de luxe items are found besides the cauldrons of various provenances. Particularly striking are the two large Celtic display wagons from Dejbjerg bog (Petersen 1888). The remains of comparable wagons are also known from two cremation burials, one from Langå on Fyn (Albrectsen 1954) and one from Kraghede in north Jutland (Klindt-Jensen 1950).[2] Cast bronze belts form a slightly larger but less splendid group. There are seven in all, divided between six find places in north Jutland (Müller 1900a; Werner 1952; Becker 1957) (figure 2.4). Whether these belts were imported or made locally has been much debated, and their date has been put between pRIA Period IIIa (Middle La Tène in European terms) and the ERIA.[3] The belts were first securely dated in the local context by the grave find from Try Skole, where associated finds place the whole grave assemblage in

Figure 2.4   Selected artefacts of the Later pre-Roman Iron Age. (after Müller 1895)

the LpRIA (Becker 1957). Three belts are bog finds, one has no recorded details and three are grave finds.

Gold finger rings occur for the first time in grave finds, seven in all from six graves. The majority are found in the cemetery at Langå on south-eastern Fyn (figure 2.4; Müller 1895, type 7). They are associated with weapons and cauldrons both here and in the grave from Kraghede. As has been noted, the gold neckrings are never found in graves, while the finger rings are mostly known from such contexts (one, however, is a dry-land find) (figure 2.4; Müller 1900b, figure 1). Among the most splendid artefacts of the LpRIA are the large Celtic gold torques from Dronninglund bog in Vendsyssel (Müller 1900b, p. 140; 1933, p. 13ff.; Hedeager 1988, p. 82) (figure 2.4; Müller 1900b, figure 1).

Also in the series of imported objects of the LpRIA are the swords. Five La Tène swords have been found in bogs, in rivers or in lakes, where they are always solitary finds. A larger group is known from the early weapon graves, in which locally produced swords also appear. The swords will be dealt with as a group in a later section (pp. 121ff., 143ff.) as well as the two major weapon deposits of the pRIA at Hjortspring bog and Krogsbølle bog (pp. 67, 245). For the present it is sufficient to note that the La Tène swords are found both in bogs and in graves.

The conclusion can be drawn at this point that only the gold neckrings as a group (of three examples) occur quite without any signs of funerary deposition. The de luxe items discussed, and the brooches, are found in bogs, on dry land and in graves.[4] This distribution pattern seems to hold for the whole of Denmark. There is nothing to indicate that deposition in graves and hoards is geographically mutually exclusive.

Roman Iron Age

Roman imports and gold finds in graves   As already noted (p. 20) hoarding ceases almost completely in this period. The volume of finds from graves grows enormously, so that these two periods are the richest in archaeological material of the whole Iron Age, with about 4,000 graves from the ERIA and about 2,700 from the LRIA. Not only are the graves numerous, but the grave goods increase greatly in quantity. Besides a wide range of locally produced artefacts, personal adornments and small tools, large amounts of imported Roman goods appear (figure 2.5; Müller 1895, types

189–90, 327–8). A number of brooches and pins of silver are produced (figure 2.5; Müller 1895, types 247, 249), and finger rings (in particular) of gold (figure 2.5; Müller 1895, types 236, 240). A closer analysis of the grave material will be undertaken in the following chapter. Attention here is concentrated on the Roman bronzes and glass and the gold finger rings.

Imported bronzes, glass and gold finger rings represent the three most important groups of foreign origin in the Roman Iron Age.[5] Other gold jewellery – as well as silver jewellery – appears too, in more exclusive forms or in types which are limited to one of the periods (breloques, for instance) which will be discussed in greater detail in chapter 3.

In what follows, we shall investigate how these three artefact sets are distributed in the graves of the two periods. No account is taken of the question of whether the individual graves are closed or not and thus the possible incompleteness of the grave goods, a question essential in other circumstances. This means, to put it simply, that the distributions assessed have to be regarded as minimal with regard to the quantity of artefacts and combinations.

The individual combinations of the ERIA are shown in figure 2.6. They are evenly spread across Denmark. For the LRIA the combination of bronzes, glass and gold finger rings is given in figure 2.7. Together with the map of the other combinations (figure 2.8) a striking geographical clustering can be seen.

Altogether, one can say that in the LRIA a marked concentration of imports takes place, especially on Sjælland. Seventeen graves contain, in all, fifty-eight bronzes, thirty-seven glasses and twenty-eight gold finger rings. From the same period a number of gold neckrings and armrings are also known from graves, especially from the rich graves at Stevns (figure 2.9).

Graves which contain a greater number of different artefact types also contain a larger number of artefacts (Hedeager 1980, pp. 50f.). This accumulation of wealth involves a wide range of other artefacts, to which we shall return in chapter 3.

Hoards   Roman imports appear only occasionally in bogs, usually as types which are also known from contemporary graves (for instance, glass bottles and enamelled bronze dishes).

Three finds of jewellery form a further special group which is dated ERIA. All three contain types which are not known in contemporary graves (Norling-Christensen 1942, 1943; Liversage 1980, figure 30).

Figure 2.5 Selected artefacts of the Roman Iron Age. (after Müller 1895)

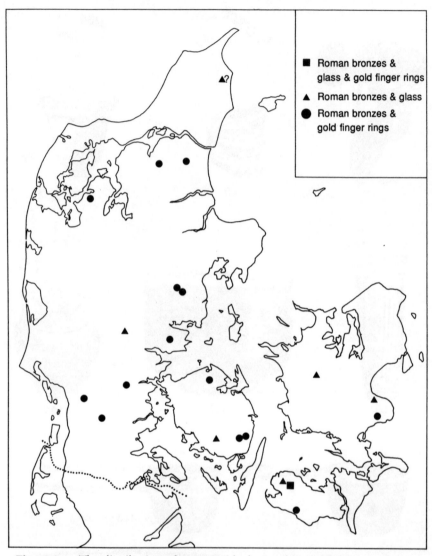

Figure 2.6 The distribution of graves with the combination of Roman bronzes, glass and gold finger rings of the ERIA.

Germanic Iron Age

The composition of the hoards The gold hoards form the largest group of finds of the EGIA (figure 2.10). They include all forms of

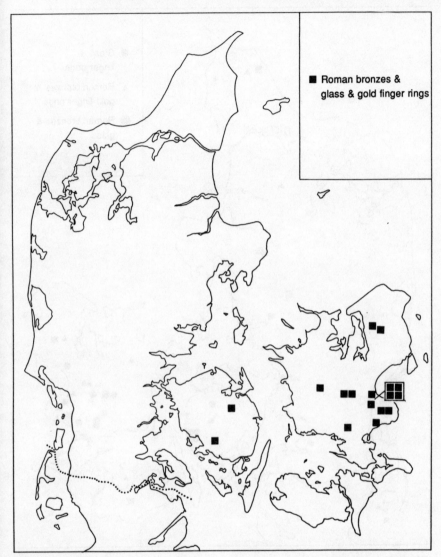

Figure 2.7 The distribution of graves with the combination of Roman bronzes, glass and gold finger rings of the LRIA.

rings: finger, arm- and neckrings, together with hackgold and bars. Bracteates too are a common find, while gold coins are a rather less frequent phenomenon. The so-called de luxe brooches of silver or gilded silver or bronze, also belong to this set. There are no other

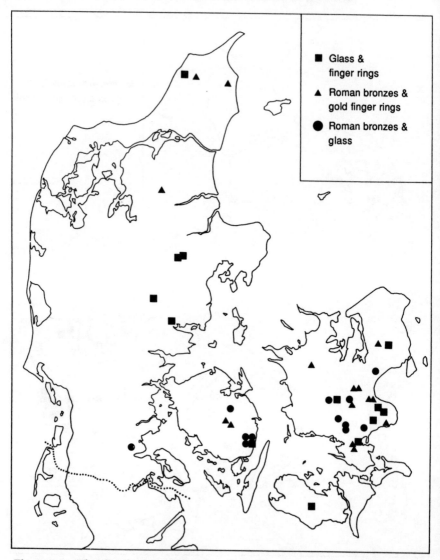

Figure 2.8 The distribution of graves with the combination of Roman bronzes, glass and gold finger rings of the LRIA.

silver artefacts in this set, while bronze is only found in the form of the brooches noted here.

The silver hoards basically comprise four pure silver finds, all of which contain different forms of hacksilver and bars, plus silver coins and fragments of imported silver vessels (Voss 1954;

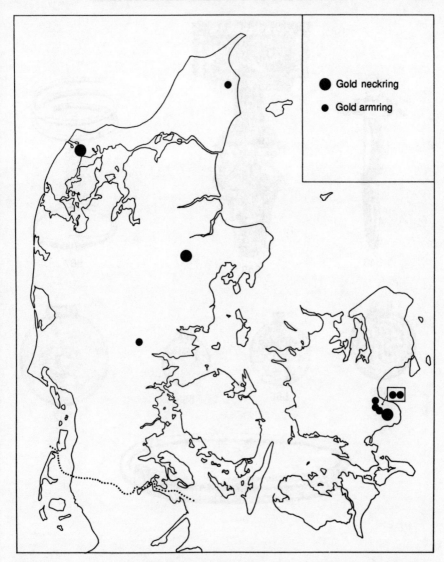

Gold neckring
Gold armring

Figure 2.9 The distribution of gold neck- and armrings of the LRIA found in graves.

Munksgaard 1955; Kromann Balling and Vang Petersen 1985). The silver, as has been noted, is used for the production of brooches, while a number of individualistic, finely crafted belt buckles with zoomorphic ornament are also known. The brooches are the only silver artefacts which occur in combination with gold artefacts.

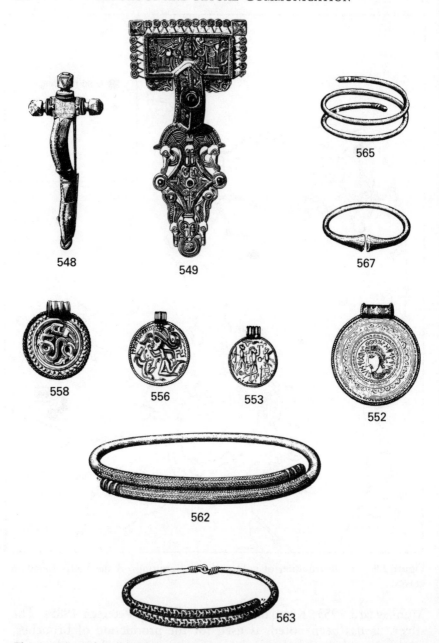

Figure 2.10   Selected artefacts of the Early Germanic Iron Age. (after Müller 1895)

Bronze artefacts include a number of different brooch types, including relief and cruciform brooches with zoomorphic ornament. These brooches are never found in combination with other artefacts, not even artefacts of gold or silver. However, gilded bronze brooches can, as noted, appear in the gold finds.

Thus the composition of the hoards is not random with respect to the inclusion of gold, silver and bronze. The individual artefact classes will now be analysed in more detail, and the grave finds brought into the picture in order to illuminate differences and similarities in depositional habits.

Brooches[6]   (1) The first brooch types to be discussed cover the whole of the period of the EGIA. Cruciform brooches are found from the end of the fourth century through the fifth century and into the sixth (Reichstein 1975) (figure 2.10; cf. Müller 1895, type 548). Silver-sheet brooches begin at the end of the fourth century and continue through the fifth century; at the end of the fifth century and in the sixth century the form is developed into the relief brooches (Schetelig 1906; Åberg 1924) (figure 2.10; cf. Müller 1895, type 549). The EGIA brooch types have a number of characteristic features which are correlated with form of deposition, associated finds and distribution.

Find circumstances: Large and small cruciform brooches, silver-sheet brooches and relief brooches are found as bog finds; in grave finds we have small cruciform brooches and a limited number of large cruciform brooches, later silver-sheet brooches and a series of other brooch types which are dated to the transition of the LRIA to the EGIA (e.g. swastika brooches, Nydam brooches, Haraldsted brooches).

Artefact set: The cruciform brooches in the bogs are always found alone; the relief brooches are usually in combination with beads, bracteates and gold finger rings. In graves containing silver-sheet brooches there is also a very uniform inventory of beads, pottery, bone combs and occasionally wooden buckets with bronze mounts.

Geographical variation is especially clear in the case of the cruciform brooches (figure 2.11). The majority of the cruciform brooches come from Jutland where they are distributed north of the Århus–Lemvig line, and in this area they are predominantly found in bogs. The small cruciform brooches from the same area come from graves, but this type is also found on the islands, where it is recovered both from graves and from hoards.[7]

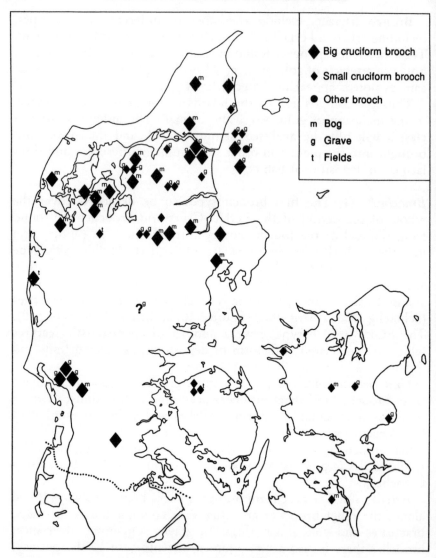

Figure 2.11   The distribution of cruciform brooches.

Chronological variation in deposition is especially clear in the cases of the silver-sheet brooches and the cruciform brooches. The earliest sheet brooches (without profile animal heads in the footplate upper borders) are found both in graves and in bogs; later sheet brooches (with profile animal heads) are only known as grave finds.

Earlier cruciform brooches (all small) are known from Jutlandic graves but from both graves and bogs on the islands. Later cruciform brooches (large ones, with animal heads) are only found in Jutland and the majority of them are found singly in bogs.

(2) Most of the brooches of LGIA are small, functional bronze brooches, the majority being bird brooches, equal-armed and duck-bill brooches, plate brooches and early tortoise brooches (cf. Ørsnes 1966, figures 47ff.). There seems to be no marked difference in use and geographical distribution among these brooches, which means also that no difference in ritual use can be traced. The absence of brooches characteristic of the LGIA in bog finds may be evidence that the majority of these were deposited in graves.

(3) If we are, finally, to survey the ritual use of brooches throughout the whole of the Iron Age the picture must be supplemented with the brooches of the EpRIA and the RIA.

Seventy brooches of the EpRIA come from graves and six from bogs (those from bogs are all from Jutland). These six are early (Period IIIa). The brooches found in graves are of iron and bronze, while those found in bogs are of bronze, but if iron brooches were deposited in bogs they would probably have rusted beyond hope of recognition and recovery and thus would not be found.

Nearly all the brooches of the ERIA and LRIA come from graves. The majority of the many graves of this period include brooches of iron, bronze and silver – in all nearly 1,550, comprising 950 from ERIA and 600 from LRIA. From the same period just four ERIA brooches are known that were found in bogs, and four or five of the LRIA.[8]

The brooches of the Iron Age were thus overwhelmingly used in connection with funerals; only in the EGIA is there a minor group whose ritual function is not linked with the burial of the dead, namely the relief brooches and the majority of the large cruciform brooches with animal heads. While the cruciform brooches are individual deposits, usually in bogs in the northern part of Jutland, the relief brooches apparently have a different pattern of deposition; the two factors in this difference is that they come from the whole country and that they are always found, in various combinations, together with bracteates, glass beads and gold finger rings. Moreover, it is in these finds that the largest numbers of bracteates are found, and the brooches themselves, of which there is never more than one per deposit, can be described as the de luxe brooches of the period. A small group of de luxe brooches can be seen alongside a larger number of small, functional bronze brooches in the LGIA too. It is unclear to what extent any of these de luxe brooches were originally deposited in graves.

Bracteates About 285 gold bracteates are known from Denmark from bogs or from dry land but never, unlike in Norway, from graves (Åberg 1924, p. 61) (figure 2.10; Müller 1895, types 552–8).

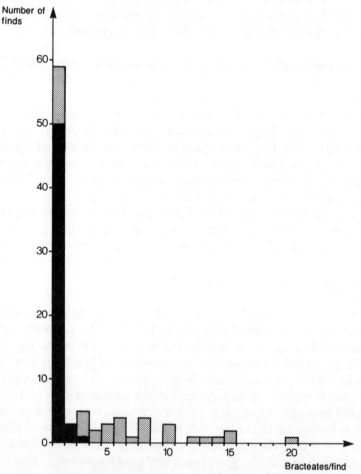

Figure 2.12 The numerical composition of bracteate finds. Bracteate finds without further associated finds are marked in black on the histogram.

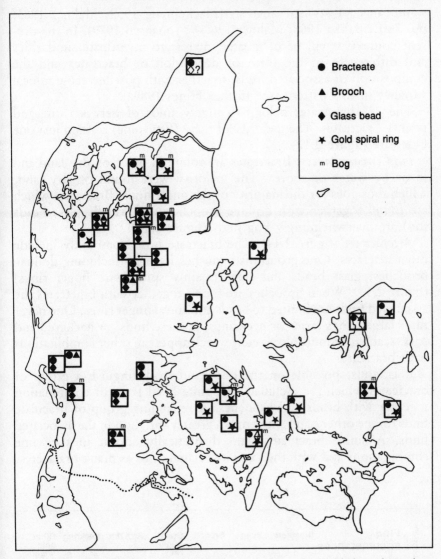

Figure 2.13 The distribution of bracteates found together with brooches, glass beads and gold spiral rings.

The chronological place of the bracteates is clearly the EGIA, and attempts have been made to subdivide the artefact class within this period. Fine-chronological dating runs into a number of methodological problems which it is unnecessary to discuss in detail here, but which are primarily related to the question of the chronological significance of stylistic analysis (Mackeprang 1952; Malmer 1963, pp. 76ff.; Bakka 1968; Malmer 1968–9; Johansen 1979). In the present context it will be of greater interest to investigate similarities and differences in the form of deposition of bracteates and the composition of associated finds, together with possible geographical variance in this pattern (see further Hines 1989a).

The 285 bracteates belong to ninety finds of between one and twenty bracteates. The majority of these (fifty-nine) contain just one bracteate (figure 2.12).

Find circumstances: Bracteates are found in bogs, on dry land and in or by water or shores. The majority were found on dry land, which thus goes for the majority of the single finds. Bracteates which are found together with de luxe brooches (and usually glass beads too) are overwhelmingly bog finds (figure 2.13).

Artefact set (figure 2.14): The bracteate finds commonly include other artefacts. One group distinguishes itself by including de luxe brooches, glass beads and rings (mainly spiral wire finger rings) (figure 2.13). When brooches are found together with bracteates the associated finds are limited to beads and spiral finger rings. One never finds larger rings (arm- or neckrings) in these finds, or hackgold and bars, scabbard mouthpieces etc., which appear in other combinations with bracteates.

It is, thus, possible on the one hand to distinguish a group of bracteates which are included in a quite fixed form of combination together with beads and brooches. A remaining group of bracteate finds on the other hand show much greater variation in the associated finds. A single bracteate could theoretically appear in the same combinations and with the same associated finds as many bracteates.

Location	Find circumstances	Bracteate	Bead	Brooch	Spiral finger ring	Arm ring	Neckring	Other gold finger rings
1	dry	12			3			
2	beach	20		1				
3	?	4						1
4	bog	8	10	1				
5	bog?	10			37		1	
6	dry	5			17			1
7	bog/meadow	7		1	31	>3	3+1/2	1

8*	dry	3	18					
9	bog	3						
10	bog/meadow	3			3			
11	dry	15			6			
12	bog	8			6			
13	dry	10	18	2				
14	dry	8	x					
15	dry	6	1					
16	bog	14	27					
17	bog	6	28	1	2			
18	bog	5	>3	1				
19	dry	3?			5			
20	dry	3			5	1		
21	dry	6	4-5					
22	bog	5	18	1	2			
23	bog	8	30	1				1
24	dry	10			11			
25	bog	13	1					
26	dry	15		1				
27	dry	6	9					
28	dry	4	5	1				
29	bog	1						
30	dry	1**			3	1/2	2x1/2	
31	dry	1			2			1
32	dry	1						1
33	dry	1			1			
34	beach	1					1	
35	bog	1			1			
36	meadow/bog	1						
37	bog	1	x	1				
38	dry	1						

* Not closed find
** Without loop

Bracteates: 1 Stenholts Vang 2 Kitnæs 3 Hjørlunde Mark 4 Maglemose 5 Bulbro 6 Killerup 7 Oure/Broholm 8 Hjørring 9 Bjørnsholm 10 Års 11 Års 12 Stenild-vad 13 Stenholt 14 Skovsborg/Silkeborg 15 Torning Vesterhede 16 Tapdrup 17 Holmgårds Mose 18 Overhornbæk 19 Lyngby 20 Hvolbæk 21 Vester Nebel 22 Kjellers Mose 23 Agerskov 24 Nørre Hvam 25 Darum 26 Skonager 27 Orten 28 Skodborghus 29 Eiby 30 Halsskov Overdrev 31 Sigerslev 32 Vedby 33 Vedby 34 Hesselagergårds Skov 35 Rynkeby 36 Apholm 37 Galsted 38 Ullerup Mark

Figure 2.14 Combinations of bracteates with: glass/amber beads, brooches, spiral finger rings, armrings, neckrings and other gold rings.

Nonetheless, the majority of the small bracteate finds (i.e. finds with one or two bracteates) lack full sets of associated finds (figure 2.12).

Thus we have a clear difference between the two groups of bracteates, large and small, in that the large group always has associated finds which the small group, in contrast, has only exceptionally, and in those exceptional cases never beads and brooches but ring gold.

Geographical variation: Bracteate finds are known from all over Denmark, but certain regional variations appear in the size of finds and their composition. Small bracteate finds (i.e. finds with one or two bracteates) are mostly from the eastern part of Sjælland, from Fyn (with the exception of south-western Fyn) and southern Jutland; more sporadically from the central and northern areas of Jutland. The centre of distribution of the larger bracteate finds is central Jutland. In the rest of the country the larger bracteate finds are found in the same areas as the small bracteate finds.

Bracteate finds with brooches and beads are numerous in central Jutland and southern Jutland. No beads or relief brooches are found combined with bracteates on Fyn. Beads are found in just one find on Sjælland. The bog finds are most common in Jutland, but are also found on Fyn and on Sjælland (figure 2.13).

Neck- and armrings of gold   Neck- and armrings, usually decorated with punched triangles and semicircles, form a substantial part of the Danish gold finds (figure 2.10; Müller 1895, types 562–7). The fine-chronological place of these items within the EGIA is uncertain, as they are never found in graves and their simple decoration is difficult to compare with other datable artefact types (Åberg 1924, pp. 63–4).

Find circumstances: The neckrings are found in equal numbers in bogs and on dry land; the majority of the armrings are dry-land finds. There is no apparent connection between find circumstances, ring types and composition.

There are no detectable fixed patterns of combination in the finds. Most of the neckrings and armrings are single finds. Exceptional are four large and special finds (from Halsskov Overdrev, Bolbro, Broholm and Hvolbæk) which bear various signs of having been put together at random (figures 2.15, 2.16).

The *geographical distribution* of neck- and armrings is more or less the same. The centre of gravity lies on south-eastern Fyn, and Lolland and south-western Sjælland can be added to this; nearly all

Location	Find circumstances	Neckring	Spiral finger ring	Ring gold	Armring	Bracteate
1	?	1				
2	dry	2x1/2	3	6	1/2	1*
3	dry	1				
4	bog	1				
5	dry	1				
6	bog	1				
7	dry	1				
8	dry	1				
9	bog?	1	37			10
10	bog	1				
11	bog?	3+1/2	31		>3	7
12	beach	1				1
13	dry	1				
14	dry	2				
15	bog	1				
16	water	1				
17	dry	1				
18	water	1				
19	meadow/bog	1				
20	bog	1				
21	bog	1				
22	bog	5				
23	bog	1				
24	dry	2				
25	dry	1**	5	1		2+1/2
26	dry	1				
27	dry	1				
28	dry	1				
29	?	1				

* Without loop
** Between neck- and armring
Gold neckrings: 1 Annisse Mark 2 Halsskov Overdrev 3 Hellested 4 Hannenov Skov 5 Vålse 6 Vejlebyskov 7 Sappesborg 8 Hjallelse Hestehave 9 Bolbro 10 Røjrup 11 Oure Broholm 12 Hesselagergårds Skov 13 Baltinggårds Skov 14 Sallingelunde 15 Bjernemark 16 Thorsen/Vornæs Skov 17 Nyborg By's Jord 18 Øland 19 Rålsminde 20 Støtterupgård 21 Sparregård 22 Fræer Nordmark 23 Stundstrup 24 Tåstrup 25 Hvolbæk 26 Silkeborg Vestskov 27 Strårupgård 28 Roager 29 Bedsted

Figure 2.15 Combinations of gold neckrings with: gold spiral finger rings, other ring gold, armrings and bracteates.

Location	Find circumstances	Armring	Spiral arm ring	Ring gold	Bracteate	Neckring
1	?	2				
2	dry	2				
3	dry	1/2	3	6	1*	2x1/2
4	dry	1				
5	dry	1**				
6	dry	1				
7	dry	1				
8	dry	1/2				
9	bog	2+4x1/2				
10	bog	2				
11	dry	1				
12	dry	1				
13	dry	1				
14	dry	1	2			
15	bog?	>3	31		7	3+1/2
16	bog	1	3			
17	dry	1*				
18	dry	1/2				
19	dry	2				
20	dry	1/2				
21	beach	2				
22	dry	1				
23	dry	1				
24	dry	1				
25	bog	1				
26	bog?	1				
27	beach	4+1/2				

* Without loop
** Made of 1/2 neckring
Gold armrings: 1 Between Hunnested and Lynæs 2 Tømmerup 3 Halsskov Overdrev 4 Enø 5 Teglstrup 6 Højkærgård 7 Erikstrup 8 Østofte 9 Maglesvinge
10 Naglesti 11 Våbensted 12 Bøgebjerg 13 Strib Banegård 14 Nørre Lyndelse
15 Oure/Broholm   16 Gudme   17 Rynkeby   18 Baltinggård   19 Svindinge
20 Nyborg   21 Bangsbo   Strand   22 Villerup   23 Vineterp   24 Havredal
25 Tebbestrup Kjær 26 Balskov 27 Lendstrup

Figure 2.16 Combinations of gold spiral armrings, penannular armrings with
expanded terminals and other armrings with: ring gold (wire), bracteates and
neckrings.

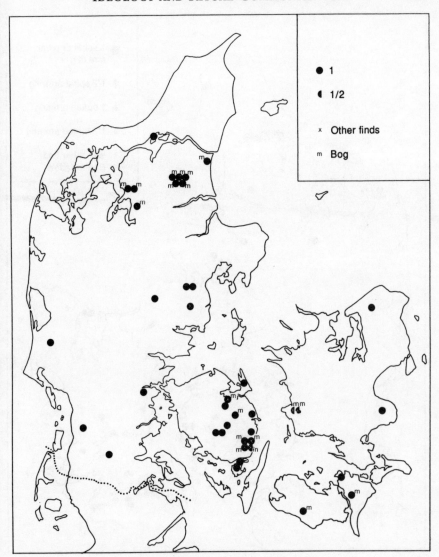

Figure 2.17 The distribution of gold neckrings of the EGIA.

of the finds from Jutland come from the north-east (figures 2.17, 2.18).

Neckrings and armrings are thus absolutely distinct from the finds of beads, brooches and bracteates, and are not inter-associated with one another. Most of them are 'pure' finds with either one or more

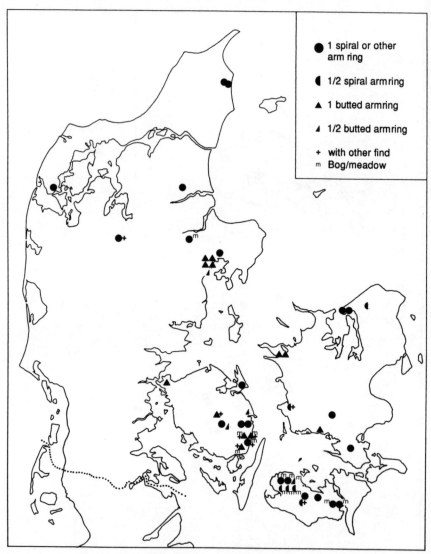

Figure 2.18   The distribution of gold armrings of the EGIA.

neckrings or armrings alone. Their geographical distribution is, Fyn excepted, virtually complementary to that of the bracteate finds and of relief brooches (cf. figure 2.13). The map of the gold neck- and armrings of the LRIA is also useful for comparison (figure 2.9).

Ring gold, hackgold and bars A great quantity of the gold of the Germanic Period was deposited in the form of ring gold, hackgold and bars. Ring gold comprises undecorated spiral rings of a form which shows that they were not dress accessories. Ring gold, hackgold and bars cannot be separated classificationally. The weight of the gold has been considered in an attempt to get an overview of this diffuse find group.

The total weight, about 45 kg, of the gold of the Germanic Period has been mapped as it occurs, *herred* by *herred*, and divided into six weight classes which are given in figure 2.19.[9]

Find circumstances: Ring gold is found both on dry land and in bogs, but the majority is from dry land. Small finds tend not to be bog finds.

Geographical distribution: Ring gold is known from the islands

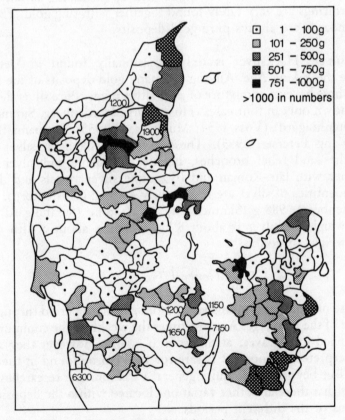

Figure 2.19 The gross weight of gold per *herred*, EGIA.

and from eastern and north-eastern Jutland. It appears much more sporadically in western, north-western and southern Jutland. A greater proportion of the gold was worked into ring gold on south-western Sjælland and in central Fyn than in the remainder of the country. In all only about a quarter of Danish Germanic Period gold is in the form of ring gold or hackgold.

Find combinations for ring gold seem rather random. As has been shown above, however, ring gold and hackgold is *not* found with neckrings, armrings or the larger bracteate finds in which the associated finds are relief brooches and beads (including only smaller rings). The ring gold group is, as noted, very heterogeneous and it is difficult therefore to classify and analyse the individual ring forms in particular detail. It frequently appears that ring gold tends to be associated only with itself; bracteates, gold coins, scabbard mouthpieces, etc., may also be present. Broken-up (including halved) neck- and armrings are very rarely found together with ring gold. The ring gold hoards are always pure gold deposits.

Hacksilver Hacksilver is only occasionally found in Denmark before the Viking Age. Among the many gold deposits of the EGIA only three have an admixture of pure silver items. Pure silver deposits are known only in four cases (Høstentorp, Hardenberg, Simmersted and Stenhøjgård) (Voss 1954; Munksgaard 1955; Kromann Balling and Vang Petersen 1985). These contain broken-up silver sheet brooches and relief brooches, buckles, pendants and silver coins together with late-Roman and Byzantine silver vessels and dishes. The quantities of silver are respectively 4.45 kg (Høstentorp), 490 g (Hardenberg), 988 g (Simmersted) and 1.28 kg (Stenhøjgård). The total weight of silver is about 8 kg, which is about a fifth of the total weight of gold.

General Trends

The use of material symbols varies from period to period through the course of the Iron Age. At some times the wealth of the community is channelled into graves, at others into hoards, however they are to be interpreted for now; it is rare for these to be found at the same time. But beyond these quite general variations the researches have shown that there are other variations located within the depositional patterns of the different periods.

In the EpRIA the grave finds include double-boss brooches, dress pins, belt hooks, iron pins (sometimes with bronze heads) and large and small looped rings. The hoards contain a series of different neckring types, including crown, knobbed and slender neckrings, armrings, bronze pins and large and small looped rings. The weapon finds from Krogsbølle and Hjortspring also belong to this period (Becker 1948).

The majority of the artefact types which are known from this period come either from graves or hoards; only the various forms of looped ring and relatively few larger spiral armrings, besides pottery, appear in both contexts. Closer analysis, however, has shown that those types which appear in hoards in one area are not also found in graves in the same area; they effectively exclude one another on a geographical basis. Such a picture is only a little hazy in the case of the small looped rings with transverse loop.

The overwhelming majority of hoards from this period are bog deposits. This holds for the large neckrings and the slender rings, the armrings and both large and small looped rings.

The picture changes in the LpRIA. Only the small number of gold neckrings of the period and the small bronze bull figures are now found exclusively as hoard finds, and lances, javelins and shields are exclusively grave goods. Imported cauldrons such as the Gundestrup piece, wagons such as the one from Dejbjerg, gold finger rings, La Tène swords, brooches, bronze belts and pottery are found in both contexts.

No geographical pattern can now be found, with a tendency for types found as grave goods in a particular area not also to be deposited in hoards in that area. There is also no sign of bog finds dominating among the hoards. The only exception is the few small bronze bull figures which are predominantly found in bogs. Brooches of the LpRIA are occasionally found in bogs, but the types are the same as those found in graves. It is of course difficult to determine whether any individual deposits of brooches took place on dry land since they can be mistaken for the remains of possible graves.

In the LpRIA as a whole the use of material symbols seems not to be random, but at the same time it seems to be free from the ritual regulations and restrictions that were striking in the previous period.

With the ERIA and further through the LRIA the pattern of deposition changes again, as investment is now virtually restricted to funerary rituals. The grave inventories become rich, varied and distinctly marked by consumer goods such as Roman luxury items, weapons and jewellery, the latter including gold rings for the neck, arm and finger.

Although the hoard finds, with the exception of the major weapon deposits, are very few, there are still some. The few jewellery finds of the ERIA form one little group, which includes some jewellery types which are not known in graves. The relatively large number of single finds of both Roman and locally produced bronze statuettes belong to the same period, along with sporadic finds of Roman glass from the bogs, bronze vessels and individual brooches. The statuettes are never found in the graves, and, unlike the bull figures of the LpRIA, are found both in bogs and on dry land. Among the Roman bronzes and glass found in bogs are types which are not represented in graves. Individual deposition of Roman artefacts can, as is the case with the brooches, only be recognized as such when they are found in bogs; on dry land it is always possible that they come from destroyed graves.

The great weapon deposits, which begin around the end of the ERIA and the beginning of the LRIA, contain a series of artefacts which are also found in contemporary graves and which include brooches, coins and gold rings as well as certain types of weapon. Other finds in these deposits include riding equipment, helmets, bows and arrows and finely crafted silver shield bosses.

Quite apart from the great war-booty offerings, the hoard finds, despite their paucity, show in their contents that, although they are not apparently linked to any systematic ritual practice, there were items in the artefact stock of the Roman Iron Age which were not used as grave goods. Conscious selection must then have been exercised, whether with regard to those things that were to follow the dead into the ground or with regard to those things which were deposited in some other way.

Finally the practice of placing pots out in the bogs carries steadily on, probably as local food offerings.

In the EGIA hoard finds come very much to the fore. In these all types of gold rings are found (neck-, arm- and finger rings), hacksilver and hackgold, bars, coins, bracteates, brooches and beads of both gold and glass. Concurrently the grave finds fade away: the grave goods become few and are mostly brooches, pottery, knives, combs and beads of clay or glass.

Besides the glass beads, the occurrence of which in hoards is limited to relatively simple deposits, brooches are the only artefact class which appears both in graves and in hoards. But the types which appear in graves are generally different from those which are placed in hoards. The two most distinct groups are the large cruciform bronze brooches and the relief brooches respectively. The majority of both the large cruciform brooches and the relief brooches are found alone in bogs; in the case of the relief brooches there is an exception in that they can be deposited along with glass beads and bracteates. The sheet brooches divide into an early group from graves, bogs and dry land, and a later group which is associated with the graves.

The EGIA is thus the only period in which brooch types which are used in the graves are substantially different from those which are deposited in the bogs. On the other hand, it is only brooches which are found at the same time both in bogs and in graves, and, further, only they have a clear association with the bogs. None of the precious metal finds has any specific association with either bog areas or dry land.

The LGIA is distinguished by persistently sparing investment. Apart from a few individual weapons, brooches are now virtually the only class which is found in the very small number of graves. To this can be added the brooches of the period from both bogs and dry land (possibly from destroyed graves?). The brooches found in bogs, the number of which is very limited, comprise a limited selection of the types which are known from the graves and the dry-land finds.

Any form of traditional ritual investment seems to have come to an end in the LGIA.

Reviewing the material of the Iron Age in a great sweep like this makes it clear that the use of material symbols is not absolutely random. Whether the hoards are to be interpreted as religious or secular, it is evident that the same artefact types are not found both here and in the graves, the LpRIA excepted. The two forms of deposit thus are mutually exclusive in all periods other than the LpRIA. This is the case at least with the more prestigious artefacts; but the deposition of artefacts which must primarily have reflected the local sphere, such as pots (bog pots and food offerings) and brooches, seems to continue through most of the Iron Age.

The use of material symbols is particularly strong in two periods, namely the RIA and EGIA; in the Roman Iron Age wealth is overwhelmingly invested in connection with funerary rituals. Certainly the number of graves with Roman imports is more or less the same in the LRIA as the ERIA, just as the actual number of bronze artefacts is, but there is a massive increase and concentration of wealth in graves in the LRIA, in the form of Roman glass and gold rings and of a wide range of other accessories, including jewellery. There are apparently no natural limits to the quantity of grave goods, and there appear to be no fixed bounds to the composition and contents of a grave inventory. Just one consideration seems to be determinative: the quantity of valuable items. It is here then, in the richest graves, that for the first and only time in the Iron Age gold neckrings and armrings are found; and these jewellery types turn out to play an important role in the ritual deposits of the Germanic Period.

This accumulation culminates at the end of the LRIA, and subsequently wealth is channelled away from the graves. The range of material forms changes too. The personal and prestigious drinking equipment now disappears entirely and only the brooches and gold rings remain. And new material such as the bracteates and 'payment gold' comes in. The brooches now clearly seem to have specifically symbolical significance: not only the distinguished relief brooches but to a marked degree the bronze cruciform brooches too.

The Interpretation of Hoarding

There are two periods in which the great majority of the archaeologically recoverable wealth was deposited in hoards: the EpRIA and EGIA. The interpretation of these deposits is thus essential for the understanding of changes in ritual deposition throughout the Iron Age as a whole. I shall therefore discuss the interpretation of the hoard deposits of these two periods separately.

The Earlier pre-Roman Iron Age (EpRIA)

The finds of rings of the EpRIA are usually simply interpreted as votive deposits (Brøndsted 1966, pp. 21–2). In Smederup bog in eastern Jutland a plank-built well was found not far from the place where a great quantity of rings were dug up. This well is regarded as a votive well (like the votive wells of the Late Bronze Age) and thus may emphasize the sacred character of the bog (Vebæk 1944).

The majority of the artefact types which were deposited in hoards were dealt with in the analyses of neckrings, armrings and looped rings (above, pp. 37ff.). Among these, a distinction can be found between types which appear exclusively in hoards and types which are also known in graves. In the former group belong the large neckrings (crown and knobbed neckrings), the slender neckrings, the large looped rings and the thin spiral armrings; in the other group are the small looped rings and a small number of spiral armrings.

There are several characteristic features in the form of deposition. Knobbed and crown neckrings are always deposited alone, the slender neckrings often in multiples and – as something characteristic of the three large finds of rings noted above – also together with slender spiral armrings and looped rings; however, the slender arm- and neckrings are not deposited together. It is typical that the large neckrings are not deposited together with the slender rings and thus that they do not appear in the large ring finds noted here. This can hardly be attributed to chronological factors alone, as among other things one of the early cast neckrings with transverse moulding is known from a grave in southern Jutland by which it is demonstrably contemporary with the three major ring deposits noted. A geographical variation might underlie the contrast in Jutland, but not on the islands.[10]

The majority of the finds of pre-Roman rings are Jutlandic finds; the large neckrings are predominantly from bogs to the south and south-west, the slender neckrings, armrings and looped rings are predominantly to the north-east. This geographical divergence can be perceived to a degree in the inventory of grave goods, in which, for instance, the large looped rings are only found towards the south, along with, among other things, triangular belt hooks, while double brooches (for instance), certain pin types, and so on, come from the northern and north-eastern parts of Jutland (Becker 1961, figures 227–30).

The general picture then is that those types which are deposited in the bogs in one area are not deposited at the same time in graves in that area. The small looped rings are the only group which falls outside this general pattern of deposition as they occur in both hoard finds and grave finds in northern Jutland. The picture is less clear on the islands, as grave finds are absent here and general relationships in the development of investments cannot therefore be deduced.

Nonetheless we may venture the conclusion that the apparent regularity which sets its mark upon the pattern of deposition and which means, among other things, that the composition of the ring finds cannot be random, must imply that the original motive for the deposition of the hoards was religious: there is no realistic case for identifying traders' hoards or treasure hoards.

The Earlier Germanic Iron Age (EGIA)

Bog finds have usually been regarded as sacrificial deposits (e.g. Worsaae 1866; Engelhardt 1867; Müller 1897; Petersen 1890), and finds from dry land as treasure (e.g. Bolin 1926; Stjernquist 1962–3, pp. 588ff.; Geisslinger 1967, pp. 9ff.; for an overview of research history see Stjernquist and Geisslinger).

This interpretation however is difficult to maintain with regard to the hoards of the EGIA; artefacts which according to find circumstances would be interpreted as religious can be found in contexts in which the motive for deposition would be regarded as secular, and vice versa. The interpretation of the extraordinary quantity of precious-metal finds of the Germanic Iron Age, the majority of them of gold, has consequently been less sure. Worsaae was the first to regard the gold finds as religious for this reason, referring to the description by the Greek geographer Strabo (63 BC–AD 20) of the Gaulish practice of sinking gold and silver in bogs (Worsaae 1866, pp. 58ff.). Through this interpretation the gold-rich areas came to appear as the most peaceful and well-off zones, with clear signs of flourishing trade.

Against this interpretation, Bolin thought in 1926 that it was possible to show a connection between coin-dated deposits and periods of war from historical times in most of Europe (Bolin 1926, pp. 196ff., 1929 pp. 95ff.). In the case of Denmark too, it was possible to demonstrate correlation between treasure hoards and those areas that were plundered during the Swedish wars of the seventeenth century; by means of the latest coins in the hoards the harrying of the Swedish army through Denmark can be traced (Skovmand 1942, pp. 185ff.). This interpretation of treasure hoards brought with it a radical change in the view of the gold deposits of the Germanic Period; gold-rich areas were now regarded as areas of war and turmoil, albeit still rich ones. The gold deposits were thus interpreted *en bloc* as secular deposits.

The latest scholar to attempt to interpret the gold deposits of the Germanic Period on an archaeological basis has been Geisslinger, and his conclusion was quite simply that no such interpretation can be made, either on the basis of an analysis of the find circumstances or on the basis of the composition of the find (Geisslinger 1967, p. 136).

This great body of finds of the EGIA is followed at a distance of several centuries by the many silver deposits of the Viking Period. With the Viking Period we are well on our way into the historical era, and thus an increasing possibility of turning our eyes towards the first written accounts. These have been used by the Russian medieval historian Aron Gurevitj in an attempt to interpret the Scandinavian treasure hoards (Gurevitj 1970). He does not reject Bolin's war theory, but at the same time he draws attention to the fact that this interpretation only provides a motive for deposition; it says nothing of why no recovery of the material took place. It is consequently always unclear whether the purpose was a temporary or a permanent deposition. In the first case, the treasure would be hidden (and forgotten!); in the second case it could have been intended for a later use in the life to come (Gurevitj 1970, p. 85). In other words Gurevitj divides the traditional question into two: the motive for deposition and the motive for a recovery that never happened.

It is natural that Gurevitj as an historian uses the written sources first and foremost in order to interpret the treasure hoards of the Viking Period. Various episodes are recorded in the sagas in which gold and silver is buried in the ground. Gurevitj refers, for example, to the famous Icelandic poet Egill Skalla-Grimsson, who had been given several chests of silver by the King of England. Together with a couple of slaves he took the chests to a secret place on his land, buried them and killed the slaves. Gurevitj mentions several examples of treasures of gold and silver which were buried in the ground or thrown into the sea. The written accounts however give no indication of the treasures being recovered, and Gurevitj therefore concludes that the evidence is that the Northmen kept their wealth in the ground in order to preserve it, so that they could bring it with them to the world of the dead in the same way as it was necessary to be accompanied by weapons, equipment, ships, carts, horses, dogs and so on. In contrast to the grave goods, which were first provided at the funeral, a man did what he could during his life to make sure that he would have some part of his worldly wealth with him in the life to come either by burying it himself or sinking it in open water (Gurevitj 1970, pp. 85–6).

Gurevitj's interpretation naturally applies first and foremost to the treasure hoards of the Viking Period, and although there are many similarities with the gold deposits of the Germanic Period they need not, of course, be interpreted identically, even though this is inevitably tempting with two almost equivalent sets of finds just a few centuries apart in date. One of the points made by Gurevitj is that gold and silver were deposited without any funerary connection, while weapons and other equipment were placed in graves. This is indeed the situation in the Viking Period, but not in the Germanic Iron Age of Denmark, where all forms of prestige items and wealth are absent from graves. This indicates that there may rather be some common ritual basis to this relationship, in that the hoards effectively replace the graves as the focus of investment at the transition from the LRIA to the EGIA. A common ritual background might be hidden here, with only the form of deposition changing.

By introducing Gurevitj's interpretation, we extend the scope for understanding the precious-metal deposits of the Germanic Period. These could have been deposited as hidden treasure, the purpose of which originally was that this should come back into circulation; they could be gifts to the gods; or they could be deposited with the goal of securing their existence for their owner for when he or she eventually came to the world of the dead.

What, however, does the archaeological material say? Do we have any opportunity to probe more deeply into the motive(s) which underlay the gold deposits of the EGIA?

Treasure hoards are meant to be temporary deposits in the ground; votive hoards are meant to stay there. It would seem, then, undeniably to be most logical to deposit treasure in such a way that it can be relatively easily recovered, not something one can easily imagine to be the case with bog deposits. In contrast, there is no logical basis for supposing that votive deposits could not just as well be deposited on dry land as in bogs. The terminological distinction 'bog find/dryland find' is thus a simple description of the find place, and says nothing clear about the character of the find (Stjernquist 1962–3). As noted, find circumstances give no definite indication of the motive for deposition, and the only other possible point of entry into the problem is through the finds themselves. Is it possible to detect any characteristic relationships in their intrinsic composition? In other words is it possible to observe any form of system among the gold deposits which could tell us anything of the motive for deposition?

If all deposits were identified as 'treasure', that is as temporarily secreted valuables which the owner had to hide in times of trouble or which an individual wished to keep safe for other reasons, they could be expected, in principle, to contain every sort of valuable, whether neckrings, armrings, bracteates, coins, payment gold or the especially fine brooches; in other words, everything which one would be afraid of losing, everything of negotiable value.

But there is simply no sign of the sort of haphazard and unsystematic mixture of objects which would provide a basis for such an interpretation. Indeed, characteristic features in the composition of the hoards have become clear in the analyses above. Thus both the neckrings and the armrings are deposited alone, in pairs, whole or halved and up to five together, but only under very special circumstances in combination with anything else. These special circumstances are cases of combinations with finds whose composition otherwise gives evidence of random assemblage. There is also a degree of methodicalness in the bracteate finds: large bracteate finds (i.e. deposits with more than two bracteates) always contain other objects, while those finds which contain just one or two bracteates may also contain ring gold but usually have the bracteates alone. By contrast, the large bracteate sets are a fixed element in finds which also contain a de luxe brooch and sometimes beads, while others of the large bracteate assemblages are a part of finds where the context is quite different, with an apparently far more random assemblage of items such as ring gold, hackgold, scabbard mouthpieces, etc. Theoretically, both small and large numbers of bracteates should be findable in the same patterns of combination and with the same associated finds, but this is clearly not the case. There are thus no grounds either for interpreting all the gold finds as one, simply as hidden – and lost – treasure. The large bracteate finds with brooches at least, and the majority of the armrings and neckrings, must have been placed in the earth for some other reason than simple temporary safe-keeping. They have a character which indicates rather that they were religiously motivated.[11]

This leaves the large group of gold finds which include hackgold, ring gold and bars, the composition of which is apparently much more consistently the product of random selection. These are usually found alone, but they can be found in combination with nearly all other gold artefact classes, including neckrings, armrings and bracteates, which may be cut into pieces quite unlike in the other finds. The major gold finds which stand out here are ones from Halsskov Overdrev, Broholm, Bulbro and Hvolbæk. All these finds can be distinguished from those already described by their apparently random composition, which makes an interpretation as treasure hoards much more plausible.

Thus we have a picture of the gold hoards which can be divided into two interpretative categories: one group of religious character and the other of secular character.

How then does this categorization relate to find circumstances? Is it the case that the group which is interpreted as non-religious deposits is found principally where the objects would be most easily recovered, that is on dry land? Are bog deposits predominant in the group of supposedly religious deposits?

None of the groups in question has any uniform association with either bogs or dry land, but certain tendencies may be seen. Most clearly linked to the bogs are those deposits which comprise bracteates associated with relief brooches and beads. Small ring finds, like the small bracteate finds, seem to be most strongly represented on dry land. For all other groups, neckrings, armrings, hackgold, bars and ring gold, it is apparently a matter of chance whether they were deposited on dry land or in a bog.

How then may we explain the deposition of what we would preferably interpret here as treasure hoards in places – such as bog areas – so inaccessible for their proper owners, who should have intended to get the goods back again? If we return to Gurevitj's interpretation, it could be that two different motives actually lurk behind the group of so-called non-religious deposits. One of them would be the temporary safe-keeping of valuables, which in periods of war or strife could be as much as the collected wealth of some village or clan. The other motive would be religious, but unlike the deposits of neckrings (for instance) would involve randomly assembled objects which reflect the wealth of the individual and which were deposited in secrecy in order to secure their continued existence for the owner in the life to come. These would therefore reflect the composition and function of valuables in real life very much more than the 'official' votive deposits would. It is thus also understandable that these deposits did not always take place on dry land, where others could relatively easily take possession of the material and bring it back into circulation.

If this interpretation is accepted, it must mean that there are deposits among the gold hoards of the Germanic Iron Age which are there for three different reasons. We have first the deposits which have an official, religious character, namely the neckrings and armrings, the large bracteate finds and the brooches; second, the deposits of valuables which were made in order to secure for their owner the use of these in a life to come and which therefore also fall into the religious – albeit private – sphere; and third the group which was decidedly meant as a temporary deposit. It has not proved possible to see any difference archaeologically between the second and third groups (which was not in fact to be expected) but it is nevertheless quite probable that from time to time people would have hidden their valuables in the ground. Treasure hoards, however, cannot be attributed exclusively to times of trouble as Bolin proposed. If this were so, one would also expect the times of war in the LRIA to have brought about deposits of, for example, valuable Roman drinking sets, which simply is not the case.

Thus the motives for ritual deposition are varied as well. On the one hand we see the result of a truly public sacrifice to the gods of the golden rings, and on the other the result of a hidden and secret practice. But the idea behind what are interpreted here as the official ritual deposits seems, naturally enough, closely related to the community's rules of gift giving in general.

The contractual character of gift giving is known from the Viking Period and from the warrior aristocracy of the early Middle Ages. If the receiver was more powerful than the giver, the principle was that he reciprocated with favours; if the two parties were equal he reciprocated with gifts in return; but if the recipient was of lower rank than the giver the gift contracted him to provide services. It is probably in this light that we should see and understand the gold sacrifices of the Germanic Period. Through the official deposits of fine jewellery the giver (man) was of lower rank than the recipient (the gods), who were expected to repay the sacrifice of the splendid jewellery with favours. The private deposits, in contrast, are composed of artefacts which were used, among other things, for payment. By preserving their negotiable currency (or at least some of it) in the earth, people managed both to have a more secure hiding place than a chest or a bed, and at the same time to have secured their valuables for the life hereafter.

Ritual, Ideology and Social Change: An Hypothesis

Rituals are an important part of a community's self-consciousness, and they are an important part of the social life and identity of the individual. If rituals remain unchanged we are only too ready to assume that everything else in the community is unchanging too. But this need not be the case. On the contrary, rituals may distort the real world through a spiritual, or ideological, statement that everything is as it was. On the other hand, rituals can also be used in an attempt to establish a new self-consciousness, a new ideology. The rituals can thus have both an active, innovative role and an actively conservative role in the development of society.

However, ritual communication is by nature preferentially conservative and preservative, for rituals build upon tradition, and only through repetition does a particular (symbolic) event become a ritual. There is therefore good reason to direct our attention to those periods of the Iron Age in which ritual communication shifts direction: this could mean that a new ideology and a new self-consciousness is under construction (figure 2.20).

In the earliest part of the Iron Age, ritual activities were normally a continuation of later Bronze-Age practice: that is, under-emphasized funerary ritual and votive offerings of bronze rings in the bogs. Large, uniform cemeteries played a part in emphasizing the common identity of individual local communities. The grave inventory was

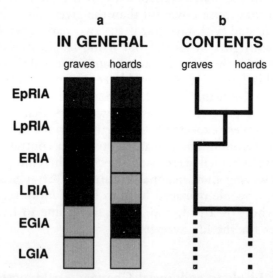

Figure 2.20 Schematic diagram of: (a) the varying presence of the archaeological material in graves and hoards from the individual periods of the Iron Age (darker boxes show greater numbers); (b) agreement or difference in the contents of graves and hoards, divided according to the same main periods.

uniform and spare, and no one had special status or pre-eminence marked through burial practice.

One may justifiably express surprise at the fact that iron was not used in the ritual practices instead of bronze. Iron was a raw material which, unlike copper and tin, the elements of bronze, could be obtained locally. The bronze, in contrast, represented a symbolic contact with the alien. It was a result of and a symbol of a wide-branching network of exchange relationships and alliances which stretched far into central Europe. In the earliest centuries of the Iron Age these exchange relationships had nearly ceased to exist, and iron had superseded bronze as the most important metal, but it was unable to supersede the network of exchange systems which were the necessary precondition for bronze supplies. Bronze as a metal and bronze as a symbol were thus inseparably linked throughout the Bronze Age. As a metal, bronze could be superseded by iron, but not as a symbol. And it was precisely the symbolical significance of bronze that was demonstrated through the votive deposits. In the absence of anything else, the bronze rings at the beginning of the Iron Age represented the only thing of foreign origin, and it was these that had been associated with ritual practice for centuries.

In the LpRIA votive practices continue, but now with a more varied and exotic range. The funerary rituals are still uniform and inconspicuous, but one particular group marks its special place. These are the warriors who, besides weapons, might also have the same exotic artefacts with them in their graves as were being used as sacrificial gifts. The sharp differentiation between ritual investment in grave goods and in votive deposition is lost, and a small group (of warriors) appropriated, or were invested with, the same signs of value that otherwise were granted to the gods. A number of individuals were now, apparently, established on an equal footing with the gods through these ritual practices, in which military pre-eminence and ideological distinction are fused.

At the transition to the ERIA there is a shift in ritual investment, apparently a very abrupt one. The large, probably collective, votive deposits cease, and only individual households carry the tradition on in the visible form of individual brooches, bog pots and food offerings. On the other hand, investment of great quantities of foreign Roman luxury goods, as well as locally produced objects, is made in the burial rituals, not simply in warrior graves but also in women's graves and men's graves without weapons. As far as it is possible to judge, it is single individuals as well as larger groups, kindreds or classes, who emphasize a special position in this way for the whole of the Roman Iron Age. The new structure – or ideology – which is first visible in the EpRIA now has taken over completely, and we have to suppose that particular individuals are securing and emphasizing their economic and political pre-eminence through ideological legitimization.

The picture changes in the EGIA. Ritual investment in the graves ceases, and votive deposits proliferate. The material that is sacrificed to the gods or put away in the ground or in a bog in order to be there for the owner in the life to come is now locally produced, although the metal (gold) and the intermittently splendid craftwork emphasizes its exclusive character. If the interpretation is valid, the inferred division between the public rituals on the one hand, with their clearly religious character, and the individual, secret sacrifices of precious metal on the other is something new in the religious world. The individual has now parted himself in some way from the clan, and himself discharges some of the religious practices which are to secure for those concerned a position in the next life. As in the EpRIA, the official rituals now have a conservative function. The clan, or groups, no longer need to demonstrate their special place through great conspicuous funerary manifestations. Rather, the new elite sought the favour of the gods through splendid gifts which both contracted and secured the individual by the burial of means of payment.

Bearing in mind the theoretical considerations with which the chapter begins, the following working hypothesis can be constructed on the basis of the foregoing interpretations. In the EpRIA the public rituals have a conservative function, as they emphasize continuity back into the Bronze Age. The grave rites display commonality and conformity. The changes which take place in the LpRIA must be an expression of individual families or persons separating themselves from this commonality and aligning themselves with the gods through their burial rites. The people who were thus equipped, either by their kindred or by the community, with the same tokens of worth as were the gods, were also warriors. A new military/political function is thus ritually legitimized. This development continues in the Roman Iron Age, but the rituals and the ceremonial practices are now exclusively associated with graves. It is now not only the most distinguished warriors who are the focus of the public ceremonies, but also men without weapons, and not least women, and it is not only individual people, but at least as far as the LRIA is concerned a larger group, an elite, which is thus distinguished. The rituals are not conservative but rather play an innovative role in the establishment of a new social order. Only when this order is fixed and unchallengeable can the rituals revert to a conservative function, and this happens in the EGIA. The new elite sacrifices to the gods and its ancestors, for it was they who took care of the established order of society and the world. The rituals are, however, more varied than before, as both public and private sacrifices and self-securing rites are performed. In the LGIA the whole business seems to stop: neither graves nor votive hoards show anything more than the slightest material trace of a social elite, perhaps because the social, political and economic situation was relatively stable.

The changes indicated in the ritual use of valuable objects throughout the Iron Age may thus show that the rituals played an active role in the processes of social and economic change; they were not simply a passive reflection of them. It further appears that investment in grave furnishing is a particular element in the establishment and legitimization of the elite, which now communicates with the gods and ancestors on behalf of the community. And finally, when all symbolical practices which involve the destruction of valuables cease, this is perhaps to be viewed as an expression of a stable social and political system.

With regard to Bloch's theory, in this way the actively legitimizing function of the rituals with regard to new positions of status is confirmed. The rituals appear, however, in Bloch's terms also to function conservatively, as they are first institutionalized and subsequently obstruct further social change. They form a barrier that can be crossed if a difference between personal status and ritually defined status is introduced. In connection with the origins of the state (see chapter 3, p. 83) this takes the form of religion becoming an institution and thus no longer an obstacle to political leadership. The gods and man are separated; rituals and sacrifices take on a more institutionalized character. It may be this development which is reflected by the transition from the LRIA to the EGIA. With regard to the general theoretical starting-point, the studies of rituals and ideologies have confirmed the concept of ideology as no set, passive reflection of changes in the economic basis of society, but rather as something taking an active part in the processes of social and political change, in the same way as it can shift from being an active agent in social reproduction to being a passive, ideological institution.

NOTES

1 This study does not comprise *all* artefact classes, but only the largest and the most salient, selected by personal intuition and also on the basis of a more comprehensive set of data investigated.

2 To this can be added a similar wagon from the settlement at Fredbjerg in north-west Jutland. On the basis of stratigraphical evidence this is dated to the first century AD, although the wagon must be somewhat older (Jensen 1980b, p. 212). Doubts have been expressed as to the Celtic origins of the wagons, and it has been suggested instead that the wagon might have been locally made (Jensen 1980b, p. 213). Fragments of a similar wagon may be included in a grave find from Nørre Broby on Fyn, dated to the first century AD (Hedeager and Kristiansen 1985).

3 The earlier dating is attributable to Klindt-Jensen 1953, pp. 54ff., matching Becker's Period IIIa; the late dating is attributable to Müller 1900a and Werner 1952. Becker 1957 dates this to pRIA Period III in the local context.

4 The Fredbjerg wagon was found at the stall end of a building of the first century AD. It is interpreted as a worn-out and abandoned item; there is nothing to indicate that it had been sacrificed (Jensen 1980b, p. 213). The Fredbjerg wagon would have been more than a century old at this point, and thus does not have a place in the picture of deposition of the LpRIA.

5 The gold rings are in fact locally produced, but the gold is imported.

6 For a definition of sheet brooches, Nydam brooches and cruciform brooches, see Hansen 1969, n. 173.

7 Variations in the distribution of Haraldsted and Nydam brooches are not dealt with in this context, as both types are associated with graves (cf. Jensen 1979, figure 4). A number of Haraldsted brooches have also been found recently in Jutland, at Sejlflod (Nielsen 1980).

8 The major weapon deposits include brooches which are not counted in here.

9 The figures for weights have been gleaned from the registers of the National Museum. The corresponding figures given by Geisslinger (1967) are correct when finds with weights given in grammes in the register are concerned, but wrong when Geisslinger gives a weight in grammes for a weight recorded in *lod*.

10 Becker 1956, p. 59 and 1961, pp. 248ff. distinguishes south Jutlandic and mid-Jutlandic groups in the pottery and the bronzes. Becker does not, however, deal with the large cast neckrings, and thus takes up no position on the question of the relationship between this group and the local groups. A dating to Period II is suggested (1961, p. 276), while the local groups are only defined in relation to Period I.

11 John Hines has recently, on the basis of an analysis of the bracteates, put forward a convincing interpretation of finds of bracteates, beads and relief brooches as 'surrogate burials' (Hines 1989a).

3

Social and Political Systems

Theories on the Centralization of Power

Political Centralization and Archaic State Formation

Between the collapse of the clan-based chieftain society of the Bronze Age (Kristiansen 1978b, 1982) and the early state society of the Viking Age which was consolidated in the Middle Ages we find those changes which mark the transition from tribal society to state society in northern Europe. The transition from what we recognize as primitive society to civilization has naturally been the subject of extensive anthropological theorizing and modelling, especially among neo-evolutionists and cultural materialists. I shall now give a short overview of the most relevant theories concerning the origin of the state.

The definitive characteristics of early state structure fall into two main groups, one based on stratification and the other on the structure of power itself (Cohen 1978; Cohen and Service, eds, 1978; Haas 1982). In definitions based upon stratification it is the connection between state formation and the establishment of permanent social classes that is particularly emphasized. Marx and Engels are the pre-eminent representatives of this, and they are followed by a large group of Marxist or Marxist-inspired anthropologists. For them, the state is the result of class formation, in which particular groups in the community come into a position to maintain control over privileges won. Fried remodels this definition around the question of fundamentally unequal access to basic resources for groups or individuals (Fried 1960, 1967).

In definitions based upon the structure of power, however, the state is seen as a centralized and hierarchical system of relationships of authority, in which local polities have lost autonomy and local leaders are subordinated to a central one. This conception of the state can be traced to, for instance, Morgan 1877 and Spencer 1897. Service applies this definition, but adds to it one further characteristic: monopolization of the physical exercise of power (Service 1975, 1978).

These two views of the characteristic features of state formation are not incompatible; they are, simply, two different expressions of what the *definitive* features are. But beyond the very general formulation which resides in these definitions it is very difficult to find common ground in the definitions of the term 'state'. Recognizing the somewhat fluid transitions between societies which find themselves in the process of political centralization, some have also chosen to use terms such as 'proto-state' – in contrast to 'state' – in order to emphasize the polysemy of the term 'state' (Cohen 1978, p. 4), and further to divide the early state (the proto-state) into three types: the rudimentary type, the typical type and a transitional form (Claessen 1978, p. 589).

The rudimentary type of early state is defined by a dominance of kinship relations and familial ties in political life, the limited existence of permanent specialists, *ad hoc* forms of taxation and social oppositions which are modulated by reciprocity and direct contact between ruler and population.

In the typical early state the principle of inheritance within the kinship groups is modified by competition and selection, by which individuals outside kinship groups play a leading role as officials and servants of government administration and in which redistribution and reciprocity dominate the relationships between the social strata.

In the phase of transition of the early state, the administrative apparatus is dominated by selected servants, and kinship relations have come to play only a marginal role in the leadership of the country. The preconditions for the appearance of private property rights over the means of production, market economy and open class rivalry are present in the community.

Although this classification looks reasonable, it inevitably contains fluid distinctions, such as in the case of heritable service rather than selection, and on the question of the definition of permanent specialists, taxation systems etc. (Claessen 1978, p. 589).

The many theoretical works which treat of the process of state formation can also be divided into two major groups, one laying primary stress on conflict, the other on integration (Service 1978, pp. 21ff.).

Conflict theories are of three different types: one, in which the conflict between individuals is attributed decisive significance; another in which it is the conflict between different communities which is stressed; and a third which focuses on the conflict between classes or groups within the individual community. The Marxist understanding of the significance of class conflict in state formation is the most important of these conflict theories. Under this, the state is understood to be a repressive apparatus whose role is to secure the interests of the elite, which includes control of the means of production (Engels 1891, 4th edn). After the time of Marx and Engels this theory has been applied, re-formed and developed (*inter alia* Herrmann 1982 on an equation of military democracy with the German mode of production). The stratification of kinship groups proves to be fundamental in the works of Fried (among others) as he stresses the prime significance of the unequal access of different lineages to strategic resources and the conflicts which result. The extent of the latter cannot be controlled by a kinship-based community, and the result is that repressive mechanisms emerge external to the clan structure (Fried 1960, 1967).

The integration theories can be divided into two main groups. One of these places greatest weight upon integration conditioned by exterior circumstances (e.g. different forms of barriers) and the other upon internal organizational characteristics (e.g. major public works).

As an example of an integration theory in which exterior circumstances condition development we may take the classic works – as they have turned out to be – of Carniero (Carniero 1970; for a critical commentary see Webster 1975). His theory is based upon the effect of an excess of population which cannot move away because of geographical factors (mountains or desert). The crisis, or struggle for resources, which results leads to war and conflicts of more permanent character in which the weaker groups are subordinated to the stronger. Subsequently the repressive state, with different economic classes, can develop.

Within integration theories in which stress is placed upon the significance of internal organizational features, redistribution and the organization of public works are to the fore as two important factors in early state formation. In the redistributive system, long-distance

86   SOCIAL AND POLITICAL SYSTEMS

trade is attributed critical importance, as this conditions the development of a bureaucracy for controlling the redistribution of goods and
services (e.g. Polanyi 1968). On the importance of the organizational
effect of public works, Wittfogel's theory of the development of a
state apparatus on the basis of bureaucratic control of water-supply
systems is generally familiar (Wittfogel 1957).

There are theories without number in which the process of state
formation is explained as the result of, *inter alia*, population pressure,
war, long-distance trade, geographical circumstances, conquest,
defence, bureaucracy or internal conflicts. A closer analysis of both
theories and data indicates that none of these factors is sufficient in
itself; indeed not once does any one of them necessarily precede
state formation (Cohen 1978, p. 70).

We must rather conceive of state formation as a systemic process,
whose preconditions usually vary from community to community,
even though the result of the process of centralization has so many
uniform traits. The fundamental weakness in most explanatory
models is that the development of the state is not perceived as
an historical process but in terms of some static entity which can
first be defined only when it has taken place. Alternatively, then,
the process of state formation can be illuminated by looking at
the following *necessary* and *sufficient* conditions (Runciman 1982,
p. 361): (1) specialization of leadership; (2) centralization of power;
(3) permanence of structure, or at least a certain measure of stability;
and (4) liberation from a real or fictive kinship structure as the basis
of the hierarchy of power.

All four of these essentials concern the social organization of the
community and thus, also, the structure of power. Three, and only
three, forms of power can be distinguished, and these will always
enter into different combinations with one another (Runciman 1982,
p. 361): (1) possession of or control over the sources and distribution
of wealth and therewith the ability to offer or withhold the means
of subsistence; (2) attribution by subjects and/or fellow-citizens of
superior honour or prestige, whether derived from sacred or secular
personal or institutional charisma, and therewith the ability to attract
and retain a following; (3) command of the technical and organizational means of physical coercion and therewith the ability to
impose obedience by force. A combination of these three forms of
power is the precondition of our being able to speak of a process of
state formation: that is to say *power must combine economic productivity with ideological legitimization and military organization.*

None of the three factors listed is adequate on its own to produce a centralized community with the character of a state.

It has to be emphasized at the same time that we are dealing here with an historical process in which transitional forms are to be expected, with these elements under development (in early or archaic states: see the discussion of Claessen and Skalnik 1978; Herrmann 1982; Kristiansen 1991). It is precisely the strength of archaeology that, unlike anthropology, it allows the documentation and explanation of state formation as an historical process.

As has already been stressed, political power, ideology, exchange and social organization are not autonomous institutions in pre-state societies. It is only in capitalist societies that the difference between functions falls together with the difference between institutions – in which economy, politics, religion, kinship, art and so on are separated (Godelier 1978, p. 765). The liberation and institutionalization of these functions characterize the transition from tribal to state society, a process which, as has been stated, is believed to have begun in the course of the Iron Age.

It also follows from this that in tribal society, that is, in a chiefdom, both production and reproduction are organized through kinship groups (or conversely that kinship groups are defined by production and exchange relationships). Control is rooted in the kinship structure, which has not yet been transformed into a class structure that permits an upper class to withdraw itself from the traditional kinship duties; it is this development which defines entirely new relationships of power and thus new conditions for social life with regard to inequality and the capacity to resist exploitation (Kristiansen 1991).

Prestige Goods Systems

The transition between tribal society and early state structure is, therefore, fluid, and it is only when the four conditions listed above are fulfilled that the term 'state' ('archaic state', 'early state', 'proto-state') can be employed.

Within the tribal structure, both exploitation and hierarchy can extend to considerable dimensions, which can also include certain forms of tribute. Through an historical process of change, traditional rights are broken down and the path is cleared for re-organization in a more permanent state structure. A continuous sequence is thus involved in which the state represents a formalization of hierarchy and exploitation, which makes the process, if not irreversible, at least realistically beyond the point of return to a tribal structure (Kristiansen 1991).

The new powerful elite of the state structure is supported by ideological legitimization coupled with economic and military control. One of the ways in which the tribal structure can be dissolved and a new elite can establish itself outside the traditional bounds of kinship relations is through the use of prestige goods. In this 'prestige goods system', as it is defined by Ekholm, Friedman and Rowlands, prestige goods are the basic economic operator (Friedman and Rowlands 1977; Ekholm 1972, 1977; Terray 1975, 1977).

By 'prestige goods' is understood objects which are not necessary for continued existence but which are essential in order to maintain the social and political organization of the community by means of payments, such as dowries and political 'gifts', for certain religious or medical activities, consecration rituals, fines, at funerals and so on. Control of prestige goods thus also means control of social reproduction.

The development of a prestige goods system based upon monopoly and upon control over foreign luxury goods requires a system of alliance which replaces, or complements, previous control based upon kinship relations. Monopolization of prestige goods is thus a new form of control which is different from the traditional ritual-economic form in which prestige goods functioned solely as luxury and ceremonial objects and thus were only in circulation among the elite. In that system their primary role was to confirm the status of the leaders and their close connection with the divine (Friedman and Rowlands 1977). In contrast, under the prestige goods system, luxury items take their place in a mechanism for the redistribution of goods and services between the leader and his allies. Here the prestige goods are used to create dependency and alliances, for instance when they are exchanged for women through dowry, or for slaves (that is for people who have lost their connection with a kindred through transferral from their own group to a new one, namely that which pays and that which they have come under obligation to); both forms thus provide the opportunity for control over several people, in other words, over several producers.

The basic significance of prestige goods in the establishment of the new political system is also a development of the representation of a new ideology by these foreign and exotic goods. The monopoly of the elite has to be ideologically anchored and grounded in religion in order for it to be possible to create that legitimization of the elite which is necessary during the splitting up of the tribal structure and the establishment of a new, economically based elite.

The economic foundation for the prestige goods system is always local production, but supplemented with those extra elements which the system provides in the form, for example, of women and slaves/thralls (labour). The matrilineal character of this system will often encourage a tendency to send sons out from the leading groups to found new settlements and cultivate new land: 'Matrilinearity, with its elaborate alliance network and with its relatively autonomous local groups, is an expansionist form of organization that continually demands external areas from which to attract producers' (Ekholm 1977, p. 125). The prestige goods system is strongly expansive in character, and its existence is also dependent upon the scope for expansion and for intensification in basic reproduction. This is how the continually growing demand for surplus is met. But a continually growing surplus is not secured through the colonization and culti-vation of new land alone, but rather, and more than anything else, through war, conflict and conquest. A prestige goods system is thus unstable, characterized by conflicts and continual change.

It is also, naturally enough, dependent upon the importation of foreign luxury items. If the monopoly is broken, the imports can fail; and if it becomes no longer possible to achieve the necessary surplus it is rarely possible to maintain political control. The prestige goods system, with its hierarchical construction, with competing centres and subcentres (see e.g. Frankenstein and Rowlands 1978; Hedeager 1978a, c, 1980), is therefore also unstable in this respect.

The great consumption of foreign luxuries which inheres in this social form is concurrently strongly personalized. Prestige goods were personal: they could not be bought but had to be obtained through personal relationships and connections, either when the elite received them from far away or when the elite undertook their local redistribution. These personally associated prestige goods were of significance as long as the phase of establishment was in process, but if the new development culminated in greater permanency of social division they lost their symbolical significance and thus their innovative character. The legitimization and consolidation of the elite brought with it scope for the changing of rituals and their direction away from specific personal associations.

Prestige goods systems, one could say, exist in the transition from tribal society to early states, and this situation can contain elements of either part. Because of its very expansive character and its vulnerability to failures of supply this situation must necessarily be short-lived; it either leads on to the establishment of a social and political order in the community which is characteristic of the early state structure, or, if the whole prestige goods system is segmented and thus falls apart, back to the tribal structure.

Military Organization

Elite control of military organization plays a decisive role in the establishment of an early state structure. In what follows I shall give an account of the compositional elements which together constitute the *character* of war and conflict (after Turney-High 1949).

The function of weapons The purpose of battle is victory, and victory is won only by attack. Strength in attack lies in the combination of weapons and mobility; by contrast, mobility and defence are ultimately irreconcilable (cf. the trench warfare of the First World War, with locked front lines).

A weapon set comprising a javelin, lance and shield is the most effective combination as it fulfils three functions: a shock effect with a throwing weapon, a hand-held weapon for close combat and a shield for protection. The sword can replace or supplement the lance as a hand-held weapon, but its effectiveness, that is its killing power, is less than that of the lance.

The effectiveness of a weapon is dependent first and foremost upon the way in which it is used rather than upon its type. Effectiveness is not however a question of training and specialization in weapon skills alone; just as important are organization, tactics and co-operation.

Organization Warfare and battle are fundamentally social phenomena, which require leadership, co-operation and organization; weapons are the tools for fighting actual battles.

The capacity of the individual community to wage war or to go into battle is defined by the relationship between the function of the leader and the discipline and co-operation of the warriors. The greater the degree of specialization the greater is the need for organization, leadership and co-operation.

Military organization is grounded in social organization, which in some circumstances can itself be in the process of change – a situation that I will explore in more depth later. The function of leadership in war and the function of leadership in peace may fall together but they do not have to. Permanent military/political leadership can emerge in situations of continual conflict or threat of war, and this can be of decisive significance for the establishment of control by the elite over military organization, for instance through relatively permanent warrior groups or classes.

In 'primitive' war the function of leadership is weak, and hierarchy within the war band is poorly developed. Social pressure from the community and loss of prestige are the only repressive mechanisms acting upon warriors who give up the fight at the wrong time or who do not wish to fight. The 'primitive' warrior fights first and foremost for his own family, and possibly for his village, for his reputation and his prestige.

If, however, the leader can link a group of warriors to himself personally through some oath of allegiance or suchlike, a group which he honours with tribute and gifts (e.g. with 'prestige goods'), the warrior will fight first and foremost for him. The first step is thus taken on the path towards liberation from the kinship structure as the determinative economic, political and military principle.

The highly specialized waging of war thus requires a political and organizational power apparatus whose development reflects ever more centralized political and military organization. Monopolization of the exercise of power, which has been used as the definitive characteristic of state formation in a number of cases (Service 1975, 1978; see also p. 84 above), may thus be regarded as the result of an already developed central political structure with a permanent, specialist warrior group, a bodyguard or retinue, whose shared interest is also the leader's: these form a new warrior aristocracy.

Motive All wars and all battles have a motive. The tribal warrior will fight first and foremost for his own prestige and his clan's, be that through some particularly heroic action or through the winning of valuables which also create prestige when given away. The motive for battle thus hardly passes beyond the reproduction and prestige of the clan or the tribe, and so its military effectiveness is likewise limited.

The motive may, however, also be of more directly economic character: the conquest of new land, for instance, or plundering, slave-raiding and so on. The conquest of settled land requires a major, co-operative military effort, in which the demand for team-work, tactics, planning, co-ordination, leadership etc. is great. The warrior can still function as an individual, but his identification must also comprise some major territorial, and political, entity. The true subordination of a conquered territory with a view to making the population tributary is irreconcilable with a political structure which is based upon kinship alone. Territorial conquest and the subordination of larger groups of people can first be effected when the conquerors have at their disposal a political and military power apparatus which can be introduced to follow up the victory.

However, plundering, pillage, slave-raiding and the extortion of 'payments for peace' do not require the same power apparatus. The profit motive here is 'cash', and the relevant military organization need not comprise anything more than a series of individuals with a leader, possibly organized in some form of war band. Their tactic is surprise attack, their mobility is great, and time, place and circumstance are all the attackers are concerned with.

Opposed to this is the pitched battle in which two groups fight until one has won. Very much greater military organization is required here, and the motive for battle will often be of truly territorial character, although there may be battle over resources other than land: for instance, trade routes, iron-producing areas etc. When the motive is the desire for territorial expansion, the aim of the battle is to conquer, that is to kill or capture as many from the ranks of the enemy as possible. War now becomes terribly bloodthirsty and demands the lives of large numbers. With this, the character of battle changes; it is now far from the athletic, often ritualized armed sports displays of the tribal societies, in which death is the exception. Now a man strikes at the enemy, instead of taking part in a dance.[1]

In addition to the two above-mentioned motives for battle, the economic and the prestige-related, there is the religious motive. Through rituals, dreams, prophecies and so on, the gods can declare that a particular battle is to be undertaken or avoided, that a particular person shall be leader etc. War and military activity will usually be swathed in rituals and surrounded by a whole series of symbols.

Battle creates heroes, and heroes have social status and prestige but do not necessarily have political power. The hierarchy of status and the hierarchy of power are not always the same. Warrior status is a position of prestige, the risk of death being balanced by the hero worship of the community. If the warriors directed their violence inwards against their own community they would lose the prestige which only their own community could give them (Clastres 1977, pp. 217ff.; Knudsen 1982, pp. 62ff.).

A dualism of power of this kind, however it is actually constituted, is the best guarantee that political centralization – and monopolization – will not reach the fullest possible extent. Political/military leadership can, however, take on a permanent character, for instance in situations of constant pressure from external enemies. In such cases, dualism in the function of leadership, which can come to involve a ritual leader in peace and a military leader in war, would be difficult to maintain. Military/political alliances over larger areas can also emerge as a result of the sharing of some external threat, and the result can be larger political entities (Turney-High 1971, p. 232).

The potential of military organization lies, in other words, in the development of a more centralized and powerful leadership structure and of hierarchies of authority and in an incipient specialization in different warrior functions.

The precondition for such a development, however, has to lie in the economy, in the capacity of the leadership to exact tribute and to pay for war gear, ships and so on. In other words the leader must have direct control over basic resources such as land and labour. But when the function of military leadership is made independent of religious power, potential centralization, monopolization and accumulation in the political sector and potential control over the social reproduction of the community have been created. The consequence, however, is completely dependent upon social organization.

Grave Goods and Social Organization

Theoretical and Methodological Framework

The analysis of political and social systems has a starting-point in the grave finds. The preceding chapter has shown that we can assume that at least a certain proportion of the hoard finds are expressions of fixed ritual behaviour. The same holds true for the grave finds, but in a different way. While the ritual deposits (i.e. offerings of valuables) have first and foremost a collective/general purpose – dialogue between the community and the gods – the grave finds have first and foremost a personal one – the individual's or family's dialogue with the gods and with the community without. Thus the grave finds reflect the characteristics of social structure itself very much more extensively than do the hoards. Grave and hoard finds thus complement one another and cannot be understood or explained in isolation.

The analyses which follow are based upon the theory that socially dominant groups, representing the dominant relations of production, will attempt to legitimize their dominance through an ideology for the whole community; this attempt will, among other things, be expressed in symbols, social norms, rules and rituals. As described above (pp. 27ff.), the rituals are not conceived of as a passive reflection of the community but rather as an active factor, which is employed by competing individuals and social groups in order to establish and legitimize their dominance by making communal their principles for the organization of the community. This means that ideology can comprise both opposition and harmony at different levels. This might be found between competing social groups or between different activities in the community: for instance, the application of agricultural production partly to basic reproduction and partly for the establishment of political alliances through feasting, gift exchange and so on. If production, for example, falls below the level required for basic reproduction, this threatens the alliances of the dominant groups which are based upon surplus; stresses then emerge which can eventually lead to a gradual restructuring of the community.

The social, economic and ideological structures thus modify one another in a dynamic interplay of exchange whose driving force lies in the social and politico-ideological structures; but the potential and limits of these structures reside in the economic structure and the ecology.

This dynamic may, among other things, find expression in either the strengthening or the weakening of different sides of the community, according to its complexity and stability. Ideology may reflect, distort or usurp, according to who uses it, and for what. In a study of burials it is therefore an essential task to try to clarify the relationship between social reality and its ideological interpretation.

It is important to note that we have furnished ourselves here with a difficult definition and interpretation of 'reality'. For the Iron-Age population there was certainly no difference between social and ritual/ideological reality. We, however, are attempting to probe back behind the norms and rituals of Iron-Age society as historical anthropologists, to reach something which we regard as 'objective' social and economic reality. By pairing this with its ritual interpretation in the context of burials, we hope to be able to reach a deeper understanding of the effective historical forces and processes.

This presupposes that we are in a position to understand and interpret the original signal sent out by Iron-Age society – or even by parts of it. One way in which we attempt to do this is by setting the finds in the context of history, which includes regional peculiarities in funerary ritual, grave goods and so on. Through comparative analyses the attempt is then made to schematize the variations in order to understand and explain their general background.

In order to avoid false interpretations it is essential to consider several variables so that the results of separate analyses can be set against one another and the interpretations tested. First, however, a systematization of the relevant factors has to be constructed. This is done on the basic premise that the funerary rituals primarily serve some purpose in the living community. The following relationships can be noted (after Pearson 1982, p. 110).

1   The relationship between the living and the dead:

    (a) the delimitation of cemeteries and their placement in relation to settlement (fields, buildings, roads);
    (b) the relationship between the dwellings of the living and the dead; how much is invested by way of material, labour etc.

2   The relationship between different social groups among the living:

    (a) the classification of the dead: what roles and group identities are reflected in the rituals of the living concerning the dead;
    (b) which material symbols (grave furnishings) are given with the dead and why; for example, whether certain social groups are either emphasized or slighted through burial (men/women, adult/child; warrior/farmer/chieftain etc.).

3   The relationship between the living and the past:

    (a) are new monuments built or are old ones used, and how long is there continuity?

(b) continuity or change in the rituals.

The interplay between these factors will frequently be able to reveal crucial points in the relationship between ideology and the social and economic situations. Such points concern variation over time and space and whether the communities involved are stable (characterized by continuity in rituals and eventually by limited investment in ritual symbols), or in flux (with shifting and aggressive displays in burials).

There are two points in particular to be revealed in what follows, namely the question of the distribution of, and control by means of, the wealth of the community, and the question of military organization. The topic of basic production is left to the following chapter.

Is there, then, a new elite establishing itself through the use and control of foreign prestige goods in the Roman Iron Age? What is meant by this in effect is whether it is in this period of the Iron Age, catalysed by prestige goods, that the traditional tribal structure is broken down and a new order of society takes shape – an order of society which contains within itself the first element of early state structure.

Is it, beyond this, possible to illuminate the development of early military/political leadership and thus also the establishment of the retinue? In this connection it will be most relevant to investigate how prestige goods, as the material expressions of status and power, are linked to the weapon-grave milieu. It is further necessary to take account of the significance of the great weapon hoards, which includes the motives of battle and the form of military organization they express.

I shall focus upon two of the archaeological find groups as indicators of 'wealth' and 'power': prestige goods and weapons. But it is also essential to investigate what degree of permanency there is in this structure. How and when, for instance, are there clear shifts in ritual behaviour in connection with burials? And is this linked to clearly defined geographical zones or does it rather cut right across these and define particular social groups?

A total of 9,650 grave finds from the Iron Age has been recorded (figures 1.6–7);[2] their distribution is shown, period by period, in the maps in figures 3.1–5. It is these graves which are the basis for the analyses which follow.

All in all, the burial forms of the Iron Age compose a variegated

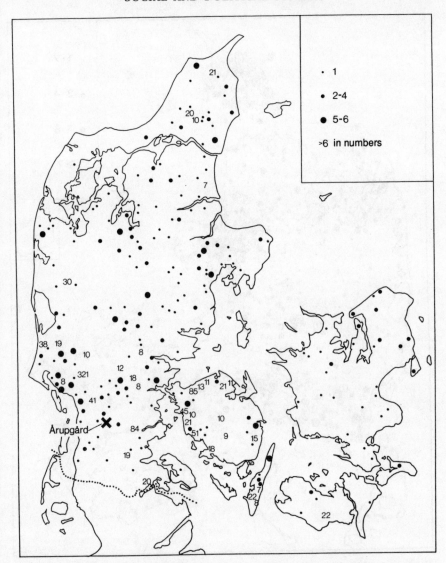

Figure 3.1 The distribution of graves of the pRIA. (The barrow cemetery at
Årupgaard with 1500 graves is only marked on the map, as no publication is yet
available.) The majority of the Jutlandic graves are to be dated pRIA Period I. All
pRIA graves are cremations, and a preponderance of the south Jutlandic graves for
Period I are clustered in barrow cemeteries. The cremation graves of the pRIA
comprise all types: urned graves with or without stone settings, urned cremation
pits and cremation patches. The graves may be clustered into larger cemeteries, in
isolation, or in small groups. There are also secondary burials in barrows.

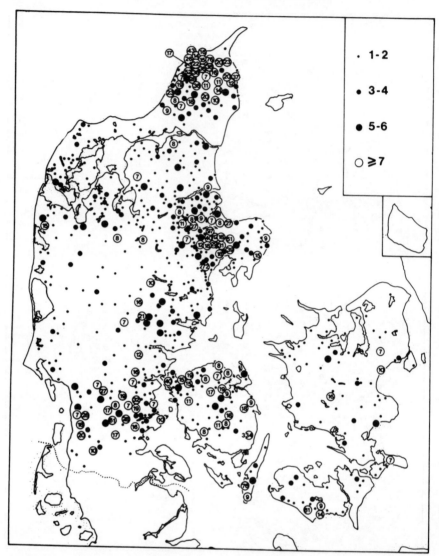

Figure 3.2 The distribution of graves of the ERIA. This is the richest period for finds, and most graves are from Jutland or Fyn. Grave form now includes both cremations and inhumations. Inhumations are dominant on Sjælland and in north and central Jutland while the cremation rite is dominant on Lolland, on Fyn and in southern Jutland. Grave form is now strongly localized in its characteristics. In north and north-west Jutland large stone cists are common (Brøndsted 1966, p. 139; Lysdahl 1971). A special form of flat grave is also known from north Jutland, without a stone structure but originally with a tent-shaped superstructure (Friis 1963). In central and east Jutland large flat-grave cemeteries are common. These

and diverse picture, with local and regional peculiarities. Most striking is the change from the pRIA to the ERIA. Cremation, formerly
the only rite, is displaced by a combination of inhumation and
cremation with marked regional differences. The second striking
change lies at the transition from the LRIA to the EGIA, at which
point the number of graves falls markedly across the whole country.

Grave types and grave construction, however, are not the only
variables in funerary rituals. A wide range of additional features are
found which are not always equally well recorded. Examples of this
are the alignment and depth of inhumation graves, the placement
and alignment of the body, the location of grave goods, age and sex
identification, etc. These data are partially dependent upon the nature
of the archaeological research and partially upon the state of preservation of the skeletons. The optimal quantity of information is
therefore much more frequently obtainable from inhumations than
from cremations.

Common to all recorded graves is the presence of grave goods.
This is thus the only variable whose information value is largely
independent of differences in burial ritual, and so is the one on
which the following analyses are built.[3]

In order to investigate the use of material symbols in the graves two
methods have been applied: qualitative analysis (called combination
analysis here) and quantitative analysis (called NAT-analysis here).

Combination analyses can be applied both to closed grave finds
and to grave finds for which uncertain or missing find information
leaves open the possibility that less than the whole assemblage was
recorded.[4] If one simply studies special combinations it is of course

---

Figure 3.2 continued   graves, the so-called pot graves, have no stone structures,
although individual stones may line the coffin, or the coffin may be covered by a
stone plate. In the southern part of Jutland, where cremations are in the majority,
some deep inhumations are found, both with and without stone packing around
the coffin (Brøndsted 1966, pp. 138ff.). The Jutlandic cremation graves comprise
all types: urned cremations, urned cremation pits and cremation patches. Inhumations and cremations may occur side by side in cemeteries. Cremations are
predominant in southern Jutland, as on Fyn, Langeland and Lolland. They are
frequently clustered in cemeteries where on occasion inhumations may appear as a
minority rite. On Sjælland, where the number of graves is quite low, inhumation
is most common. There may be a few stones around the coffin, and stones may
overlie the coffin. Burials in barrows, both primary and secondary, are known
from Jutland in particular (Brøndsted 1966, p. 138; Hedeager 1985).

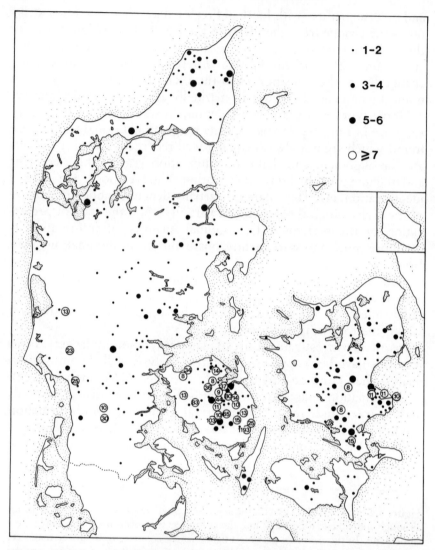

Figure 3.3 The distribution of graves of the LRIA. The majority of the grave finds are now from Fyn and Sjælland, while Jutland, Langeland and Lolland/Falster are weakly represented. In Jutland and on Sjælland, Lolland and Falster inhumation is now quite dominant although there is still some cremation, especially in southern Jutland. On Fyn, however, cremation is still predominant; there are some inhumations, but only a very limited number. In north Jutland there were still burials – or reburials – in stone cists, although not a great number. Otherwise, local traditions live on within the Jutlandic grave types, only in very blurred form. There are scattered primary and secondary burials in barrows (Brøndsted 1966, p. 183; Hedeager 1985).

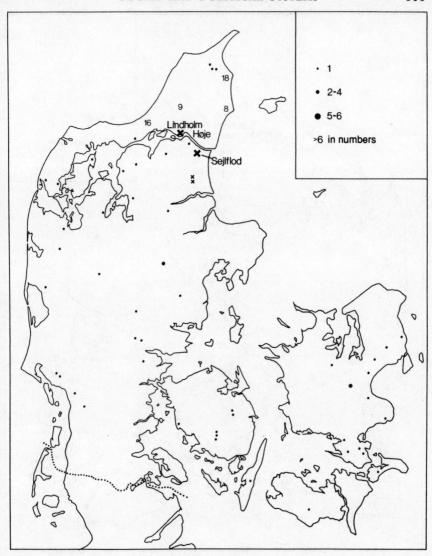

Figure 3.4 The distribution of graves of the EGIA. Most of the grave finds by now are from north Jutland, where cremation dominates, frequently deposited below a small barrow and on occasion surrounded by a rim of stones. The graves may cluster in cemeteries or be dispersed as isolated graves. In the remainder of Jutland and on Fyn both cremations and inhumations are found; on Sjælland, however, only inhumations are found.

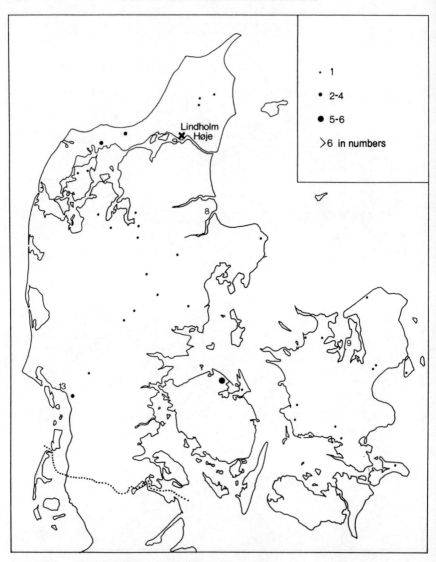

Figure 3.5 The distribution of graves of the LGIA. The relationship between inhumation and cremation on the whole follows the EGIA pattern. In the large cemetery of Lindholm Høje by the Limfjord the first ship monuments are found: stones placed around the graves in the form of a ship. Urned graves are a minority amongst the cremations in both halves of the Germanic Iron Age (Ramskou 1976).

essential to study only definitely closed finds. But if the goal is to clarify general tendencies in combinations the less secure finds should also be included; if one or two items from some finds are missing it is of no consequence as long as these graves are randomly distributed. That can be tested against the closed finds. The combination analyses have the further advantage that particular groupings and combinations can be placed immediately onto distribution maps which reflect local, regional and possibly supra-regional similarities and differences (Hedeager and Kristiansen 1981). Finally, the composition of the grave inventory can be directly compared with that of the hoard finds, which have also been investigated by means of combination analysis.

Quantitative analyses have already been applied to the Roman Iron-Age graves of eastern Denmark (Hedeager 1978b, c, 1980). These require a data set of definitely closed grave finds. The principle is that the number of different artefact types in each grave is counted so that one glass bead, two bronze brooches or three gold rings, for instance, all count as one NAT (NAT = Number of Artefact Types).

The purpose of this method is quite the opposite to that of the combination analyses, that is to eliminate the many local and regional differences in the composition of grave assemblages. It provides a general instrument for measuring wealth and social differentiation in grave furnishing. Further, an objectivity is obtained which is absent, for instance, in a value-based points system under which 'valuable' artefacts are of themselves sufficient to classify a grave as rich.

This method, however, requires well-documented data as only definitely closed finds can be used. Uncertain grave finds could thoroughly distort and falsify the value of NAT measurements. Compared with the combination analyses, therefore, only a small proportion of the grave finds can be used, and this limitation can produce regional biases as the quality of information – and thus certainty in the relevant details – varies directly with archaeological industry (cf. Hedeager 1985).

These two methods thus supplement one another. The combination analysis shows qualitative differentiation in the composition of grave assemblages while NAT analyses show quantitative differentiation. The first method provides a good starting-point for a discussion of the employment of status symbols and the meaning of local and regional traditions, while the NAT method is well suited to the illumination of variation in wealth and social complexity, as, for instance, they are reflected in the quantity of status indicators. This will, of course, be shown more clearly in what follows.

General NAT Analysis

Comparative analyses of grave goods require a certain amount of standardization and quantification. Are valuable objects, for instance, distributed across a broad spectrum of graves or concentrated in a few? Are the weapon graves richly furnished in comparison with other graves? Is the distribution of wealth equal for men and women or can we find gender-determined differences in grave furnishing? Are there geographical and/or chronological differences?

As has been stated, standardization and quantification can be put into effect with the aid of NAT measurements. The number of different artefact types is counted, so that 'fine' artefacts do not define a grave as rich by their own virtue if that grave does not at the same time contain other objects which produce a high NAT value.

Of course this method is very coarse, but it does bring diverse data into a common formula and makes possible the reasoned comparison of cremations with inhumations. The method takes no account of the number of artefacts of the same type, but only of the number of different artefact types (which means, here, artefacts with different functions). In the context of the cremations it can be difficult, if not impossible, to determine whether brooch fragments come from one or more brooches, whether there is one or more glass bead, and so on, and in both cremations and inhumations counting the number of pots is often awkward. With the NAT measurements no differentiation is made between a single sherd and several complete pots, or between one brooch fragment and several complete brooches.

The NAT measurements, which for reasons of clarity are presented in diagrammatic form as histograms, are thus to be interpreted primarily as expressions of difference and similarity in the complexity and composition of grave assemblages.

As we have already noted, find circumstances and, thus, the quality of information are varied, depending on the level of archaeological industry. Large, well-excavated cemeteries contrast with scattered, isolated finds which have come by chance into a museum without any sort of scholarly investigation. An inconspicuous grave with no grave goods, or only a few found by chance, will naturally be less likely to have been recorded archaeologically and to have had its location subsequently investigated than a grave whose contents were richer and therefore more conspicuous. A comparison with well-excavated cemeteries in which all graves have been recorded, even the least impressive and the most poorly furnished ones, shows that the number of scattered, isolated and also poorly furnished graves is under-representative. This observation should then (to some extent) be taken account of in the ultimate evaluation of the NAT scores of individual areas and periods.

In what follows, the NAT histograms for the periods ERIA and LRIA are presented *amt* by *amt* (county by county), although Sjælland (Zealand) is treated as one unit.[5] For the EpRIA, only the individual barrow cemeteries are presented diagrammatically, and for the LpRIA individual rich areas. For both the EGIA and the LGIA the number of closed grave finds is so limited that it provides no basis for the construction of histograms.

The general NAT scores subsequently provide a starting-point for a particular evaluation of graves with Roman imports, gold, weapons and iron knives. The selection of these artefact classes in particular is determined by the consideration that they represent three fundamental, and different, categories of object: foreign prestige objects such as imports and gold (irrespective of whether it were worked locally), weapons and locally produced minor artefacts, such as iron knives, which are personal accessories. The intention is to investigate the relationship between the complexity of the grave assemblages (NAT) and different symbols of status and/or wealth.

The NAT histograms show the complexity of composition in grave assemblages. A high NAT value is not, however, a direct statement of wealth. A grave with an NAT value of 1 could, theoretically, contain three gold rings or three Roman buckets and nothing else. The diagrams nevertheless contain crucial information concerning equal and unequal access to particular objects, which may provide a basis for an interpretation of social structure.

Were access to supposedly valuable objects equal for all the members of the community, imported objects and gold artefacts should be evenly spread through the graves; in other words, they should be most common in the largest NAT groups (that is those with the lowest NAT scores). If, however, the valuable objects are grouped and principally found in the smallest NAT groups (i.e. those with the highest NAT scores) this should indicate a degree of monopolization which emphasizes the prestige value of these objects.

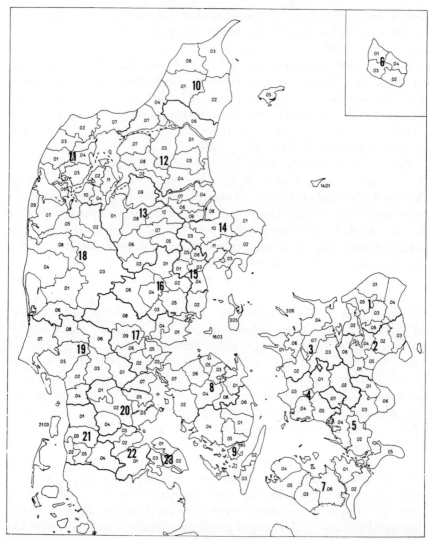

Figure 3.6   Danish county (*amt*) and district (*herred*) numbers.

These hypotheses will be tested through an investigation of the
NAT values of graves with Roman imports and gold.

Specific NAT Analysis

Imports Over the whole country the quantity of graves with
imports rises with the NAT values (figures 3.7–9). The higher the

1. Frederiksborg Amt
1.01 Holbo
1.02 Horns
1.03 Lynge-
Frederiksborg
1.04 Lynge-
Kronborg
1.05 Strø
1.06 Ølstykke

2. Københavns Amt
2.01 Ramsø
2.02 Smørum
2.03 Sokkelund
2.04 Sømme
2.05 Tune
2.06 Volborg

3. Holbæk Amt
3.01 Ars
3.02 Løve
3.03 Merløse
3.04 Ods
3.05 Samsø
3.06 Skippinge
3.07 Tuse

4. Sorø Amt
4.01 Alsted
4.02 Ringsted
4.03 Slagelse
4.04 V.-Flakkebjerg
4.05 Ø.-Flakkebjerg

5. Præstø Amt
5.01 Bjæverskov
5.02 Bårse
5.03 Fakse
5.04 Hammer
5.05 Mønbo
5.06 Stevns
5.07 Tybjerg

6. Bornholms Amt
6.01 Bornh.s Nørre
6.02 Bornh.s Sønder
6.03 Bornh.s Vester
6.04 Bornh.s Øster

7. Maribo Amt
7.01 Falsters Nørre
7.02 Falsters Sønder
7.03 Fuglse
7.04 Lollands Nørre
7.05 Lollands Sdr.
7.06 Musse

8. Odense Amt
8.01 Bjerge
8.02 Båg
8.03 Lunde
8.04 Odense
8.05 Skam
8.06 Skovby
8.07 Vends
8.08 Asum

9. Svendborg Amt
9.01 Gudme
9.02 Langelands Nr.
9.03 Langelands
Sdr.
9.04 Sallinge
9.05 Sunds
9.06 Vindinge
9.07 Ærø

10. Hjørring Amt
10.01 Børglum
10.02 Dronninglund
10.03 Horns
10.04 Hvetbo
10.05 Læsø
10.06 Vennebjerg
10.07 Øster-Han

11. Thisted Amt
11.01 Hassing
11.02 Hillerslev
11.03 Hundborg
11.04 Morsø Nørre
11.05 Morsø Sønder
11.06 Refs
11.07 Vester-Han

12. Ålborg Amt
12.01 Fleskum
12.02 Gislum
12.03 Hellum
12.04 Hindsted
12.05 Hornum
12.06 Kær
12.07 Slet
12.08 Ars

13. Viborg Amt
13.01 Fjends
13.02 Harre
13.03 Hids
13.04 Hindborg
13.05 Houlbjerg
13.06 Lysgård
13.07 Middelsom
13.08 Nørlyng
13.09 Rinds
13.10 Rødding
13.11 Salling Nørre
13.12 Sønderlyng

14. Randers Amt
14.01 Djurs Nørre
14.02 Djurs Sønder
14.03 Galten
14.04 Gjerlev
14.05 Mols
14.06 Nørhald
14.07 Onsild
14.08 Rougsø
14.09 Støvring
14.10 Sønderhald
14.11 Øster-Lisbjerg

15. Århus Amt
15.01 Framlev
15.02 Hads
15.03 Hasle
15.04 Ning
15.05 Sabro
15.06 V.-Lisbjerg

16. Skanderborg Amt
16.01 Gjern
16.02 Hjelmslev
16.03 Nim
16.04 Tyrsting
16.05 Voer
16.06 Vrads

17. Vejle Amt
17.01 Bjerre
17.02 Brusk
17.03 Elbo

17.04 Hatting
17.05 Holmans
17.06 Jerlev
17.07 N.-Tyrstrup
17.08 Nørvang
17.09 Tørrild

18. Ringkøbing Amt
18.01 Bølling
18.02 Ginding
18.03 Hammerum
18.04 Hind
18.05 Hjerm
18.06 Nørre-Horne
18.07 Skodborg
18.08 Ulfborg
18.09 Vandfuld

19. Ribe Amt
19.01 Anst
19.02 Gørding
19.03 Malt
19.04 Ribe
19.05 Skast
19.06 Slavs
19.07 Vester-Horne
19.08 Øster-Horne

20. Haderslev Amt
20.01 Frøs
20.02 Gram
20.03 Haderslev
20.04 N.-Rangstrup
20.05 S.-Tyrstrup

21. Tønder Amt
21.01 Hviding
21.02 Højer
21.03 Lø
21.04 Slogs
21.05 Tønder

22. Åbenrå Amt
22.01 Lundtoft
22.02 Rise
22.03 S.-Rangstrup

23. Sønderborg Amt
23.01 Als Nørre
23.02 Als Sønder
23.03 Nybøl

Figure 3.6   continued

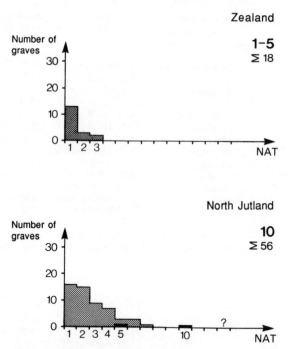

Figure 3.7 Grave finds with Roman imports marked on the NAT histograms for Sjælland (1–5) and north Jutland (10) of the LpRIA.

NAT value, the fewer the grave finds but the greater the quantity of imports. The NAT histograms also show that high NAT values can be found without imports; imports are thus not an absolute precondition for high NAT values.

The number of graves with imports and the percentage of the number of graves they comprise is greater in the LRIA than the ERIA (figures 3.10–11), and graves with imports with low NAT scores are more frequent in the LRIA than in the ERIA. Compared with the LpRIA, the number of recorded closed graves with imports is 152 (LRIA) and forty (ERIA), but only between seven and eleven for the LpRIA. There are none in the EGIA and LGIA.

The geographical centre of distribution of imports shifts from period to period. In the LpRIA the graves with imports are dispersed; however, the cemetery of Langå in Svendborg *amt* is the richest. In the ERIA the centre of gravity lies on Lolland and on

Figure 3.8 Grave finds with imports (Roman bronzes and glass) marked on the NAT histograms for the ERIA.

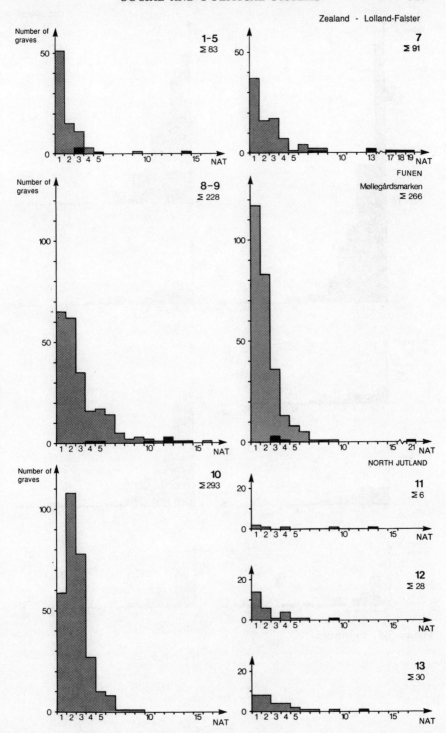

Zealand - Lolland-Falster

FUNEN

Møllegårdsmarken

NORTH JUTLAND

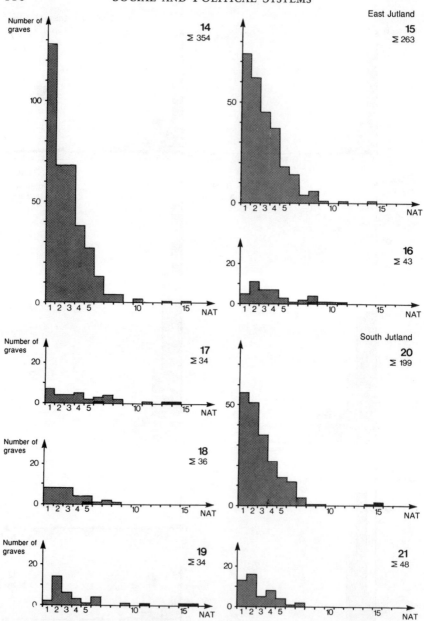

Figure 3.8   continued

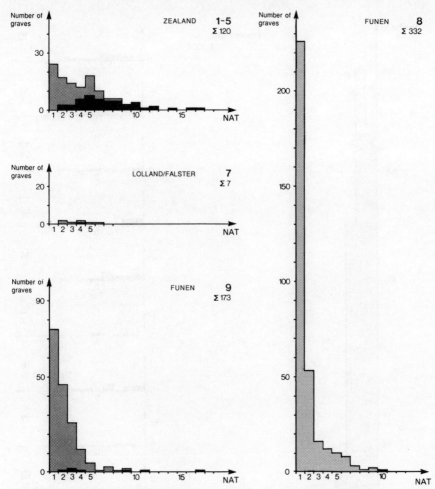

Figure 3.9 Grave finds with imports (Roman bronzes and glass) marked on the NAT histograms for the LRIA.

Fyn. The Møllegårdsmarken cemetery has a limited number of graves with imports. In the LRIA the centre of gravity has shifted to Sjælland, and a concentration emerges in Svendborg *amt* on Fyn, where Møllegårdsmarken is well represented. In the whole of Jutland a distinct decrease in the number of graves with imports can be seen from the ERIA to the LRIA. In the ERIA, imports are especially concentrated in the southern and south-eastern part of Jutland, but in the LRIA imports have almost completely disappeared.

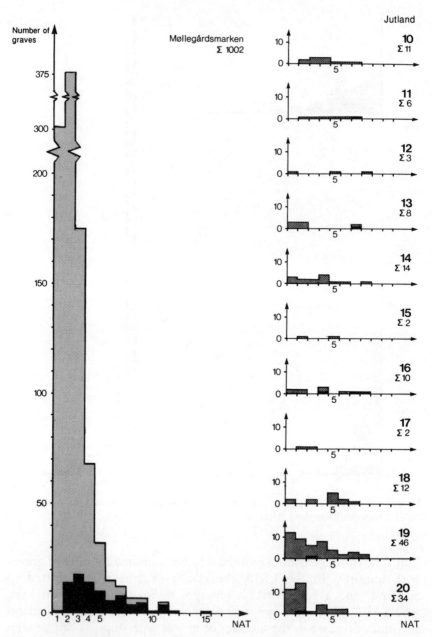

Figure 3.9   continued

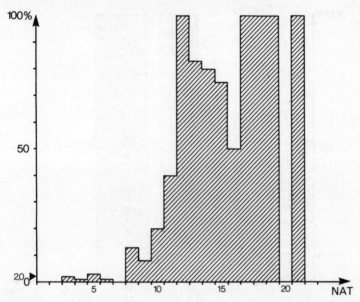

Figure 3.10 Grave finds with imports, calculated as a percentage of all closed graves for each NAT value. Two per cent of the closed graves of the ERIA have imports (i.e. 40 out of 2,001 graves).

Gold In the ERIA and LRIA a general correlation between high NAT scores and the presence of gold in the graves can be seen. The number of graves with gold is quite steady; sixty-eight of the ERIA and fifty-five of the LRIA. In both periods they comprise about 3 per cent of all closed grave finds (figures 3.12–13).

When the percentage of graves with gold and graves with imports is compared with the numbers of graves, the following points can be observed.

1 With higher NAT scores, more graves contain gold and imports, though certain chronological shifts can be discerned.
2 Graves with imports are less strongly represented in the ERIA than graves with gold, a situation which is reversed in the LRIA; in other words, graves with gold are more common in the ERIA, as are graves with imports in the LRIA.
3 In the ERIA, gold is better represented than imports among the lower NAT values, but the opposite is the case in the LRIA.

Beyond the general tendency for the number of graves with gold and imports to remain proportional to the NAT scores, it can also be seen that the more gold or imports there are, the more these are

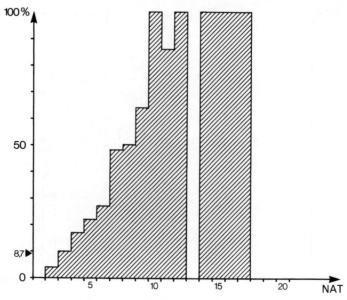

Figure 3.11 Graves with imports, calculated as a percentage of all closed graves for each NAT value. Nine per cent of the closed graves of the LRIA have imports (i.e. 152 out of 1,750 graves).

distributed down to the lower NAT scores. This applies to gold in the ERIA and to imports in the LRIA. These, in effect, swap places between the ERIA and the LRIA.

The distribution of gold contains major geographical variations. In the ERIA, the greatest concentration is found on Lolland and on Fyn. In the LRIA, the centre of gravity has moved over to Sjælland, while at the same time there is a marked decline in the number of graves with gold from the ERIA to the LRIA in the rest of the country.

Taken together with the geographical distribution, there is always one general relationship to be seen: that is that those areas which are rich in imports are also rich in gold. This observation holds for the LpRIA, the ERIA and the LRIA. In the LRIA, however, Fyn is an exception, as here imports are much more frequent than gold, and so to, to a degree, is Jutland, where the graves with gold are more common than the graves with imports.

The geographical centre of gravity thus shifts from period to period. Fyn, especially Svendborg *amt*, has a special position, as

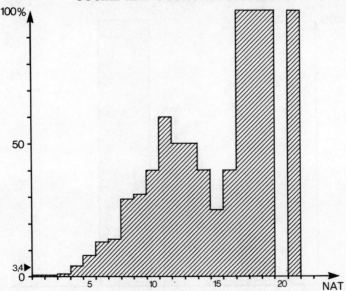

Figure 3.12 Graves with gold, calculated as a percentage of all closed graves of the ERIA for each NAT value. Three per cent of the closed graves of the ERIA contain gold (i.e. 68 out of 2,001 graves).

graves with imports dominate right through the LpRIA, the ERIA and the LRIA. Gold, however, is giving ground in the LRIA.

Weapons and spurs Weapon graves first appear in the LpRIA in Jutland and on Fyn, especially in Hjorring and Svendborg *amts*. Generally they lie among the graves with the highest NAT values, but can also be found among the lower values.

In the ERIA, the number of weapon graves climbs markedly, and now such graves are known over the whole country. They comprise about 7 per cent of all graves (figure 3.14). Geographically the centres of distribution are found in Svendborg, Randers and Haderslev *amts*. In the *amts* of southern Jutland the richest graves are weapon graves; however, weapons are not found in such graves in the rest of the country. Thus it is only in a particular area that there is a correlation between graves with high NAT scores and the presence of weapons. Areas with *many* weapon graves thus do not necessarily have *rich* weapon graves.

In the ERIA, the number of weapon graves declines quite markedly to form just 2 per cent of the whole corpus of grave finds

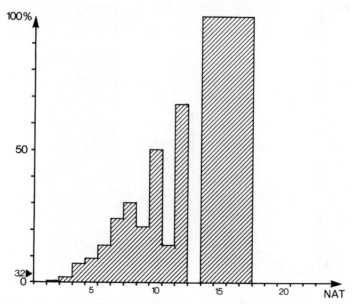

Figure 3.13   Graves with gold, calculated as a percentage of all closed graves of the LRIA for each NAT value. Three per cent of the closed graves of the LRIA contain gold (i.e. 55 out of 1,750 graves).

(figure 3.15). Weapon graves are known from the whole country, and regional differences have disappeared.

Weapon graves are quite unknown in the EGIA and LGIA.

Iron knives   Iron knives are one of the most common grave goods. They first appear in graves of the LpRIA, and have their greatest distribution in the ERIA, but are missing in graves of the EGIA and LGIA. Two points to be noted with reference to iron knives are (1) that in areas where they are common they are found across the range of NAT scores and their numbers are regularly proportional to the number of graves, and (2) that graves with high NAT values on Sjælland and Lolland/Falster lack iron knives.

About 52 per cent of all closed graves of the ERIA contain iron knives; in the LRIA only about 12 per cent (figures 3.16–17). The lowest NAT categories are well represented in the ERIA and knives are not found among the very highest NAT values. In the LRIA a tendency is visible towards a correlation of higher NAT scores with a greater representation of iron knives, but here too the better furnished graves often lack knives.

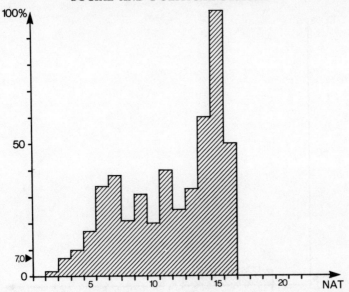

Figure 3.14 Grave finds with weapons, calculated as a percentage of all closed graves for each NAT value in the ERIA. Seven per cent of the closed grave finds contain weapons and/or spurs (i.e. 139 out of 2,001 graves).

The distribution of iron knives can thus be interpreted as 'random', as they follow the course of the NAT histogram. The same holds for other more humble artefact classes, such as locally produced small artefacts (e.g. combs, awls, spindle-whorls, pottery etc.) and various forms of dress accessories and jewels (e.g. belt buckles, simple pins, vitreous or clay beads etc.).

NAT: Power and Wealth

On the strength of the analyses above, certain general tendencies can be noted. Unsurprisingly, imports and gold are particularly linked to the better furnished graves, those with the highest NAT scores. This is only partially the case for weapons and certainly not the case with iron knives and other locally produced artefacts. We can conclude that the composition of grave assemblages is the result of selectivity. The question then is: what does this selectivity reflect?

The NAT measurements are, as I have said, a fictive scale of value, which does not show the real quantity of 'luxury goods' (imports and gold) in the individual graves. It is, however, possible to show a correlation between the NAT scores and the actual quantity of

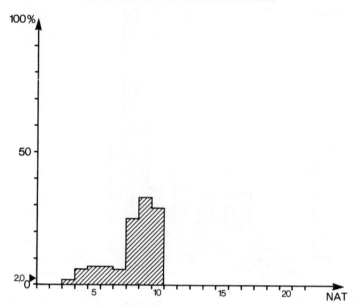

Figure 3.15 Grave finds with weapons, calculated as a percentage of all closed graves for each NAT value in the LRIA. Two per cent of the closed grave finds contain weapons (i.e. 34 out of 1,750 graves).

luxury goods per grave (figure 3.18) (Hedeager 1978a, p. 352; 1980, pp. 50f.). Graves with high NAT values thus have a large number of luxury goods, while graves with low NAT values have a correspondingly lower quantity of the same goods. When a grave with a high NAT value, for example, contains gold rings and imported bronze, it contains more objects than a grave with a lower NAT value. A quantity of certain things thus implies a matching quantity of other things (luxury objects). Iron knives, bone combs and other common utilitarian objects, however, do not follow this pattern; they are found rather only as single examples, or in very small numbers, in each grave, irrespective of its wealth. In the richest graves, however, iron knives are frequently supplanted by bronze knives. Figure 3.18 may thus be interpreted as a real expression of wealth, quantitatively rather than qualitatively (for which one example of any particular thing would be sufficient). It is not satisfactory simply to symbolize wealth; it has to be demonstrated, in the simplest semiotic manner. Furthermore, the quantity of luxury objects is regularly proportional to the NAT values, even if the imports are excepted.

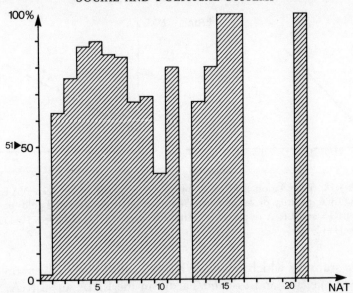

Figure 3.16 Grave finds with iron knives, calculated as a percentage of all closed graves for each NAT value in the ERIA. Fifty-two per cent of the closed graves contain iron knives (i.e. 1,034 out of 2,001 graves).

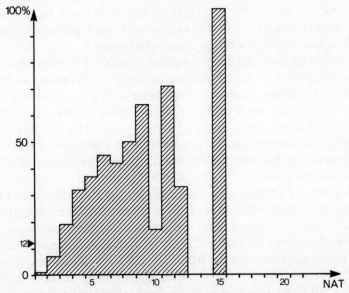

Figure 3.17 Grave finds with iron knives, calculated as a percentage of all closed graves for each NAT value in the LRIA. Twelve per cent of the closed graves contain iron knives (i.e. 215 out of 1,750 graves).

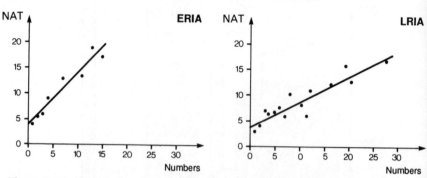

Figure 3.18 Correlation diagram showing the relationship between NAT scores and the total quantity of 'luxury items' (Roman imports, silver and gold) per grave in the ERIA and LRIA respectively. (after Hedeager 1978a, c, figures 10–11; 1980, figures 11–12)

The study to which reference has been made here covers only the areas of Sjælland and Lolland/Falster in the ERIA and LRIA, but a parallel correlation between high NAT scores and many luxury objects is repeated over the whole country. In areas where only one or very few graves with imports or gold have been found, it is not necessary for these graves also to be highest placed according to NAT values, although more often than not they will be. By contrast such graves with low NAT values never contain more than one single imported item or one single gold ring.

The distribution of luxury objects in the NAT histograms can also reveal something of the conditions required for obtaining such items. It has been shown that the more imports or gold there was overall in the graves, the more graves with low NAT scores got some share of these: that is, luxury goods 'move down'. The greatest absolute quantity of luxury goods, however, is consistently found in the graves with the highest NAT scores. This pattern contrasts with that of the locally produced material, which is found evenly distributed in all graves. *Therefore, the accumulation and distribution of luxury objects was controlled.* Those who controlled the collection and distribution (the highest NAT values) could accumulate to an almost unlimited degree; the more this group had at its disposal, the more they could distribute to the lower groups. This correlation between NAT and wealth also means that the number of different grave goods (NAT) to a certain extent reflects the number of positions of status among the deceased. The more one had, the greater the status, power and wealth one could mobilize.

It is also worth noting that Roman products are never copied locally, unlike the situation found in the Bronze Age (Thrane 1975, figures 131–2). This shows that the status value of these items lay principally in their foreign origin. The elite may also, as well as monopolizing long-distance trade and distribution, have controlled local craft production and prevented imitations.

The control over long-distance trade and distribution by the elite makes it unlikely that any form of 'free' market trade existed. If there were equal access for all to buy and sell, one would expect a much more extensive distribution of luxury objects. It would then have been possible to 'save up for' one prestigious silver dish, for example. But such a dish never turns up alone in a simple grave group. It will only be found together with a series of other luxury objects. These questions, however, are taken up again later.

Combination Analysis: Weapons and Other Items

Through combination analysis, various groups can be placed straight onto a distribution map which reflects local, regional and in some cases supra-regional similarities and differences in grave goods. In contrast to the NAT analyses, the combination analyses include all graves, not only the definitely closed finds, although closedness naturally has an effect when particular combinations come to be assessed. In this way possible regional biases, reflecting differences in the intensity of excavation, are eliminated.

It is of course of primary interest to look at those groups of artefacts which have already been investigated by means of NAT analyses.

Weapon graves The sword, shield, javelin, lance and occasionally the axe and arrowheads belong to the weapon set. Spurs, which may also find a place in the warrior's equipment, will be dealt with separately. The distribution of weapon graves in the LpRIA, ERIA and LRIA is shown in figures 3.19–21.[6]

In respect of combinations of weapons,[7] the contents of weapon graves vary greatly, from a full set with sword, shield, javelin and lance to just one single weapon or a shield alone. Graves with a full weapon set, in all periods, comprise only 10 to 15 per cent of all weapon graves.

There are ten such weapon graves in all from the LpRIA (figure 3.22). These lie in the south and southern Jutlandic areas, on eastern

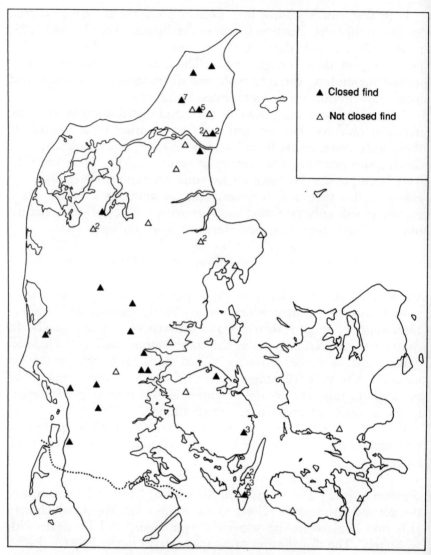

Figure 3.19   The distribution of weapon graves in the LpRIA.

Fyn and on Langeland. In the ERIA, graves with full weapon sets are particularly found in southern Jutland and south-east Jutland, scattered on Fyn, Langeland, Lolland and in the western part of the Limfjord area (figure 3.23). A total of twenty-four graves with full weapon sets are known from this period. From the LRIA only six graves are known, of which four are from Fyn (figure 3.24).

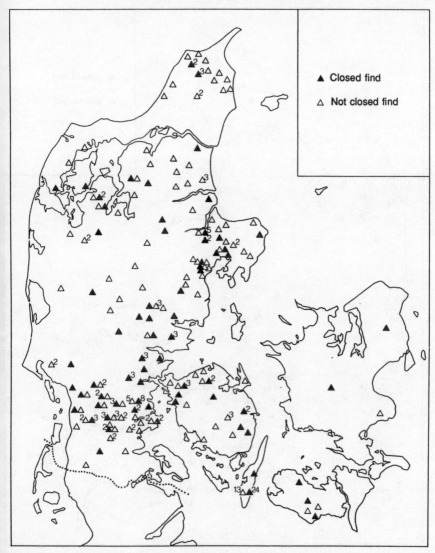

Figure 3.20   The distribution of weapon graves in the ERIA.

The combinations of weapons in all closed graves from the three periods may be classified according to the groups shown in table 3.1. This table shows that combination II is the most common in the LpRIA and ERIA but that III is the leading combination in the LRIA. The full weapon set (I) is the most weakly represented in all three periods.

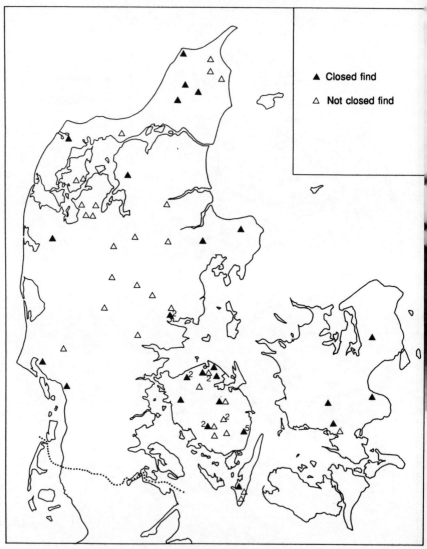

Figure 3.21 The distribution of weapon graves in the LRIA.

The information in italics on table 3.1 shows further the sub-division of the weapon sets in groups II and III. From this we can see that in group II the combination of sword with javelin and/or lance is the most common in the LpRIA and that of shield with javelin and/or lance in the ERIA and LRIA. In group III swords

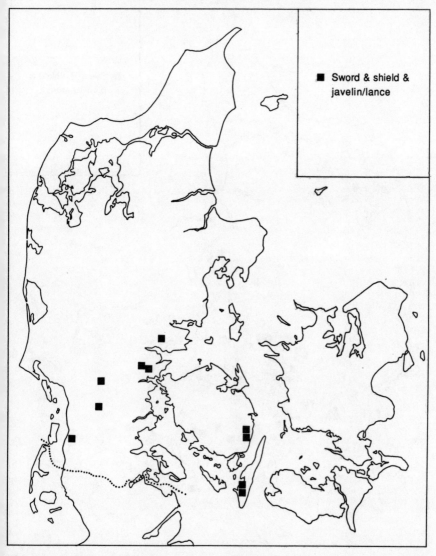

Figure 3.22 The distribution of weapon graves with full weapon sets (sword, shield, javelin/lance) in the LpRIA.

and javelins and/or lances have an equal place in the LpRIA, while shields dominate in the other periods. The most frequent of all weapon groups is the combination of shield with javelin and/or lance in the ERIA.

We can, then, draw the following conclusions on the composition

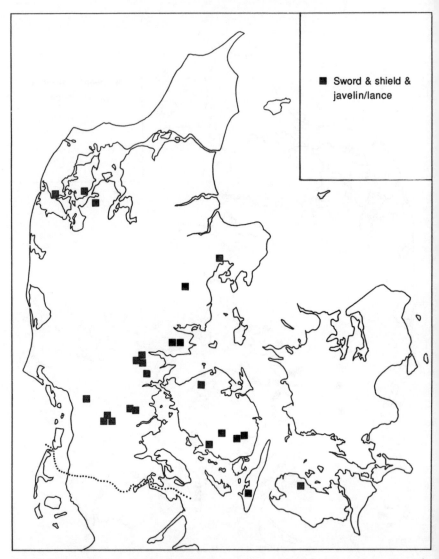

Figure 3.23 The distribution of weapon graves with full weapon sets (sword, shield, javelin/lance) in the ERIA.

of weapon sets: that the combination shield with javelin and/or lance is the most frequent (found in fifty-seven graves in all); that swords are virtually never found in more than one example per grave; that spearheads are quite regularly found in pairs, in sets of up to three indeed in the LRIA, which has to be explained in terms of the

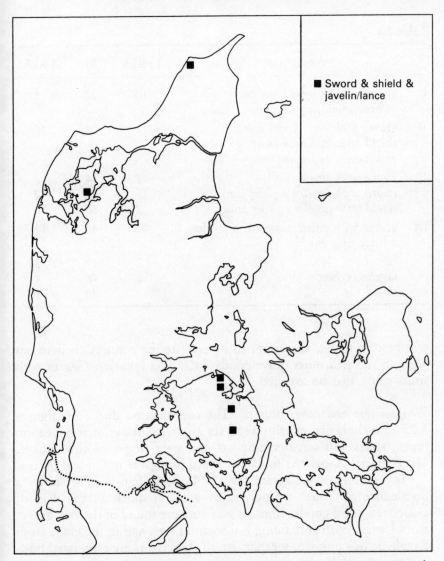

■ Sword & shield & javelin/lance

Figure 3.24 The distribution of weapon graves with full weapon sets (sword, shield, javelin/lance) in the LRIA.

different function of javelins and lances; and that group III virtually never contains anything more than single weapons (a javelin or lance can, exceptionally, be found in doublets in the ERIA). In contrast to luxury objects such as gold rings and Roman imports, weapons appear only in the necessary quantity according to their function. It

Table 3.1

	Combination	LpRIA	ERIA	LRIA
I	graves with full weapon set: sword, shield, javelin and/or lance	10	20	5
II	graves with sword and shield, shield and javelin or lance, or sword and javelin or lance	17	58	10
	sword with shield	*2*	*4*	*3*
	sword with javelin and/or lance	*13*	*4*	*2*
	shield with javelin and/or lance	*2*	*50*	*5*
III	graves with either a sword, a javelin, a lance or a shield	14	47	12
	sword	*7*	*12*	*2*
	javelin or lance	*6*	*16*	*4*
	shield	*1*	*19*	*6*

will be of interest, therefore, to investigate the connection between weapon sets and other grave goods, including luxuries. Graves with spurs must also be assessed.

Weapon sets and other objects The combination diagrams (figures 3.25–8) include arrowheads and axes as well as the common weapon types; spurs and scissors, imports and gold rings are also shown. More special associated finds are added alongside individual graves.

The combination diagram for the LpRIA (figure 3.25) shows a dominance of 'pure' weapon finds without much in the way of associated grave goods. Imports and gold are found in the two graves from Langå, both containing full weapon sets, and in the grave from Kraghede belonging to weapon group II. Scissors are associated finds in some cases, but spurs do not yet appear.

The combination diagram for the ERIA (figure 3.26) shows a greater frequency of associated finds. With few exceptions, imports are found in weapon graves with full weapon sets. The same goes for gold rings, for spurs and to an extent for scissors too. Other valuable artefacts such as, for instance, drinking horn mounts are often deposited in weapon graves belonging to group I. In a few cases spurs are also found in graves of group II, but never in graves

Sword	Shield	Javelin/ lance	Spurs	Scissors	Roman import	Gold	NAT
4	1-2	1	-	-	3	2	9
1	1	1	-	-	1	1	9
1	1	1	-	-	-	-	4
1	1	1	-	-	-	-	6
1	1	1	-	-	-	-	5
1	1	1	-	-	?	-	10
1	1	1	-	-	-	-	7
1	1	1	-	-	-	-	5
1	1	1	-	-	-	-	7
1	1	1	-	-	-	-	5
1	1	-	-	1	-	-	6
1	1	-	-	-	-	-	7
?	-	1	-	-	-	-	5
1	-	1	-	-	-	-	6
1	-	1	-	-	-	-	10
1	-	1	-	1	1	1	6
1	-	1	-	1	-	-	6
1	-	1	-	-	-	-	2
1	-	1	-	-	-	-	4
1	-	1	-	-	-	-	3
1	-	1	-	-	-	-	5
1	-	1	-	-	-	-	4
1	-	?	-	-	-	-	5
1	-	1	-	-	-	-	2
-	1	1	-	-	-	-	4
-	1	1	-	-	-	-	3
1	-	-	-	-	-	-	2
1	-	-	-	-	1	-	4
1	-	-	-	-	-	-	5
1	-	-	-	-	-	-	4
1	-	-	-	-	-	-	4
1	-	-	-	-	-	-	4
1	-	-	-	-	-	-	2
-	-	1	-	-	-	-	4
-	-	1	-	-	-	-	4
-	-	1	-	1	-	-	5
-	-	1	-	-	-	-	2
-	-	?	-	-	-	-	3
-	-	?	-	-	-	-	5
-	1	-	-	-	-	-	4

Figure 3.25 Combination diagram for weapon graves with: spurs, iron scissors, Roman imports and gold. LpRIA.

Sword	Shield	Javelin/ lance	Spurs	Scissors	Roman import	Gold	NAT
1	1	2	2	-	-	-	6
2	1	2	2	-	4	1	14
1	1	1	1	1	3	-	13
1	1	2	2	1	1	1	12
1	1	2	2	-	-	-	15
1	1	2	2	1	1	2	13
1	1	1	2	-	-	-	11
1	1	1	1	-	-	-	7
1	1	2	6	1	(6)	2	(16)
1	1	2	2	-	?	-	(15)
1	1	1	4	-	x	1	(15)
1	1	2	4	1	x	-	(14)
1-2	1	1	-	-	-	-	6
1	1	1	-	1	-	-	9
1	x	2	-	1	-	-	8
1	1	1	-	-	-	-	6
1	1	1	-	-	-	-	8
1	1	1	-	-	-	1	7
1	1	1	-	-	-	-	6
1	x	2	-	-	-	-	7
1	x	-	-	-	-	-	4
1	1	-	-	-	-	1	4
1	1	-	-	-	-	-	7
1	x	-	2	1	(8)	-	(15)
1	-	1	-	-	-	-	3
1	-	1	-	-	-	-	2
?	-	2	-	-	x	1	14
1	-	1	-	-	-	-	7
-	1	1	-	-	-	-	6
-	1	1	-	-	-	-	4
-	1	1	-	-	-	-	6
-	1	1	2	1	-	-	8
-	(2)	2	-	-	-	-	6
-	1	1	-	-	-	-	7
-	1	1	-	-	-	-	6
-	1	1	-	-	-	-	2
-	1	1	-	-	-	-	3
-	1	1	-	-	-	-	4
-	1	1	-	-	-	-	3
-	1	1	-	-	-	-	5
-	1	1	-	-	-	-	3
-	1	1	-	-	-	-	3
-	1	1	-	-	-	-	5
-	1	1	-	-	-	-	5
-	1	1	-	-	-	-	2
-	1	1	-	-	-	-	4
-	1	1	-	-	-	-	9

Figure 3.26 Combination diagram for weapon graves with: spurs, iron scissors, Roman imports and gold. ERIA.

Sword	Shield	Javelin/lance	Spurs	Scissors	Roman import	Gold	NAT
-	1	1	-	1	-	-	9
-	1	1	-	-	-	-	4
-	1	1	-	-	-	-	6
-	1	1	-	-	-	-	9
-	1	2	2	-	-	-	6
-	1	1	-	-	-	-	3
-	1	1	-	-	-	-	6
-	1	2	-	-	-	-	7
-	?	2	-	-	-	-	6
-	1	1	-	-	-	-	5
-	1	1	-	-	-	-	5
-	1	1	-	-	-	-	5
-	?	1	-	-	-	-	4
-	x	2	2	-	-	-	8
-	1	1	-	-	-	-	6
-	2	2	-	-	-	-	4
-	1	1	-	-	-	-	6
-	1	1	-	-	-	-	5
-	1	1	-	-	-	-	5
-	?	1	-	-	-	-	5
-	1	2	-	-	-	-	7
-	1	1	-	-	-	-	5
-	1	1	-	-	-	-	6
-	1	1	-	-	-	-	6
-	2	1	-	-	-	-	4
-	2	1	-	-	-	-	5
-	1	1	-	-	-	-	4
-	1	1	1-2	-	-	-	4
-	1	1	-	-	-	-	6
-	1	1	-	-	-	-	6
-	1	1	-	-	-	-	5
-	1	1	-	-	-	-	7
1	-	-	-	-	-	-	1
1	-	-	-	-	-	-	3
1	-	-	-	-	-	-	3
1	-	-	-	-	-	-	2
1	-	-	-	-	-	-	6
?	-	-	-	-	-	-	4
1	-	-	-	-	-	-	6
1	-	-	-	1	-	-	7
?	-	-	-	-	-	-	6
1	-	-	-	-	-	-	6
1	-	-	-	-	-	-	10
x	-	-	-	-	-	-	3

Figure 3.26 continued

Sword	Shield	Javelin/ lance	Spurs	Scissors	Roman import	Gold	NAT
-	-	2	-	-	-	-	4
-	-	1	-	1	-	-	4
-	-	1	-	-	-	-	2
-	-	1	-	-	-	-	2
-	-	1	-	-	-	-	2
-	-	1	-	-	-	-	3
-	-	1	-	-	-	-	4
-	-	1	-	-	-	-	4
-	-	1	?	-	-	-	3
-	-	1	-	-	-	-	3
-	-	1	-	-	-	-	3
-	-	2	-	1	-	-	6
-	-	1	-	-	-	-	3
-	-	1	-	-	-	-	2
-	-	1	-	-	-	-	2
-	-	1	-	-	-	-	3
-	1	-	-	-	-	-	4
-	1	-	-	-	-	-	3
-	x	-	-	-	-	-	3
-	x	-	-	-	-	-	1
-	1	-	-	-	-	-	3
-	1	-	-	-	-	-	2
-	1	-	-	-	-	-	6
-	1	-	-	-	-	-	2
-	1	-	-	-	-	-	3
-	1	-	-	-	-	-	3
-	1	-	-	-	-	-	5
-	1	-	-	-	-	-	4
-	?	-	-	-	-	-	6
-	1	-	-	-	-	-	5
-	x	-	-	-	-	-	5
-	1	-	-	-	-	-	5
-	1	-	-	-	-	-	3
-	?	-	-	-	-	-	2
-	x	-	-	-	-	-	3

Figure 3.26   continued

of group III. Graves with spurs may also, however, be without weapons (figure 3.27), but the other grave goods match – iron scissors apart – those of weapon group I.

The combination diagram for the LRIA (figure 3.28) shows a much more mixed and random picture. Imports and gold rings are found in all kinds of weapon graves. Spurs by themselves are found in just one grave, and there is also just one grave with spurs that

Sword	Shield	Javelin/ lance	Spurs	Scissors	Roman import	Gold	NAT
-	-	-	3	-	(10)	-	14
-	-	-	1	-	-	-	3
-	-	-	1	-	4	-	12
-	-	-	1	-	-	-	2
-	-	-	2?	-	-	-	6
-	-	-	2	-	-	1	3
-	-	-	1	-	-	1	6
-	-	-	2	-	-	1	7
-	-	-	2	-	-	-	4
-	-	-	1	-	2	2	11
-	-	-	2	-	-	1	7
-	-	-	1	-	-	-	6
-	-	-	2	-	-	-	5
-	-	-	2	-	-	-	5
-	-	-	4	-	-	-	5

Figure 3.27 Combination diagram for graves with spurs but no weapons with: Roman imports and gold. ERIA.

lacks weapons.[8] We may provisionally conclude that weapon graves belonging to group I are normally accompanied by imports and/or gold, most frequently in the ERIA and LRIA; that iron scissors sometimes appear in weapon graves of the LpRIA and LRIA, but most frequently in the ERIA, especially among the better furnished weapon graves (group I); that spurs predominantly belong to weapon graves of group I in the ERIA; that most weapon graves belonging to groups II and III in the LpRIA and ERIA are 'pure' weapon graves, without associated finds; and that the LRIA differs in that weapon graves of all three groups are associated with gold or imports.

In the previous section the location of the weapon graves within the NAT diagrams was investigated. It would be appropriate therefore to investigate too the NAT values of weapon graves belonging to groups I, II and III respectively. This has been done for the three periods in the diagrams of figures 3.29–31, in which the presence of gold/imports is also shown. It transpires from this that gold and imports are linked with weapon group I in both the LpRIA and the ERIA, but that the picture is unclear in the LRIA.

To sum up, in the LpRIA, for the first time, one can see in the weapon graves a division into different groups of warriors with a warrior aristocracy at the top. Wealth in these graves is represented by just a few weapon graves from Langå on Fyn and Kraghede in

Sword	Shield	Javelin/ lance	Spurs	Scissors	Roman import	Gold	NAT
1	2	1	2	1	1	-	10
1	1	1	-	-	-	1	4
1	1	1	-	-	-	-	4
1	1	2	-	-	-	1	5
2	1	-	-	-	-	1	8
1	1	-	-	-	1	-	7
1	1	-	-	-	-	1	5
1	-	1	-	-	-	-	6
1	-	2	-	-	-	1	6
-	1	1	-	-	-	-	6
-	1	3	-	-	-	-	4
-	2	1	-	1	2	1	7
-	1	2	-	-	-	-	4
1	-	-	-	-	-	-	5
1	-	-	-	-	-	-	3
-	-	1	-	-	-	-	5
-	-	1	-	1	-	-	5
-	-	1	-	-	-	-	3
-	-	1	-	-	1	1	8
-	1	-	-	-	1	1	4
-	1	-	-	-	3	-	8
-	x	-	-	1	-	-	5
-	1	-	-	-	-	-	3
-	1	-	-	-	-	-	3
-	?	-	-	-	-	-	6

Figure 3.28 Combination diagram for weapon graves with: spurs, iron scissors, Roman imports and gold. LRIA.

north Jutland. These graves are quite different from the other graves of the period either with or without weapons. They contain, uniquely in this country, parts of Celtic wagons. Linked with these graves, however, is the grave from Husby in southern Schleswig, immediately south of the Danish border (Raddatz 1967a). This is a cremation grave in a cauldron (of the Brå type) with a wagon and the equipment for two horses, but without weapons.

In the ERIA, the division into warrior groups or 'warrior classes' appears more clearly. This is interpreted as an expression of the consolidation of the structure. The accumulation of gold/imports is linked to graves with spurs and full weapon sets or graves with spurs and no weapons in the southern and south-eastern parts of Jutland. These graves are also the richest from Jutland.

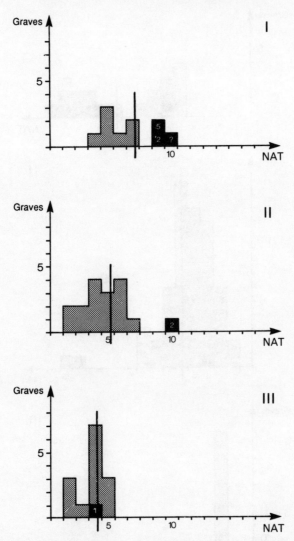

Figure 3.29 The distribution of weapon graves in weapon combinations I, II and III according to NAT values. Roman imports and gold are noted by numbers. The mean NAT value is given on the histograms. LpRIA.

In the LRIA, a military 'order of rank' is no longer marked in the weapon graves, either because it had gone or because it was no longer necessary to do so. Gold/imports are found scattered through the weapon graves and their accumulation seems to have no connection with the composition of weapon sets.

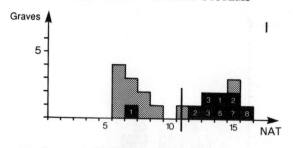

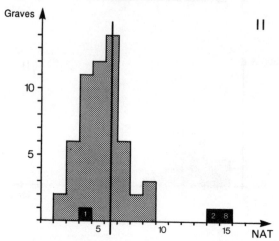

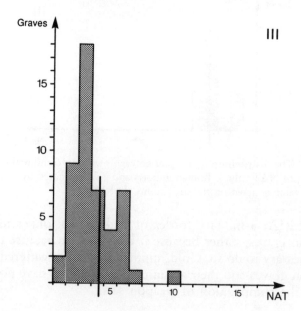

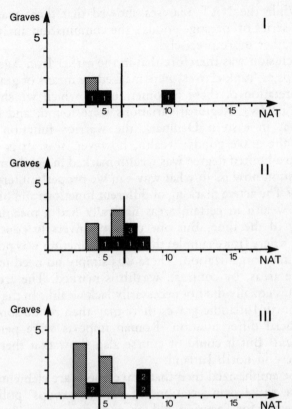

Figure 3.31 The distribution of weapon graves in weapon combinations I, II and III according to NAT values. Roman imports and gold are noted by numbers. The mean NAT value is given on the histograms. LRIA.

Social Ranks

The qualitative analysis of weapon graves in particular has shown that a series of recurrent combinations can be found. From this the weapon graves can be divided into three groups. It can also be shown that the NAT analyses agree well with the combination

Figure 3.30 (**opposite**) The distribution of weapon graves in weapon combinations I, II and III according to NAT values. Roman imports and gold are noted by numbers. The mean NAT value is given on the histograms. ERIA.

analyses. While the NAT analyses showed that there was unequal access to a series of 'prestige goods', the combination analyses made the point rather more precisely.

The conclusion was therefore that in the earlier Iron Age different social groups or 'rank classes' were marked by means of grave goods. The interpretation of these is something to which we shall return (pp. 159ff. below). Regional variations were found, and it is most striking that in eastern Denmark the warrior function was not marked in the grave goods; wealth, however, was. It is also clear that only to a limited degree was wealth marked in northern Jutland.

The question now is, in what way can we properly interpret these differences? The active marking of different functions and of different degrees of wealth in certain areas naturally had a meaning in the community of the time. But one cannot conversely conclude that those areas where (for example) the warrior function was not marked had no military organization. There was simply no need to mark it. In the same areas, by contrast, wealth is marked. The areas which do not do this equally did not necessarily lack wealth. In the uniformity of the north Jutlandic graves there may then reside some refusal to mark social differentiation. Roman imports were perhaps not *comme il faut*. But it could of course also show that there was no share in these in north Jutland.

It must be emphasized then that grave goods are elements in some very precise ritual manifestations of various groups' political and social strategies for securing old or new positions. This is most manifest in what is signalled by being given; less manifest in what is signalled by being withheld.

In order to achieve greater clarity with regard to the meaning of this, in the next section we shall look more closely at some other ways of signalling similarities and differences through funerary rituals.

Burial Ritual and Social Identity

Burial Ritual

A very much greater quantity of information inheres within burial rituals than a one-sided analysis of the grave goods can express. Many variables play a part in characterizing the 'social person' of the deceased, and among these the following are of especial importance (Binford 1972, pp. 210ff.).

1   Different treatment of the body

   (a) various ways of decking out the body;
   (b) the treatment of the body: e.g. cremation, mummification
        etc.;
   (c) different placement in the grave.

2   Different treatment of the coffin

   (a) the form of the coffin;
   (b) the alignment of the coffin;
   (c) location in the cemetery or, perhaps, by buildings.

3   Differences in the items which are deposited with the dead

   (a) different forms of grave goods;
   (b) different quantities of grave goods;
   (c) different types which are found in different quantities.

On the basis of a study of a number of ethnographically well-investigated primitive communities (forty in all) a connection has been demonstrated between the complexity of funerary rituals and the organizational complexity of the individual community. This investigation has shown that complex funerary rituals are positively correlated with complex societies, but that the opposite does not necessarily hold (Binford 1972).

Do these observations imply too that there is a connection between the different variables (the above points 1–3)? We must now address this question.

Up to this point we have analysed the grave goods, but in what follows we shall investigate whether a connection can be seen between these results and variation in other rituals. An analysis of this is, however, heavily dependent upon factors such as the state of preservation, the method of excavation and so on. Thus the data concerning burial rites are much more vulnerable and sensitive to external factors than is the grave furnishing itself.

As noted, the picture of grave form, grave types and furnishing from the Roman Iron Age is more varied and complex than from any other prehistoric period (the Viking Period excepted). What is most evident in the funerary rituals is the simultaneous presence of inhumations and cremations, often in the same areas. The question now is whether grave forms are also used to mark similarities and differences between people within or across local areas. Do some areas use funerary rituals in a more complex way than others?

Inhumation versus Cremation

These two forms of burial are not equally common across the whole country; in fact, great regional variation can be seen. The traditional cremation rite, which had been the sole rite throughout the pRIA, continues in some areas, but in others is almost entirely superseded by the new inhumation rite.

As a result, in the ERIA, cremation continues to dominate in the whole of the southern part of Jutland (*amts* 17, 19–23), on Fyn (*amts* 8–9) and on Lolland/Falster (*amt* 7); in the rest of the country the new burial form with unburnt bodies has been adopted extensively (figure 3.32a). The variance from *amt* to *amt* is certainly great; where cremation is strongest it accounts for about 90 per cent of all graves (i.e. the *amts* in southern Jutland and the *amts* of Svendborg and Maribo); where it is weakest it accounts for only 10 to 15 per cent (Sjælland (1–5) and the *amts* of Hjørring, Århus, Skanderborg and Ringkøbing).

In the LRIA the cremation rite dominates only on Fyn (8–9) and in Vejle (17) and Skanderborg (16) *amts*; on Fyn it is in fact almost exclusive (90–98 per cent) (figure 3.32b); by contrast inhumations are absolutely dominant on Sjælland (1–5) and in Randers (14) and Viborg (13) *amts* (92 to 98 per cent). Some *amts* have so few LRIA graves that they have to be kept right out of the calculations.

Within both of these burial forms one can find innumerable local and regional peculiarities. Among the inhumations the most striking are the stone cists of northern Jutland and the inhumation graves with tent-shaped superstructures from the same place. In east Jutland it is the large, almost square, plank coffins surrounded by a small frame of buttressing stones (the so-called east Jutlandic pot graves), while long, narrow, stone-packed cuts with log coffins are especially found in southern Jutland. Alignment varies; in Jutland the coffins/cists are normally aligned west–east and the deceased lies with the head to the west; on Sjælland, Lolland/Falster they are always north–south, in the ERIA with the head to the north (northeast), in the LRIA to the south. On Fyn the graves are aligned in every direction: in the ERIA, however, the deceased never has the head to the south and rarely to the east; in the LRIA, the head is

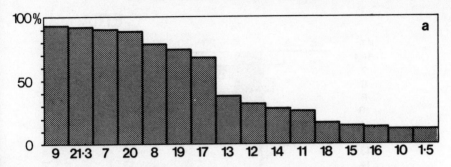

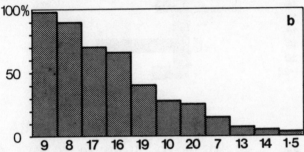

Figure 3.32 Cremations as a percentage of all graves per *amt* in (a) the ERIA and (b) the LRIA (*amt* numbers are shown on figure 3.6). In the case of the LRIA, *amts* 11, 12, 15, 18 and 21–23 are omitted as the volume of finds is too low. Otherwise, see the table.

rarely to the north and the east. We can thus see that there is one alignment in Jutland, another on Sjælland, Lolland and Falster, and that Fyn is a mixed area, following the tendencies both of Jutland and of Sjælland.

Regional peculiarities are not so striking among the cremations; urn graves, cremation pits and cremation patches are found everywhere, but vary in their proportions to one another.

What is critical is not so much the form that local and regional variations take but the fact that they are so clearly present. This shows with absolute certainty that burial form was a very definite factor within the funerary rituals and was used to confirm local and regional identity and difference. On this basis it will also be of interest to see whether certain burial rites run across regional traditions to produce a set of graves more similar to one another than they are similar to the other graves in their own local area. We will look first at graves with prestige goods and weapons.

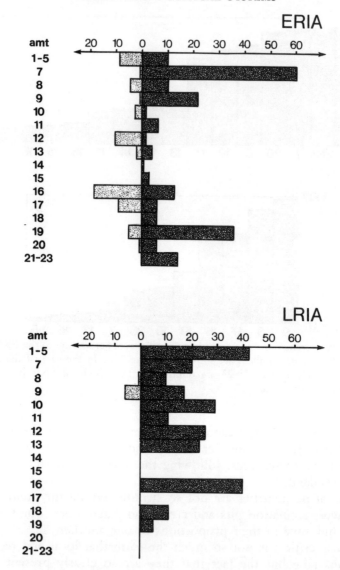

■ Cremations
■ Inhumations

Figure 3.33 The percentile proportion of cremations and inhumations containing Roman imports and/or gold in (a) the ERIA and (b) the LRIA calculated by *amt* (*amt* numbers are shown on figure 3.6). The numerical scores are, for the ERIA, 35 cremations and 80 inhumations with imports/gold, and for the LRIA, 94 cremations (all on Fyn, mostly at Møllegårdsmarken) and 101 inhumations.

Prestige Goods and Weapons

Prestige goods in the ERIA   Prestige goods in the ERIA (defined as Roman imports and gold) belong to the new period just like the inhumation rite. Does this mean that form and content are correlated? Or do prestige goods appear just as strongly in cremations?

On figure 3.33 the percentile contents of prestige goods is calculated for either burial form. It transpires from this that the rich graves of the ERIA, *amt* by *amt* are inhumations; the exceptions are north Jutland (i.e. Hjørring (10) and Ålborg (12), and the central Jutlandic *amts* Skanderborg (16) and Vejle (17)). There is also a small group of graves which are exceptionally rich and the contents of which have much in common (Hedeager and Kristiansen 1981).

The distribution of these especially rich graves (with more than 10 NAT) is shown on the map in figure 3.34. It transpires that both inhumations and cremations are included; in local terms it is only on Lolland that the rich graves are exclusively inhumations. These belong to the so-called princely graves of the Lübsow type, which are nearly all inhumations. Among these, the level of conformity is striking, both in burial form and in contents (this group in Denmark is composed of Hoby, Juellinge 1 and 4, Nørre Broby, Dollerup, Espe, Skrøbeshave) (Eggers 1949/50).

The princely graves are quite clearly defined by rather random and subjective criteria (Gebühr 1974), but this does not change the fact that great congruence can be observed among these rich graves, a congruence which overrides regional peculiarities. Their background lay in direct personal contacts and connections. The evidence for this is a series of apparently insignificant and valueless petty items. These turn up in the Lübsow graves and recur in several of the rich Danish women's graves (Hedeager and Kristiansen 1981).

The next group of graves to be discussed are the weapon graves of the ERIA. Counted among these are graves with at least one of the following objects: sword, javelin, lance, shield or spurs. Weapons are found in 155 cremations and eighty-two inhumations, and the percentile proportion of the two burial forms is given for each *amt* in figure 3.35. It appears that cremations form a larger proportion than inhumations in nearly every district.

Three spatial groups are immediately detectable. The first includes Sjælland, Lolland and Fyn (*amts* 1–9), where cremations are nearly exclusive. The second comprises the northern and central parts of

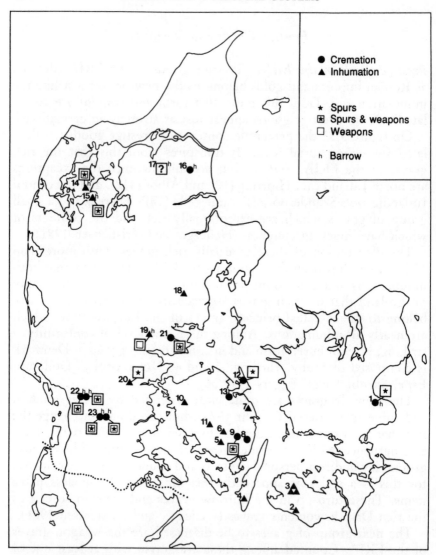

Figure 3.34 The distribution of 'rich' graves in the ERIA, defined as graves with a NAT score above 10 which contain gold and/or Roman imports (cf. also figure 2.6). 1 Himlingøje; 2 Hoby; 3 Juellinge (three graves); 4 Nordenbrogård; 5 Blidegn; 6 Espe; 7 Skrøbeshave; 8 Møllegårdsmarken; 9 Ellerup; 10 Faurskov I; 11 Nørre Broby; 12 Martofte; 13 Vejrupgård; 14 Store Kongehøj; 15 Lynghøjgård; 16 Blemstrup; 17 Byrsted; 18 Karolinehøj Mark; 19 Agersbøl Hovedgård; 20 Dollerup; 21 Bjergelide; 22 Brokjær Mark (two graves); 23 Kastrup (two graves).

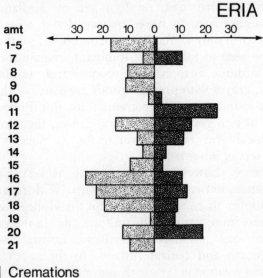

Figure 3.35 The percentile proportion of cremations and inhumations of the ERIA containing weapons, calculated by *amt* (*amt* numbers are given on figure 3.6). The numerical scores are 155 cremations and 82 inhumations.

Jutland (*amts* 10–16 and 18), where inhumations are predominant. The third area comprises the southern and south-eastern parts of Jutland (*amts* 17–23). A division into the three categories of weapon graves mentioned previously – graves with spurs and weapons (A), graves with spurs without weapons (B) and weapon graves without spurs (C) – has shown that in southern and south-eastern Jutland categories A and C are particularly found among the cremations and category B among the inhumations. There is no difference between any other places in the correlation of the three weapon-grave categories with any particular burial form.

This means, to put it another way, that inhumation graves with spurs (B) in the south and southern Jutlandic area alone follow neither the burial form of the other weapon graves in the area nor the area's general burial practice, in which between 80 and 100 per cent of all graves are cremations (cf. figures 3.33a, 3.35).

We shall finally have a look at the rich graves with weapons. On the map in figure 3.34 the weapon graves have been added. The rich weapon graves lie, as has already been described, primarily in the south and the southern Jutlandic area, but some are found in the west of the Limfjord area, on Fyn and on Sjælland. In Jutland prestige goods are virtually never associated with weapon graves and on Fyn they form only a minor proportion. On Fyn the rich weapon graves can be seen to follow the dominant cremation rite, while the rich graves without weapons are predominantly inhumations.

In general, graves with prestige goods are usually inhumations and weapons are found primarily in cremations. But if one considers the whole mass of rich graves and weapon graves, they conform on the whole to local and regional variations as regards burial form (cremation versus inhumation).

In some areas, however, the burial rite is very clearly used to signal differences between different groups. With regard to the rich graves this applies to eastern Fyn (except for Møllegårdsmarken) and Lolland, where inhumation is the uniform rite. In the case of weapon graves, cremations dominate on Sjælland, Lolland and Fyn, inhumations in north and central Jutland. In the south and southern Jutlandic areas weapon graves with and without spurs are cremations but graves with spurs and no weapons are inhumations.

The signalling of differences between selected groups and the rest of the community is, then, greatest on eastern Fyn and on Lolland, where weapon graves and rich graves are clearly differentiated both from one another and from the remainder of the community, and in southern Jutland where the graves with spurs are quite distinct from the other groups.

The many local variations in burial practice described above show that an effort was made to demonstrate regional identity. The rich graves and the weapon graves in most places conform to regional tradition in burial practice. But in the areas just noted some groups stand apart. It is typical that these are precisely those areas where most rich graves are found. In these places competition and the need to emphasize social differences was greatest.

Prestige goods in the LRIA   In the LRIA there is a shift in the distribution of graves with imports and gold to Sjælland and Fyn, and several of the Jutlandic *amts* become void of finds (cf. figure 3.32). It is shown by figure 3.33b that graves with prestige goods are now exclusively inhumations, except for on Fyn where cremations still have a marked presence.

As in the ERIA, a group of LRIA graves with especially high NAT scores (more than 10) can be distinguished. These also contain imports and gold (figure 3.36). The map shows that all of

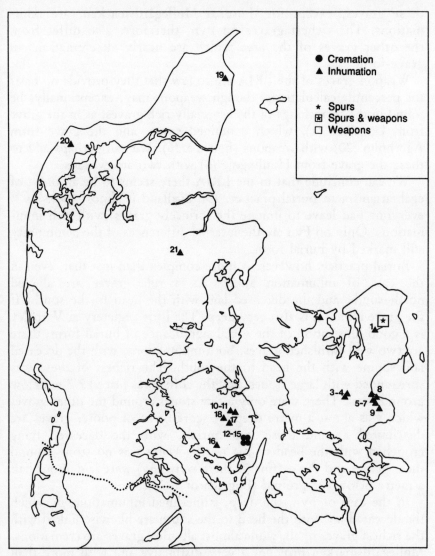

Figure 3.36 The distribution of 'rich' graves in the LRIA, defined as graves with NAT scores above 10 which contain gold and/or Roman imports (cf. also figure 2.7). 1 Uggeløse; 2 Nyrup; 3–4 Nordrup; 5–7 Himlingøje; 8 Valløby; 9 Varpelev; 10–11 Sanderumgård; 12–15 Møllegårdsmarken; 16 Hågerup; 17 Eskildstrup; 18 Årslev; 19 Donbæk; 20 Agerholm; 21 Vrangstrup.

these graves, except for those at Møllegårdsmarken, are inhumations. The richest graves on Fyn, therefore, also differ from the other graves of the area which are nearly all cremations in grave-form.

Weapon graves of the LRIA are so few that they provide no basis for percentile calculations, though weapons may, exceptionally, be found in the furnishings of the especially rich graves, as in the grave from Uggeløse (1), which contained spurs, and the grave from Agerholm (20) with weapons (figure 3.36). We can perhaps add to these the grave from Himlingøje (6) with two arrowheads.

We can conclude that in the LRIA there seems to be an onset of egalitarianism in burial practice. On Sjælland it almost looks as if everyone had leave to imitate the 'princely graves' with rich inhumations. Only on Fyn are the internal differences of the community still marked by burial form.

Burial practice, however, is more complex than just that, even in the case of inhumation alone. As a rule graves are aligned north–south, and the deceased laid with the head to the south. If the grave is rich it is also very deep. The little cemetery at Varpelev is a good illustration of the social significance of burial form; there are two well-furnished graves, both inhumations, with the deceased laid supine with the head to the south. The richest of these was surrounded with large stones, and the coffin was placed 2.7 m below ground level. There were only a few stones around the other grave, which was about a metre deep. A score or so of poorer graves are distributed around these two burials, with the deceased lying crouched with the head to the north. There was no stone around these graves and the coffins (if there were any) were laid about half a metre below the ground (Engelhardt 1877).

In the case of Fyn, the deep, stone-lined inhumations in which the deceased lay with the head to the south are likewise linked with the richest graves of all, while almost all other graves are cremations. Møllegårdsmarken provides a very distinctive site with more than 1,000 LRIA graves. There is an unusual concentration of (molten) glass on the site (from fifty-one graves) and grave goods such as sherds of *terra sigillata* and fragments of chain mail which otherwise never – or only very rarely – are found in Denmark. The cremation rite is effectively exclusive, and the tradition of using the inhumation rite in connection with the richest graves does not intrude here, either in the ERIA or the LRIA.

Cemeteries and Single Graves

As we have seen, the burial rite gives certain groups or individuals the opportunity to demonstrate their identity. It would be possible to emphasize either localized commonality with the rest of the community and, concurrently, difference from the surrounding world, or to mark difference from one's own 'nationals' and to play up an 'international' commonality with others of the same rank.

Another obvious aspect of burial practice is the location of graves: isolated, in small cemeteries or gathered into large cemeteries. All these possibilities are found in the Roman Iron Age. The next step in the investigation must therefore be an analysis of the deceased. The central question will be whether the rich graves lie alone, or perhaps in groups of a few together, or whether they stand together with other graves in the larger cemeteries. This is a very tangible way of marking commonality or difference.

Even after source-related problems are taken into account – rich graves come to the museums more readily than poor ones – it can be observed as a general tendency that areas with many graves (usually with large cemeteries) rarely contain rich graves. These are normally found in fact in parishes with only a few graves. A simple reckoning of the number of parishes with graves from the ERIA and LRIA respectively is given in figure 3.37. Graves with gold and/or Roman imports (marked in grey) occur very rarely in parishes with a lot of graves even though, statistically, they ought to be most frequent here. This especially applies to the particularly rich graves with NAT scores over 10 (marked in black) (cf. figures 3.34, 3.36). It is also typical that normally only one, or perhaps some few, rich graves are found per parish.[9]

We can conclude, then, that rich, 'status-laden' graves do not normally occur in the larger cemeteries but predominantly lie alone. Often two, three or four are grouped at one site, possibly together with a few humble or genuinely poor graves.

We shall subsequently investigate whether the rich graves and the large cemeteries are found in the same tracts of territory, albeit in different parishes, or whether the two groups are also mutually exclusive at a regional level.

A comparison of the distribution of the very rich graves (figures 3.34, 3.36) and the general distribution map (figures 3.2, 3.3) shows both coincidence and separation. In the ERIA the rich graves avoid

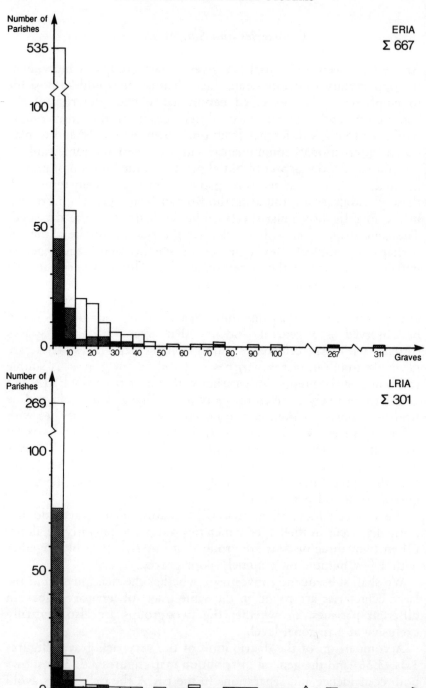

areas with many graves, that is, principally, Hjørring, Randers and Århus *amts*. On Fyn the richest graves are in Svendborg *amt*, but the centre of distribution of the humbler graves is in Odense *amt*. In southern Jutland, however, and on Langeland, the two distributions coincide, while on Lolland they are separated. In the LRIA the picture is reversed: both on Sjælland and on Fyn the richest graves are found in the areas where finds are most densely distributed.[10]

Burial Ritual and Social Identity

A connection has thus been shown to exist between variation in grave furnishing and variation in grave type (inhumation versus cremation) and burial form (isolated graves versus cemeteries).

The burial rite was therefore used for the marking of differences and similarities with others in the community. This holds both at a regional level and between different social groups. The weapon graves, for instance, are more tradition-bound than are the rich graves, which increasingly make use of the innovative inhumation rite. It clearly was quite rare for warriors to have the positions of status in which the new rite was used. And it was only in Jutland that both the political and the military leadership distinguished themselves in their grave goods.

What is most noteworthy, however, is that graves with distinctly prestigious furnishing differentiate themselves from graves in their own immediate locality, not only in terms of furnishing but also in their isolated location – a situation which holds pretty well for the whole country and for both periods. The new elite thus palpably made manifest their assumption of a special position in relation to the rest of the community.

Even so, in certain areas this rule does not apply. In north and east Jutland cemeteries occur with continuity through several centuries. Investment here is relatively subdued, and only exceptionally are Roman imports found (although gold is not infrequent).[11] In these areas the rich graves are found within the cemeteries and thus demonstrate some connection with the rest of the community.

Figure 3.37 (opposite) Histogram of the number of graves per parish in Denmark (ERIA and LRIA). Parishes which are home to at least one of the especially rich graves are marked in black; parishes which are home to at least one grave containing gold and/or Roman imports are marked in grey.

It is also noteworthy that in this area one finds the strongest manifestation of regional identity in the ERIA. This can really only be understood as a conscious demonstration of opposition here to the new tendencies towards the development of rich and powerful elites and of a preference for holding onto the older traditions with their roots in the village communities of the pRIA. However, all of these cemeteries cease at the transition to the LRIA.

Southern Jutland has an intermediary place, with strong regional traditions which are interrupted to a degree by the new rite concerning warrior graves. But there is continuity here, in contrast to Sjælland and Lolland/Falster, where there is strikingly little. There, new areas come to prominence from the LRIA onwards (figure 3.38).

We can conclude, then, that the burial rite corroborates the picture which was sketched on the basis of the NAT analyses and combination analyses. These show a society in division, marked on the one hand by strong regional traditions and on the other by new, burgeoning elites who marked their wealth and position through their burials. The change is the strongest on the islands and to some degree in east Jutland, and weakest in north Jutland. Fyn and southern Jutland take up a somewhat intermediary position. In all areas, however, the burial rite is used actively and selectively to emphasize social identity, whether to maintain old regional and 'democratic' traditions or to demonstrate new 'elite' positions of power which cut right across these.

Social Differentiation and Centralization

We shall now try, with the aid of the introductory theoretical generalizations, to probe behind the empirical generalizations and provisional interpretations of the previous sections in order to reveal something of the structures – political and social – which produced variations in material culture.

Social structure is in itself an abstraction. It consists neither of graves nor of grave goods. These are the result of processes and structures whose existence can only be interpreted and explained as concepts. This can appear tenuous, but it is the very essence of scientific analysis. Scientific analysis can be supported by deducing the theoretical consequences of the analyses undertaken in a systematic and logical manner. But only one criterion can be offered for the

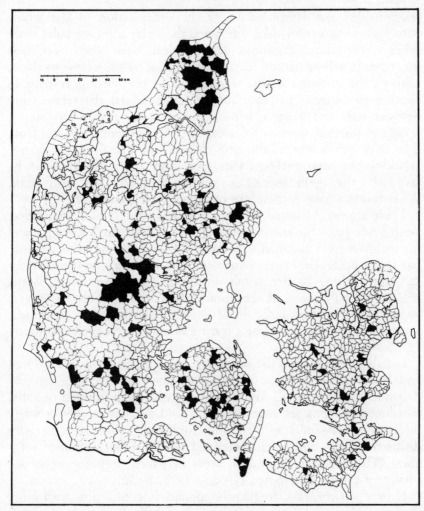

Figure 3.38   Danish parishes containing graves from both the ERIA and the LRIA (shown in black).

reliability of the results: that they give the best and most consistent explanation of the variance observed. The result can be criticized, but it can only be superseded by some better explanation.

Kinship and Social Organization

All societies have fixed rules governing marriage, the reckoning of kinship and, consequently, inheritance. In some societies, kinship relationships are determinative of the organization of the whole community; in others, like our own, they play a minor role, since other relationships, economic and political, have taken over their function. It will be natural, therefore, to start by subjecting to closer analysis the question of the significance of the kinship systems in relation to variance in grave furnishing, not least the relationship between men and women. It must, however, be emphasized that it is only possible to draw conclusions of a very general character from this. It is only when, in the next chapter, the question of property relations has been analysed that something more concrete can be said about the significance of the kindred as an economic institution. What follows here is therefore of a provisional character.

There are two forms of marriage payment: dowry and bride price. With bride price the man's kindred pays the woman's kindred, and the children enter the man's kindred. With dowry the bride's family pay to the bride; she brings valuables along with her into the marriage but they belong to her family in the event of separation. Some researchers have been of the opinion that it is possible to show a connection between large bride price payments and patrilinear society, while dowry may be a feature of matrilinear society (Goody 1973).

In patrilinear systems the woman is adopted into the man's kindred and loses rights in her own kindred. She thus becomes entirely dependent on the man's kindred. It has also been pointed out that patrilinear systems are often open to kindred connections in many directions (exogamy) and are therefore well suited to a broadly diffused alliance policy, characterized by the redistribution of valuables. This seems to appear in areas in which property rights are relatively evenly distributed (Goody 1973, p. 32).

Dowry, in contrast, frequently appears in connection with more closed (endogamous) marriage systems, in which an individual can inherit from both the man's and the woman's kindred (bilateral systems). This means that women can inherit on an equal basis with men (Ortner 1981), which is of particular importance in the inheritance of land. Such a system provides optimal opportunities for obtaining control over land and valuables through inheritance as a result of strategic marriage alliances. Such kinship and marriage systems occur particularly in communities with a more differentiated and unequal distribution of property rights, in which other groups are excluded from influence.

These researchers thus come to the conclusion that kinship and marriage systems are directly dependent upon the economic and political structures in the relevant communities. They are a symptom rather than an explanation of more basic traits of the structure of the community.

With these outlined generalizations as a starting-point, it is natural to go on to reflect upon the situation in the Roman Iron Age, looking at the variations demonstrated in burial rite.

In Jutland we see a clear connection between wealth and male burials with a military aspect. The difference between here and Sjælland, Lolland and Falster, where rich women's graves occur and the military aspect is lacking, is striking. It is easy then to link these variations with a patrilinear and exogamous kindred structure in Jutland and a matrilinear or at least bilateral and endogamous structure on the islands. There are no obvious reasons for furnishing women with rich grave goods if status was only expressed and transmitted in the man's family; there is a reason if the woman had inheritance rights.

If we follow this line of argument further, it would imply that the social structure in east Denmark was more hierarchical and property rights were more differentiated than in Jutland. Through kinship and marriage systems the attempt was made to preserve the rights acquired within the privileged groups, while at the same time the system permitted the growth, indeed maximization, of difference. In Jutland, property rights would have been more evenly distributed, and particularly linked to the man's kindred, combined with a predominantly pastoral agriculture as is also common in patrilinear society. This interpretation is at least in agreement with the emphasis in the burial rites of older, egalitarian traditions, especially in north and east Jutland, in contrast to the new and more elitist traditions in east Denmark.

The general analysis and interpretation of marriage and kinship systems thus indicates the presence of some structural differences between east and west Denmark, which we shall try to substantiate further in the following sections.

Gifts and Tribute

In a society with a certain social hierarchy, gifts, goods and services are exchanged between both equal and unequal groups in the hierarchy (horizontally and vertically). How this is done may vary. Alliances are regularly formed between equals – through marriage, for instance – as a preliminary to political, military and commercial transactions. Moving both up and down in the system, services can be both given and received, but they will often be of different character. Gifts are typically given downwards because they create dependency, while services in return often have the character of dues (political or military) or payment, for example of tribute or tax proper. The latter, however, requires some well-defined basis of taxation, while tribute can be collected less methodically.

It was our thesis that the Roman luxury goods took a central place in the development of a new social system through their function as prestige goods. We shall now attempt to interpret the function and significance of imports in the Roman Iron Age on the basis of the foregoing archaeological analyses.

One of the most striking features of the Roman imports is that the objects were never copied locally. Only the genuine article was valued, presumably because it demonstrated the owner's contact with the Roman world and showed a knowledge of Roman taste and the Roman lifestyle. The Roman artefacts represented the elite's monopoly of alliances and long-distance connections which brought it into contact with Roman culture.

Another typical feature was the possibility of accumulating to an almost unlimited degree. The Roman imports did not need to fit into fixed jewellery or weapon sets, as had, for instance, been the case in the Earlier Bronze Age, where wealth was manifested by making the individual artefacts heavier, more finely crafted and in some cases gilt (Randsborg 1974). In the Roman Iron Age, the configurations of Roman imports, gold and silver were apparently of no great significance: it was the quantity that mattered.

It may then also be remarkable that no long-term 'accumulation of capital' in the form of valuable Roman goods took place in the form of hoards (treasure deposits). The explanation may be that purchasing power was lacking. They were the visible symbolic expressions of certain political/social relationships and alliances, and were not for sale. The most illuminating explanation of these situations would therefore be that the Roman goods may have served the function of prestige goods, as described in the introduction to this chapter (pp. 87–90).

Three features are characteristic of the use of prestige goods in the Roman Iron Age. First, the Roman objects are exchanged over long distances between political leaders of equal status, evidently as a factor in alliances/marriage settlements, and they are consequently used to demonstrate the special position of their owner in the community; second, they are used locally as gifts, through which a leader creates dependent vassals from whom he can expect service in return; and third, they are invested as grave goods in order to emphasize further the special position and wealth of the kindred, for the benefit of those still living.

The prestige goods are of course not independent of economic and military structures, which will be described in due course. But we must first look a little closer at what the use of prestige goods in the Roman Iron Age can tell us of the structure of power and of possible changes to it. The evidence of both the NAT analyses and the combination analyses makes it probable that an elite monopolized both Roman imports and wealth in general. That this elite quite clearly used Roman imports to differentiate itself in some areas could also be inferred from the fact that these people allowed themselves to be buried in particularly small cemeteries.

But the analyses also show that there was both regional and chronological variation. In the ERIA, Roman imports circulated within a relatively small group of leaders of equal status who were distributed geographically at more or less equal distances; only a small proportion of the imports was sent further down the social/ political system. A number of these graves are very rich and uniform – the so-called princely grave stratum (figure 3.39) – and these must (with diplomatic gifts from the Roman Empire, among other things) represent the establishment and consolidation of a regional elite over the whole of the north Germanic area. Some areas apparently sought to oppose this development: in north and east Jutland in Denmark and in continental Europe in the west Germanic areas, that is, those areas which after a short transition formed the Roman province of Upper Germany (Hedeager 1987). Thus intrinsic oppositions between Germanic and Roman cultural traditions emerged, which can be seen at their deepest level to reflect an opposition between an egalitarian and an elitist society.

In the LRIA, the imports are concentrated in graves in particular areas; within these localities, in due course, we see a more extensive distribution. It is clear that imports are now no longer found only in the very few graves but also in graves with lower NAT scores. An earlier analysis left it probable that this structure was an expression of a redistribution of wealth from a social/political power centre with control over the imports to the vassals/clients of the area. This system appears most clearly on Sjælland, with Stevns at the centre,

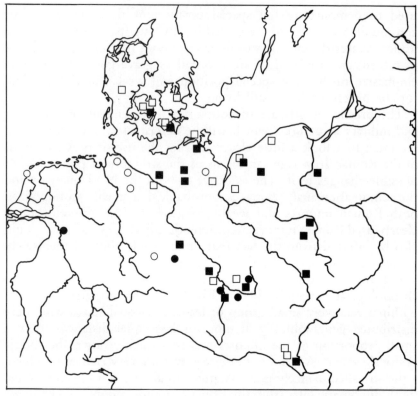

Figure 3.39 The distribution of 'princely graves' of the ERIA. (after Steuer 1982, p. 211) ○ cremation grave from first century AD; ● cremation grave from second century AD; □ inhumation grave from first century AD; ■ inhumation grave from second century AD.

and in the continental context clearly also in Thuringia (Hedeager 1980) (figure 3.40). The imports are just one expression of the existence of a prestige goods system, in which a political power centre is in a position to share out duties and protection in return for services such as tribute and loyalty.

A development like that sketched here, which appears first to disrupt the previous clan and tribal traditions of the ERIA and then to overturn the system entirely in the LRIA, unquestionably went hand in hand with military, economic and tenurial change. In the next section we shall look at changes in the military system.

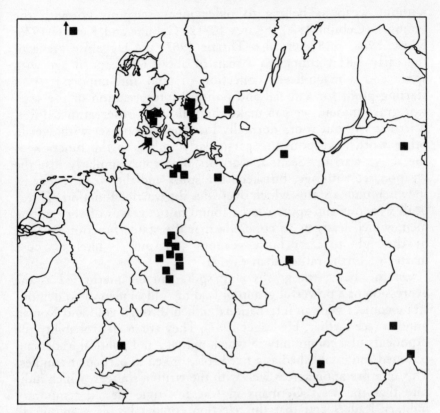

Figure 3.40 The distribution of 'princely graves' of the LRIA. (after Steuer 1982, p. 221) ■ inhumation grave.

The Weapon Grave Milieu

The familiar status-bound weapon grave milieu appears for the first time in the LpRIA, is consolidated in the ERIA and dissolved in the LRIA; the foundation of a description will therefore be located in the ERIA.

The warrior graves can be divided into three groups: (1) warrior graves with full weapon sets and spurs, frequently also containing gold and imports; (2) 'knightly' graves without weapons but containing gold and imports just like the graves of group 1; (3) other weapon graves, which as a group do not contain prestige goods and only very exceptionally spurs. Through a series of anthropological studies of graves from the north German Roman Period cemeteries of Kemnitz and Hamfeld it has been shown that sets with spurs but without weapons belong to older men; weapons go with the younger (Gebühr 1970, figures 10–12; Gebühr and Kunow 1976; Künst 1978, p. 88; cf. also Thrane 1967: the Uggeløse grave of the early LRIA contained a man of about 60 years of age with spurs and a magnificent collection of gold and imports). As a starting-point for a social and political interpretation of the warrior grave milieu, we can make the following observations. First, warriors without spurs normally lose the weapon set with age; in other words, weapons are particularly linked to the function of the active warrior. Second, warriors with spurs similarly lose the weapon set with age, but keep the spurs and the wealth; that is, they maintain a status which overrides the warrior function. Third, both weapons and spurs can be found in the graves of very young men, which leads us to conclude that the status/function marked by the right to carry both weapons and spurs is likely to be a matter of birth, rather than earned.

On this basis, the graves with spurs can be interpreted as the expression of a powerful group of leading (older) men, who demonstrate contact with an international milieu through gold and Roman imports (see further, Hedeager 1987). They are in all probability the exponents of a community in which military and political leadership is joined and established as a fixed role, linked to particular families. This interpretation agrees well with the written sources, which indicate that the west Germans in Caesar's time elected temporary military leaders and that this election could take place among all weapon-bearing men, while as early as the time of Tacitus the leader (or two leaders) was elected from a number of particular families (Thompson 1965). Here personal leadership has become of more permanent character, which agrees well with personal prestige goods following the dead into the grave.

The employment of Roman imports and gold demonstrates contact with the pan-Germanic princely grave milieu. The presence of spurs in these graves thus emphasizes the symbolic value of spurs within the west Germanic area (see further, Gebühr 1970, tables 3–4; Hedeager 1987). But the graves with spurs also imply a special position in another way, both military and economic, partly through the use of horses in battle and partly through the development of horse breeding and specialized horsemanship; this continues through the LRIA and can be seen in the evolution of new and more effective types of bridle and of a true cavalry. Smiths' graves likewise accompany this weapon grave milieu and emphasize the significance of weapon production.[12]

We can conclude from this that in the LpRIA a military/political leadership developed in the western parts of the country and was consolidated in the ERIA. Young warriors who did not themselves have access to foreign, Roman goods, must have connected themselves to this leadership. These leaders are geographically distributed at relatively even distances, so that each of them appears to have controlled an area the size of a *herred* (Hedeager and Kristiansen 1981, figure 46), while the warriors were recruited from the leading families in the villages (cf. Overbygård in Lund 1979b).[13]

The connection of scissors and 'flesh knives' with the weapon graves of Jutland and Fyn may provide a valuable clue to the local economic preconditions for the warrior grave milieu of western Denmark. The selection of these particular tools for burial can be regarded as an expression of the fundamental significance attributed to them: the sign they gave of the person's association with a more specialized side of agricultural production – namely, sheep and cattle raising and skin/leather production.[14] This may also provide an insight into some of the products which were used in alliances and in trade to the south in exchange for Roman imports. The Jutlandic weapon grave milieu takes its place in a common Germanic northwest European milieu (Hedeager 1987, figure 11.3), the establishment of which can be seen in conjunction with the Roman expansion which at the beginning of the first century AD led to the establishment of a temporary Roman border along the Elbe.

The weaponless grave milieu of eastern Denmark is similarly part of a common Germanic north-east European milieu (Hedeager 1987, figure 11.3). These differences between east and west Denmark will be discussed later.

The use of weapons to mark the status and group identity of particular people from the LpRIA onwards can be seen as the expression of certain processes of social change, in which new positions of power were marked. Conforming with this, the use of weapons in graves gradually disappears in the course of the LRIA, when the elite has been consolidated. Evidence that war still took place to a significant degree and under strong leadership is provided by the votive hoards of weapons.

The weapon grave milieu must then be regarded in the first instance as the result of a series of processes of social and political change and centralization. It is additionally remarkable that these are especially linked with the west of Denmark, just like the later votive hoards of weapons, which now ought to be looked at in this context.

The Weapon Hoards

The great bog finds lie dispersed along the eastern coast of Jutland from Angeln in the south to Randers *amt* in the north, and on Fyn (figure 3.41) (Hines 1989b). The number of warriors has been put at 'several hundred' in the case of Torsbjerg, at 200 at Ejsbøl (cf. also Ørsnes 1969a, 1984, 1988), at more than 300 at Nydam I and at Vimose at more than 500 (Steuer 1982, figure 34) (figures 3.42–6). To these can be added Illerup, a site which is not yet fully excavated, but where the number of warriors must have been particularly large. The largest of all the bog finds hitherto was Skedemose on Öland, which by Steuer's assessment must represent 500–800 men. This number is proposed on the basis of the mere 10 per cent of the original area from which finds were made, now entirely destroyed (Hagberg 1967; Ilkjær and Lønstrup 1983, p. 99).

Although many of the weapons were destroyed before sacrifice, deep cuts and blows are evidence of their use in a preceding battle. An analysis of attack and parrying cuts on swords, javelins and lances has provided an insight into the use of weapons and battle tactics (Gebühr 1977, 1980). It has, for instance, been possible to show how the javelin/lance was used as a particularly effective and dangerous hand weapon and not exclusively as a throwing weapon, an observation which fits well with the finding of a stocked spearhead at Illerup with a shaft 3 m long (Ilkjær and Lønstrup 1975, p. 109).

The function of long-range weapons, which has previously been described as a necessary tactical element in the construction of an army, is taken care of by the archers. Arrowheads are as good as absent from the graves, but they frequently appear in large numbers in the bogs. From the earliest deposit at Illerup, dated to the end of the ERIA, 150 examples have been found, from Torsbjerg 200–300 (Steuer 1982, figure 34) and from Ejsbøl 676 (Ørsnes 1968; 1988, p. 72).

The mobility of the warriors was high: their weapons and shields were light and they did not carry heavy armour, which certainly provided protection but which limited speed and freedom of movement. An example of such armour is the mailcoats, which are found in the bogs but not in any large numbers.

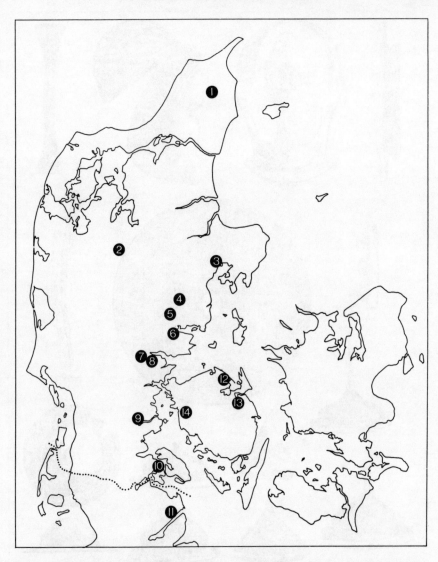

Figure 3.41 The distribution of bog finds of the ERIA, LRIA and EGIA containing weapons and/or horse gear. 1 Fuglsang = Trinnemose (no weapons); 2 Vallerbæk (dry land); 3 Hedelisker; 4 Illerup; 5 Porskjær; 6 Dollerup sø; 7 Vingsted sø; 8 Tranebjerg; 9 Ejsbøl; 10 Nydam; 11 Torsbjerg; 12 Viemose; 13 Illemose; 14 Kragehul.

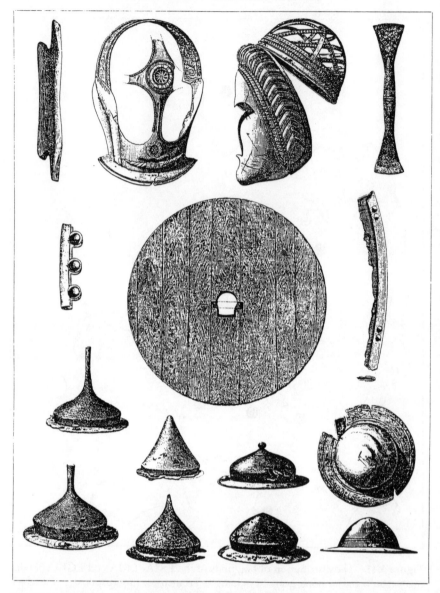

Figures 3.42–6 A selection of weapons, horse gear and other military equipment from the great bog deposits. (after Müller 1888–95).

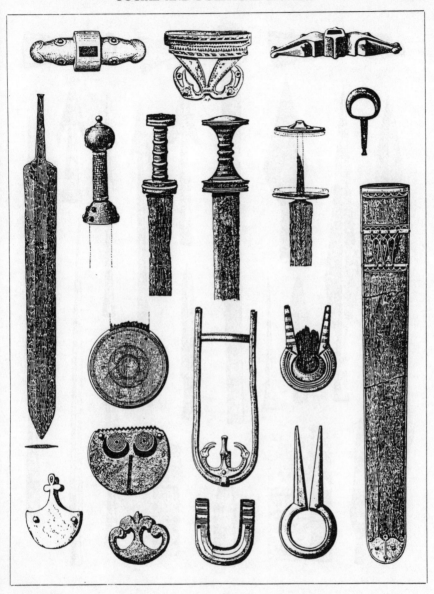

Figure 3.43

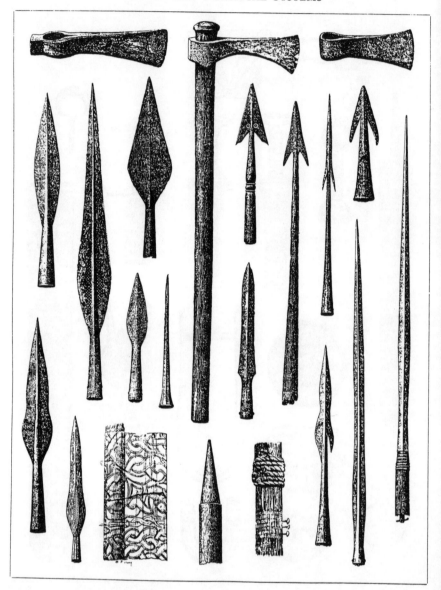

Figure 3.44

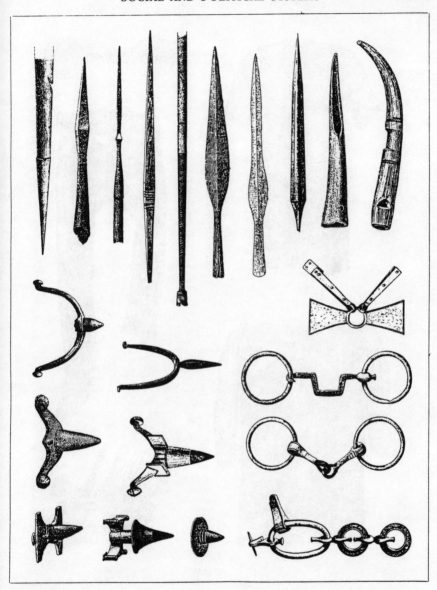

Figure 3.45

Figure 3.46

The various weapon types reflect specialized functions. At the top were the mounted leaders of the army (the officers); riding gear is evidence of specialized horsemanship and also of horse breeding. This feature seems to become more marked in the course of the LRIA. The weapon types become more diverse and more specialized, and genuine display weapons and display gear come on the scene (Raddatz 1966, 1967b). The types of bridle also develop from simple snaffle bits to large, strong, curb bits; the purpose of the latter was to prevent the horse from getting its tongue over the bit, which would result in the rider's completely losing control of his mount. The finely crafted bridle chains of bronze likewise emphasize the vital importance to the rider of keeping control of his horse; a leather bridle can, unlike a metal one, be cut in two, and in a battle the consequences of a ruined bridle would at best be that a warrior would have to fight on foot.

Unlike the grave finds, the bog finds give us some insight into the size of armies. The two find groups supplement one another. In the graves we find the warrior as a social individual, at home in his village, possibly after having fallen in battle and therefore buried with his weapons. In the bog finds we find the warriors of the battle field, now subjected to the military hierarchy. The grave finds and bog finds also show a degree of agreement between the social hierarchy and the military one. The order of rank in the graves is generally repeated in the military order of rank of the armies, although the graves do not contain prestige weapons such as in the votive find at Ejsbøl.

A closer comparison of the social order of rank in the weapon graves and the military order of rank in the war booty offerings might provide an estimate of the size of the territories that were involved. The votive deposits of weapons lie at fairly uniform intervals along the eastern coast of Jutland and on Fyn, and they divide the land into certain geographical entities which approximately match the size of *amts* in the same zones. In relation to the rich weapon graves and the territorial distribution of the graves with spurs (corresponding to the size of *herreds*) there would, according to these modules, be five to ten *herreder* (local officers) in the territory of one weapon deposit. If we consider the number of mounted warriors to be found in the different war booty offerings, the level of agreement is good.

We may suppose then that the army was composed of local military leaders (the mounted men) with their following of young warriors from the villages. That at the same time it was not a matter of randomly assembled fighters is evidenced by the uniform and professional character of the weapons. Like the structure of the army, this indicates that we are dealing here with professional soldiers.

We should also remember that the weapon graves and the war booty offerings are chronologically contiguous, with just a degree of overlap. There may, then, have been a development in political and military organization in this phase (figure 3.47). This is the next question to be considered.

Political and Military Organization

The description of the size and structure of the armies tells us two things: first, that real battles were fought in which the goal must have been territorial control; second, that there was a warrior elite around the leading chieftains (the troop or retinue) who fought for their leader rather than for their clan. These two points have extensive consequences for our comprehension of political and military organization.

A traditional, kinship-based tribal society will normally be incapable of mobilizing and maintaining a proper army. A man fought primarily for himself and for his immediate kin; in larger conflicts kindred groups could temporarily ally themselves. A 'professional' army with an order of command requires that these bonds be loosened or severed completely, so that in certain periods a man would fight for a leader who would be responsible for the partial or complete keep of the warrior and who would provide an opportunity for the warriors to keep in training. Thus the man was more of a soldier than a warrior. The precondition, then, for the larger armies which we find in some of the bog finds was that the regional leaders and their retinues could readily be joined into an order of command which was already known and practised.

When the clan or family, once the only basis of existence, is extended, or partially superseded, by bonds of loyalty to a leader, it is also implied that a man can appear as the representative of the leader in various situations, for instance in the village, the parish or the district. This man is the person who may eventually be able to mediate in the payment of tribute.

Thus it is through the troop that a leader can not only build up a more effective and professional army, but also a group of loyal retainers who, after their service was over, were furnished with suitable gifts and could look after his interests on a local basis. Both the weapon grave milieu and the war booty offerings make it probable that such a linked political and military structure may have been established and consolidated from the first century AD onwards.

As the bog finds testify, the end of the weapon grave rite shows only that the warrior function had become something taken for granted, something no longer distinguished in the graves. The military function was now, in all probability, completely subject to the political leadership, and weapons too may have fallen under central control. In any event, their uniformity shows that they were centrally produced and distributed.

In addition, when battles are fought by a professionally led army, put together out of the retinues of several regional leaders under the leadership of a single man, the motive must surely have been control of strategic resources and territories; this could mean trading posts or trade routes, but proper territorial control over the producers was also a goal.

The first large military barriers such as the one at Olmerdiget and the underwater barriers of stakes in the fjords were constructed at the end of the ERIA. These show that there were territories to defend, that the battles were concerned with these and that it was possible to mobilize not only the troops required but also the labour needed for the construction of these substantial structures.

That territories were the subject of conflict implies that a system existed under which it was possible for valuables, presumably as some form of tribute, to be appropriated by the leader. Through victory, then, one could not only take over the place of the military leader but also the administrative system which was the basis for taxation, the payment of tribute or however a surplus was then exacted; an army could not move from village to village to find its victualling. Such a system must have had a different basis.

It is not least the major weapon finds of the LRIA that show that an effective system of taxation now existed, a system which made the conquest of further areas attractive. And these must have been areas of a certain size. Sjælland, Fyn, central and south Jutland may certainly have formed independent political entities, each with its central leader, but not necessarily with control over each individual village; rather with a network of retainers all around the area, and possibly too with control over any trading posts there might have been.

Although minor raids must have taken place continually, generally the finds paint a picture of territorial battles for political control over the producers and presumably also over trading places in larger areas. In Jutland the rich outcrops of bog iron are likely too to have played an essential role (figure 3.47).

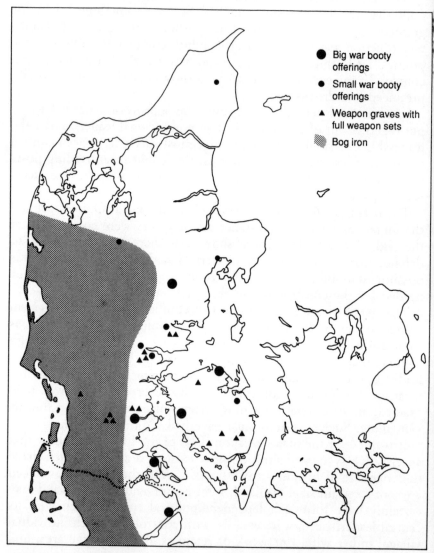

Figure 3.47 The distribution of war booty offerings (figure 3.41), weapon graves with full weapon sets of the ERIA (figure 3.23) and the presence of bog iron (i.e. potential iron-extraction areas).

Control over strategic resources and access to tribute are an essential precondition for it to be possible to maintain a troop and retinue. Thus the combined politico-military development towards control over ever larger areas had a self-enhancing effect, which subsequently led to the more effective exaction of tribute.

Traces of the Earliest State Structure: the Prestige Goods System

The four essentials which were put forward at the beginning of this chapter for the definition of an early state structure were the following: the specialization of the role of leader; the centralization of power; structural permanence; and finally an escape – either real or fictive – from the kinship structure as the basis of the hierarchy of power. The transition from a tribal structure to an early state structure will of course be gradual, as it is an historical process. Between these two appears that form which is described as the 'prestige goods system'. This is an adjunct to the 'archaic' state (Claessen and Skalnik 1978) or 'military democracy' (Herrmann 1982). A natural conclusion to this chapter, then, will be to summarize which of the structural characteristics that have been described seems to be applicable to the society of the Roman Iron Age on the basis of the investigations carried out.

The society which passes through the prestige goods system on its way from a tribal structure to an early state will be much more conspicuous archaeologically than one that follows some other route. It is natural, then, to find a starting-point in the prestige goods themselves.

What we regard as prestige goods are found in other periods of antiquity besides the Roman Iron Age, without our consequently looking to describe the society as one constructed around a prestige goods system. Prestige goods are also found in traditional chieftain societies, such as in the Early Bronze Age. In this case, however, they appear to be of a very much more ceremonial character. They find a place in fixed, normative sets of weapons (which are also ceremonial) or adornments, which, as has been noted, are made heavier, more finely crafted and gilt in order to emphasize the character of their significance, of their weight in symbolism. They are made of bronze, but their production is Scandinavian; what was foreign was the metal – the bronze and the gold – not the artefacts themselves. Many of these weapons and adornments are very worn; they have therefore been used (Kristiansen 1974b) and can thus also be considered as expressions of personal identity. Their symbolic meaning was at the same time an emphasis of relationship towards the divine and an identification with a well-defined, kinship-based, local elite. The relations of exchange in this part of antiquity do not, apparently, cross and cover great distances. The prestige goods themselves presumably took no part in any inter-regional exchange system of significance; only the metal was involved in this.

The use of prestige goods in the Roman Iron Age stands in clear contrast to the Bronze Age. The spiralling cycle of consumption, which seems to gain especial impetus at the beginning of the LRIA, is characterized by prestige goods no longer forming fixed sets of material, as in the Bronze Age, but rather by quantity being of decisive importance. In addition, the prestige goods themselves are of foreign origin; they demonstrate contact with the Roman world and find a place both in a supra-regional elite exchange system and in the internal exchange system. They give a much fuller insight into individual possession of wealth and individual contacts – in fact, over very long distances.

Symbols are however still found, clearly worn to be seen, and locally produced but of precious metal. This is most clearly evident with the snake's-head rings, be they finger rings, armrings or, occasionally, neckrings, and is certainly also the case with some of the large brooch types, such as the swastika brooches and the rosette brooches. These can be understood as individual symbols of particular social position or relationship with the elite. The situation is different with prestige goods of foreign manufacture, such as the Roman bronzes and glass. These objects are indeed personal – they are not dispersed by sale and purchase – but they do not form part of fixed sets of personal accessories. On the contrary, they can be accumulated in apparently unlimited quantities. At a local level, they take part in relations of exchange with local leaders as a factor in the construction of political alliances (vassalships) which imply political control over larger areas. The prestige goods were thus not only status symbols; they were active as creators of rank, and in legitimizing the construction of a new elite in which they represented aspirations to a Roman lifestyle.

A society in which prestige goods play an innovative role in this way must necessarily be marked by great social mobility: old structures and old elites are destroyed and new ones established. Such a process must also, if it is to succeed, be ideologically well founded. The elite monopoly – which affects access to prestige goods, which are the key to control of social reproduction – must be ideologically well founded and grounded in religion in order to be capable of splitting the traditional tribal structure.

But the prestige goods system too must of itself be very expansive in order to obtain the necessary economic bases for that expenditure which is demanded in order to maintain supply. One must expect, as a result, great physical mobility, a community marked by war and conquest, which is exactly what the archaeological evidence has indicated from the end of the ERIA through the whole of the LRIA.

But what came first – the prestige goods or the political control? Put in another way, were prestige goods used for the further development and strengthening of a form of economic and political control which was already in existence, or were they used in order to create the conditions for this? At this point in the research it is too early to answer this question definitively. It appears, as we shall see in due course (chapters 5 and 6), that these things are coincident in the sense that there is an interplay of factors of which no single one can be taken in isolation. The choice of the term 'prestige goods system' for the Roman Iron Age is governed by the fact that the Roman goods are, after all, the dominant element, and we have reasons to believe that they played an essential role, socially and ideologically, in preparing the ground for those changes which can be observed from the ERIA into the LRIA, but which also require changes both in the economy (control over the land) and in political organization (military control). Let us recapitulate, then, with a review of how many of the four preconditions for the identification of an early state structure have been fulfilled by the investigations up to this point.

Specialization of the role of leader   It is more than probable that some specialization of the leadership role took place. The fully armed warriors and knights with prestige goods at the very least indicate that from as early as the end of the LpRIA and clearly in the ERIA some political and military leadership was differentiated, just as the 'princely grave stratum' also indicates the existence of supreme political leadership in the ERIA. It is likewise worth noting that the rich graves, whether of the ERIA or the LRIA, are only exceptionally (especially on Fyn, at Møllegårdsmarken, for instance) found in the large cemeteries; rather they lie isolated or in quite small cemeteries, as if even in death their occupants continued not to identify themselves with the remainder of the community.

In this respect, it is the ERIA which shows the first signs of a specialized leadership function which comes to fulfilment in the LRIA. In the LRIA prestige goods are no longer used just to emphasize the leadership function but also to construct and maintain local political dominance by the establishment of a network of alliances with leading local men. In this we can also find signs of a centralization of economic and political power.

Centralization of power and structural permanence   From the same period, the war booty offerings also show unambiguously that there must have been a centralized structure of military-political leadership with a degree of permanence. It is worth noting that many cemeteries are abandoned at the end of the ERIA. Considering that there are still many graves in the LRIA (but not as many as in the ERIA), this must be attributed to a relocation or a break of a comprehensive character at the beginning of the LRIA. It is not possible to show fully what happened until the settlements are brought into the investigation.

If the votive hoards of the EGIA are set against the grave finds of the LRIA, with both of them regarded as material expressions of ideological activities, a pattern of permanence in structure emerges even though there is clearly a break in the votive ritual. Prestige goods in the form of Roman manufactured goods come to an end at the end of the LRIA but the use of gold for jewellery and rings continues throughout the EGIA. While previously these found their way into graves as an emphatic part of personal equipment – most noticeably in neck- , arm- and finger rings with the snake's-head motif, the gold rings are used in the EGIA as votive gifts.

The disappearance of everything of value from the graves in and from the EGIA can be interpreted in two ways. (1) When foreign goods (prestige goods) could no longer be obtained the political system collapsed. This is a natural interpretation of the 'poor' grave finds if they are not looked at in the light of the following, very much gold-rich, period. (2) The prestige goods disappeared when they had played out their role and so no longer had a place in ritual practice.

Whatever the case was, the prestige goods system as described here would predictably have a relatively short life. The cycle of consumption would come to an end in one way or the other, either because the community could no longer expand politically and economically or because the political and economic structure which was founded with the aid of the prestige goods had now been adequately consolidated. Since the votive finds of the EGIA give the impression of a phase of consolidation, in social, political and ideological terms, the second explanation is preferable.

The changes, then, are interpreted as an institutionalization of the religion and the consolidation of the elite, through which the political leadership was, at least in part, freed from the connection of rank and rituals. Instead, contact with the gods was performed in the form of sacrifices.

Escape from the kinship structure   The last of the four preconditions for speaking of incipient state formation is the partial parting of the kindred from the structure of economic and political power, so that the kinship system no longer functions as the sole economic basis for the individual. There can be no doubt that kinship and relationship to the clan continued to play a decisive role into the Middle Ages, but the social solidarity of the kinship system no longer ran from one end of society to the other. It was cut, vertically, into new social groupings, the internal relationships of which were regulated by economic and political determinants in the form of tax, military service and so on. These new groupings marked a clear distance between one another in, for instance, their funerary rituals. The new military hierarchy and the retinue also bore witness to rupture and a new social mobility. Thus in the material there are clear signs of a vertical partition of the kinship system into new politically and militarily defined groupings.

The studies of the grave finds and the hoard finds of the Iron Age presented here thus give the impression that in the course of the Roman Iron Age a development took place in which features of an early state structure, which have been defined in the chapter, can be seen in the archaeological material. But control of basic production would always have been the foundation upon which the structure of society operated, and which at the same time it modified. The graves and the votive practices will first be taken beyond the limits of ideological self-reflection when they are placed in relationship to this.

NOTES

1 Headhunting, torture and execution of captured enemies, cannibalism etc. are also found in societies with weaker organization, but the numbers killed in

these circumstances will never approach the numbers killed when two armies meet.

2 The grave finds of the ERIA and LRIA were recorded in the National Museum in Copenhagen during the years 1973–7 and in the following local museums: Vendsyssel Historiske Museum; Kulturhistorisk Museum, Randers; Forhistorisk Museum, Moesgaard; Haderslev Museum (in all cases in 1979). I have also used as supplements: Albrectsen, *Fynske Jernaldergrave II* (1956), *III* (1968), *IV* (1971) and *V* (1973); Skaarup, *Stengade II* (1976). For cross-reference, Norling-Christensen, *Katalog over Ældre Romersk jernalders Grave i Århus Amt* (1954) has been used. The grave finds of the pRIA and the EGIA and LGIA were recorded in the National Museum in 1980. As supplements I have used: Albrectsen, *Fynske Jernaldersgrave I* (1954) and Becker 1956, 1957 and 1961. The LGIA is supplemented by Ørsnes 1966 and Ramskou 1976.

3 Artefacts of organic material are not counted in these analyses because of their very variable state of preservation.

4 A 'closed find' is here defined as an archaeological find for which it is attestable (1) that the artefacts found were all deposited together and not added to at later times, and (2) that the number of artefacts found matches the number of artefacts originally deposited, that is, it can be attested that the find has remained undisturbed until excavation. Not all grave finds fulfil these criteria but, unlike the hoards, virtually all grave finds comprise objects that were deposited at a single time. Thus the grave group is affected only by the degree of uncertainty that resides in the find circumstances.

5 The choice of the *amt* as the geographic unit to work with is explained by the wish to make local differences and similarities appear as clearly as possible. Sjælland, however, is treated as one unit because geographically it is a definite entity, with a uniform burial rite. The same goes for Fyn, but here the quantity of graves is so great that again a division by *amt* is justified. Møllegårdsmarken is also treated as a separate unit.

6 The graves of the pRIA in the National Museum were all recorded, but not the smaller collections in the local museums; this means that the data set is not complete.

7 The analysis of weapon graves with full weapon sets can be carried out with all grave finds, closed or not. An analysis of the remaining weapon graves, however can only be carried out on the basis of the closed grave finds as it must be certain that one or more weapons have not been lost. The same applies to the analysis of the finds associated with weapons.

8 Both of these graves, one from Fraugde (Albrectsen 1968), the other from Uggeløse (Thrane 1967) can be attributed to the very beginning of the period and thus in their composition too clearly belong to the weapon graves of the ERIA.

9 Møllegårdsmarken is an exception here, with eight graves of the ERIA (from 266) and eighty-eight graves of the LRIA (out of 1,002).

10 See also the NAT histograms *amt* by *amt*, in which the presence of gold and imports is marked (figures 3.10, 3.11, 3.12 and 3.13).

11 Gold is, however, not found in the graves of Randers *amt*. Breloques in this area are usually of silver, unlike in the rest of the country (Hedeager and Kristiansen 1981, figure 39).

12 Swords, however, should really be treated as imports.
13 In the course of the most recent excavations at Vorbasse in central Jutland a
    small cemetery with, *inter alia*, two weapon graves has been uncovered. One
    of these has a full weapon set: two lances/javelins, a shield and a sword, and
    a Hemmoor bucket et al. (Hvass 1983).
14 This contrasts with Öland and Gotland, where leather knives are found in
    women's graves (Hagberg 1967).

4

Settlement and Economy

Settlement Structure

Introduction

Up until a few years ago the most important progress in research into the settlement structure and economy of north European Iron-Age society at a regional level had been made outside Denmark. In Norway and Sweden co-operation with cultural geographers and others had produced a series of regional and local settlement studies which contributed to greater understanding of changes in settlement, production systems and the cultural landscape in the course of the Iron Age. Cultural-geographical studies were introduced in Sweden by Lindqvist (1968, 1974) and have since been carried on by Carlsson (1979, 1984), Sporrong (1971), Widgren (1983, 1984) and Windelhed (1984). In Norway, Bjørn Myhre in particular has completed a series of fundamental investigations (Myhre 1973, 1978). The application of cultural geographers' methods has, however, been criticized (Näsman 1979).

A series of settlement-history studies on the internal structure and organization of Iron-Age society in the Mälar region has been undertaken, relying upon the systematic mapping of Iron-Age monuments there; they involve, for instance, the administrative development of parishes and districts (*herreds*) (Ambrosiani 1964; Hyenstrand 1974; Wijkander 1983). Place names too have been brought into the study of settlement history.

There have also been comprehensive studies of settlement history in north Germany during the last twenty-five years, with co-operation between natural scientists, historians and archaeologists (summarized, for instance, by Kossack et al. 1984; Haarnagel 1979; Jankuhn 1976).

At the same time, there has been a significant development of theory and methods specifically relating to the topic of settlement history, particularly in the Anglo-Saxon lands (summarized in Hodder and Orton 1976; Haggett 1965; Chisholm 1962). Site catchment and central place theories came into general use (e.g. Ellison and Harriss 1972; Grant 1986), and a large number of studies based upon the systematic application of the new methods appeared.

Only in recent years have these theoretical and methodological advances pushed their way into Danish Iron Age research, into settlement research last of all (e.g. Jacobsen 1977, unpublished dissertation, Århus University; Jensen 1978). A series of methodological symposia organized by Henrik Thrane have been pre-eminent in encouraging discussion (Thrane 1976, 1977, 1978, 1979; Thrane and Jeppesen 1983, etc.).

Research into Iron-Age settlement in Denmark is, however, still under the influence of problems defined almost two generations ago, primarily by historians. These include the question of the age and continuity of the village, and with this the age of place names, and the question of continuity in areas, on sites or on particular plots (Becker 1976). In recent years a number of archaeological projects have been directed specifically at following the continuity of present villages back in time (Jeppesen 1979, 1981; Hedeager 1982; Hedeager, Poulson and Tornbjerg 1982). At the same time, huge resources have been put into complete excavation of a number of well-preserved villages. It is here that Danish archaeology has, scientifically, conquered the greatest amount of new territory (Becker 1971, etc.; Hvass 1983, 1985b, etc.).

We can conclude, then, that to only a limited extent have ecological and economic analyses of the development of village society been undertaken, and that systematic settlement-history analyses are lacking, apart from an analysis carried out in the north-east of Fyn (Porsmose 1985). Modern zoological and botanical analyses of the relationship between settlement and the environment/field systems are also wanting. In this area, practically nothing has been done since the work of Gudmund Hatt (1949), which has been followed by Viggo Nielsen's mapping of east Denmark (1984) and Harder Sørensen's of west Denmark (1982).

The following survey must therefore primarily take the character

of an analysis of problems, aimed at putting the existing material into
a cultural-historical formula which allows more general conclusions.
Within this, especial importance will be attributed to the ecological
situation, combined with the analysis of the organization and development of the village. It is not possible at present to undertake more
systematic analyses of settlement itself, as will become evident in the
section on representativity and the following sections on place names,
soil type and continuity. Some conclusions can nevertheless be
drawn. Because the problems of representativity associated with the
settlement material are so great, this is the first factor requiring
critical evaluation.

Problems of Representativity

In chapter 1 (pp. 13–21) the representativity of various find groups
at the national level was briefly discussed, and it was concluded that
the distribution of settlements and settlement traces had to be
regarded as far from representative of the original geographical distribution (Hvass 1985a).[1]

In archaeological terms, an 'Iron-Age settlement' may be anything
from simple pits, hearths and culture layers with potsherds through
simple building traces to full villages. Altogether about 900 sites
were recorded in the National Museum's parish survey of 1978
(Hvass 1985a). The majority of known settlements are in Jutland,
and it is here too that the majority of fully excavated villages are
found: central, west and north Jutland are especially rich in finds.
On Fyn, the number of recorded sites is greater in Odense *amt*
than in Svendborg *amt*; Sjælland, Lolland and Falster are poorly
represented. Compared with, for example, the distribution maps for
Iron-Age graves (figures 3.1–5) it is instructive that in every case
Sjælland, Lolland-Falster and Svendborg *amt* are under-represented.
The picture as regards settlement excavation is also skewed; larger,
fully excavated villages are known as yet only from Jutland,
especially the centre, west and north.

The distribution map in figure 4.1 shows Iron-Age settlement
traces. The majority of the sites recorded can be dated to the pRIA
and the ERIA, fewer to the LRIA, fewer still to the EGIA and
virtually none to the LGIA. The general distribution picture thus
contains serious bias as far as chronological representativity is concerned. Among the reasons for this is that settlements from the
LRIA, EGIA and LGIA lack culture layers such as stone paving

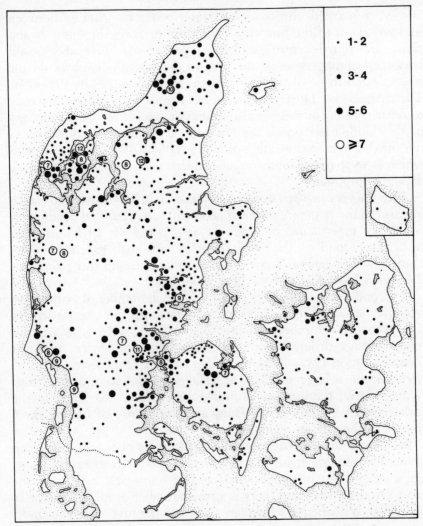

Figure 4.1 The distribution of Iron-Age settlements (Hvass 1985a, figure 25). Status: 1978.

and clay floors. The marked decrease in the number of recorded sites must not, therefore, simply be attributed to a decline in settlement in the later Iron Age (Jensen 1982).

As regards dating, there are problems with settlement pottery of the later Iron Age. The most recent study of building typology (by Dorte Mikkelsen in an Århus University dissertation in 1988) shows two very marked chronological watersheds: the first is between building types of the first and second centuries on the one side and third- and fourth-century building types on the other; the second between building types of the fifth to the seventh centuries on the one side and those of the eighth to the tenth centuries on the other. The changes that Dorte Mikkelsen has demonstrated apply not only to settlement in Jutland but also to that on the islands. A chronology of this kind, based upon the form of the buildings, will prove an inestimable help in the dating of many settlements, the pottery from which is so sparse or undistinguished that even a relatively accurate dating is impossible.

With the very marked differences not only in building construction but also in the structure of the villages and in agricultural production which are in evidence between the ERIA and the LRIA, that is, from the second to the third centuries, we shall proceed in this chapter with a general division of settlement around this point into the earlier Iron Age and the later Iron Age.

A second explanation of the relatively small number of settlements from the latter half of the Iron Age may lie in the fact that settlement was probably centralized: many small villages were grouped into fewer ones, with larger units (Porsmose 1985; S. Jensen, personal communication 1989). This must necessarily have involved the abandonment of a large number of villages in the second and third centuries AD; the number of villages, therefore, was larger in the earlier Iron Age than in the later, and the chance of finding them must also then be so much better.

We may conclude that as yet the settlements of the Iron Age can be used in settlement-history analyses only with great reservations. On a national basis, geographical and chronological bias is significant. On the other hand there is a small number of fully or partially excavated settlements which are very informative. They cannot, however, simply be assumed to be representative of all settlements.

The absence of regional settlement studies is still an acute problem. Only by these means could one put the well-excavated settlements into their settlement context and assess their general significance.

The following interpretations of settlement and economy must therefore have the character of an analysis of the problems. How far can the evidence we have take us, with regard to the important questions of settlement structure, density and continuity, expansion and regression, production systems and ecology? Because of the greatly varying information value of the basic data, it has been necessary to introduce results from place names, pollen analysis, graves and hoards. Each of these find groups has its own problems as a source, and these are discussed in the course of the survey.

Settlements, Burials and Hoards

We have seen how the settlement finds of the Iron Age are representative neither geographically nor chronologically, and it is natural, therefore, to put the other major find groups, the graves and the hoards, alongside them in order, if possible, to reveal more of the settlement pattern.

The distribution of grave finds from the ERIA and LRIA at least, and the distribution of gold hoards of the EGIA can be regarded as representative (Geisslinger 1967; Fonnesbech-Sandberg 1985; Hedeager 1985) (figures 3.2, 3.3, 4.2). This means that future finds should not be expected to change the patterns of distribution at present known, and that these therefore can be taken as representative of the prehistoric deposits (see pp. 13ff. above). But they cannot simply be supposed to represent the distribution of settlement in these three periods. It has been shown, for instance, that at least the graves from Sjælland in the LRIA are more probably an expression of the socio-political organization there than of the settlement structure (Hedeager 1978c, 1980, 1985). On the other hand there are various examples of grave finds lying in the immediate vicinity of settlements. We may suppose, then, that there is a connection between grave finds and contemporary settlements, although an absence of grave finds cannot be read as evidence of an absence of population.

The situation on the issue of the relationship of the gold hoards to the original settlement pattern is clear. Gold finds have been associable with settlements of the EGIA in relatively few cases.[2] Since gold deposits are probably both ritual and religious, and since these are found in the same areas, we may reasonably assume that these areas were also settled in the EGIA.

It appears that the distribution of graves of the pRIA, ERIA and LRIA agrees fully with that of the settlements in Jutland and partly too on Fyn (figure 4.1). It matches very well with most of the known settlements from these periods. We may presume, then, that those areas which are void of finds in the earlier Iron Age were also in fact little used. The same conclusion cannot, however, be drawn on the basis of the grave finds of Sjælland, Lolland and Falster.

We can also see that the gold hoards of the Germanic Iron Age

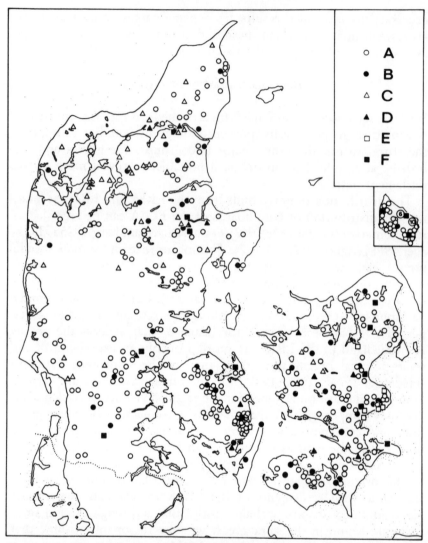

Figure 4.2 The distribution of gold caches of the EGIA. The find circumstances are given as: A fields; B formerly bog/wetland; C bog; D rivers, open water; E coast; F unknown. (Fonnesbech-Sandberg 1985, figure 18)

are found in the same areas as settlement in Jutland south of the Limfjord, but not in other parts of the country, and one should not conclude that areas without gold finds and without known settlements were abandoned in the later Iron Age. The distribution of gold hoards is, however, a good supplementary guide to the picture of settlement in the Earlier Germanic Period.

Place Names

'So there lie the place names, slumbering like soldiers in Kaiser Frederik's underground fort; they are waiting for the correct watchword, the blaring trumpet, which will rouse them from their sleep and bring them to form their serried ranks,' wrote the historian H. V. Clausen in his monograph *Studier over Danmarks Oldtidsbebyggelse* [*Studies in the Ancient Settlement of Denmark*] of 1916. To form serried ranks of place names one has to date them. But can one?

There is general agreement on the relative dating of a series of prehistorical place names. In the oldest groups are considered to be names ending in *-inge, -lev, løse* and *-sted*, and to a later group belong names ending in *-torp, -by, -holt, -rød* and more. The placing of the oldest group in the Iron Age and the next in the Viking Period is also generally agreed (e.g. Steenstrup 1894; Clausen 1916; La Cour 1927; Christensen 1938; Hald 1950; Søndergaard 1972; Christensen and Kousgård Sørensen 1972; Jørgensen 1979). The absolute dating of the earliest name endings, however, is less certain. There is a widespread view that their origins must lie before the beginning of the sixth century at the latest, but how far back before this they could go cannot be determined with certainty.

Clausen believed that the *-inge* names were the oldest. Since this element is not found in the areas of Vendsyssel, Himmerland, southeast Schleswig (including Angeln and Sundeved) and south-east Fyn (i.e. in those areas, except for south-east Fyn, from which the great migrations of Cimbri and Angles took place), they must be older than the emigrations: formed, in other words, before *c*.150 BC.

Clausen linked the *-lev* settlement to a great expansion out of Sjælland which was part of the formation of the Danish state. According to his theory, powerful Danish kings were ruling as early as 500 at Lejre by Roskilde, and the *-lev* settlements must therefore be older. The group of names in *-løse* has to be dependent on the *-lev* settlement, and is considered to be either contemporary or a little later. Finally, *-sted* must be later than *-lev* and *-løse* but earlier than *-um* and *-by*, and these could only have appeared between 700 and 800.

On the strength of old forest names and clearing names of the Viking Period and the early Middle Ages, Clausen defined the settlements of the Iron Age in relation to surrounding, wooded land.

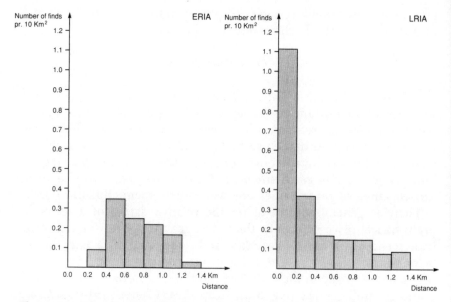

Figure 4.3 The distance between the earliest place name elements (*-lev*, *-løse*, *-sted*) and grave finds of the ERIA and LRIA respectively. The diagrams are based on surveys of Sjælland, Lolland and Falster, but the situation on Fyn is identical.

In spite of reservations and criticisms there can be no great doubt but that Clausen's studies do provide a general perspective of the main features in settlement history in as far as they illustrate the relationship between earlier and later settlement. The maps also clearly show that before the beginning of the Viking Period the land was divided into separated settlement blocks with large, unsettled areas between them (Christensen 1938).

This reconstruction implies that about half of the land was settled, and that within the settlement blocks only a small part was cultivated. Of the individual areas, east Jutland from Århus to Vejle, and north-west Jutland seem to have been most densely settled, as the forest areas here are limited to small bands around the settled areas. The larger stretches of forest and waste appear particularly on Fyn and in northern Sjælland (Christensen 1938). One recent attempt to use place names as a means of understanding Iron-Age settlement in Scandinavia is that of Brink (1988). He too concludes that the earliest place names must have been formed in the Roman Iron Age, and that it is justified to regard them as evidence for continuity of settlement from that period onwards.

But if the settled areas became fixed in the course of the Iron Age, when did the administrative divisions appear? The historian Aksel E. Christensen has compared the *herred*-maps with Clausen's settlement map and concludes that the *herred* was originally a naturally evolved Iron-Age settlement zone which took on administrative significance at a later stage. In the case of the islands the *herred* boundaries always run through the outlying farms and forest tracts which separated the old settled areas. In Jutland the situation is more complicated, as the coincidence between original settled area and *herred* is rather indistinct in some places, for instance in the large Århus block. However, in other parts of Jutland the agreement is quite clear. It should be noted that the boundaries of the *herreds* in the Middle Ages were not definitively fixed, and some division of the *herreds* took place in the late medieval period (Christensen 1938, pp. 9f.).

It has been thought that the great age of the *herreds* and the parishes is confirmed by the fact that many more Iron-Age names are parish names than are later names of the Viking Period and Middle Ages, perhaps because the old settlement areas were still dominant when the parishes and *herreds* were established. Knudsen (1939) found that: 54 per cent of *-lev* names are also parish names (150 out of 280); 46 per cent of *-um* names (114 out of 250); 26 per cent of *-by* names (166 out of 650); 14 per cent of *-torp* names (283 out of 2,000); and 9 per cent of *-rød* names (14 out of 150).

One of the most important non-linguistic means of clarifying the date of the place names is archaeology. But there is a wide range of methodological problems involved in such an interdisciplinary linkage. A number of statistical studies have been carried out with regard to Fyn and Sjælland, in particular into the relationship between well-dated archaeological finds and place name types in the immediate vicinity (Nielsen 1978, 1979; Albrectsen 1970) (figure 4.3). The results show that finds of the earlier Iron Age are strongly represented around villages with old place name endings, especially *-lev*, *-løse* and *-sted*. The later name types, *-by* and *-torp*, are not correlated with finds of the earlier Iron Age. The results thus agree well with those of place name research's own methods.

The creation and the survival of both the place names and the archaeological material are the products of complicated historical processes which may have suppressed earlier elements or which of their very nature represent only a limited or some special section of the society. Thus neither the archaeological distribution map nor the maps of the oldest place names give a comprehensive picture of the

Iron-Age settlement of this country. But each provides essential pieces of a settlement-history mosaic which can be extended further.

The Development of Settlement Structures

There are two factors which appear to be decisive in the location of Iron-Age settlements. In the first place, between 80 and 100 per cent of the village land within 1 km was arable, that is, it was not too heavy nor too wet. In the second place, the settlements are so placed that they had access to minor, wet areas which could provide (winter) fodder for the beasts. Access to water, however, seems to have been of less importance, and concomitant with this is the fact that wells were common. One can also see that those settlements that were not centrally placed in relation to larger, coherent agricultural areas did conversely have good meadow lands in their vicinity (Jacobsen 1977).

Most villages remained inside the same resource area or estate for most of the Iron Age (figure 4.4). Once an area was cultivated, its continuing exploitation was preferable in terms of production and labour, especially as the Iron-Age farmers manured the soil. A consequence of this was that the land became so densely settled that new areas with good arable land were no longer available.

A series of studies of Iron-Age settlement in various parts of the country all point the same way: that in some areas from as early as the beginning of the present era the villages were as densely sited as they are today, in other words at intervals just a few kilometres apart. These studies cover Thy (Jensen 1976, 1979; supplemented by personal communication from Jens H. Bech), Ribe area (Jensen 1980a), Vejle district (personal communication from Steen Hvass), north-west Jutland (Mathiassen 1948), eastern Fyn (Porsmose 1985) and Stevns in eastern Sjælland (personal communication from S. A. Tjornbjerg). In the broad view, we must assume that all of Denmark was settled in the course of the earlier Iron Age, with the simple exception of certain major forest areas on the steepest moraine zones.

Some shifting in settlement does, however, take place. Finds from the earliest Iron Age are distinctly linked to the light soil in west and central Jutland – just as in the Bronze Age – while finds from all other periods cluster most densely on heavier soil (Mathiassen 1948, pl. XXVIII; N. H. Andersen 1976; Jensen 1980a) (figure 4.5). We may therefore conclude that the Iron-Age population of the centuries around the beginning of our era could settle on all kinds

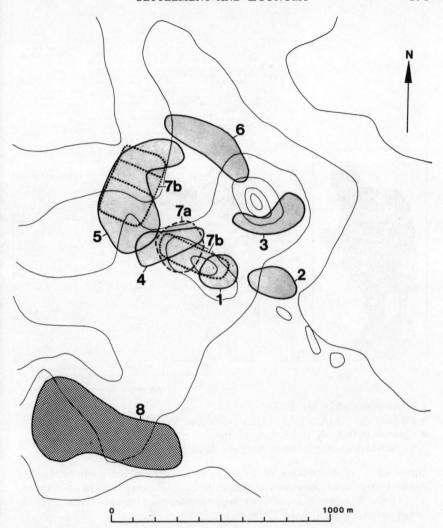

Figure 4.4 The shifting of settlement at Vorbasse in central Jutland from the first century BC to the twelfth century AD. The numbers show the location of the village in different periods. 1 First century BC; 2 First century AD; 3 Second century AD; 4 Third century AD; 5 Fourth–fifth centuries AD; 6 Sixth–seventh centuries AD; 7a Eighth–tenth centuries AD; 7b Eleventh century AD; 8 From the eleventh century to the present.

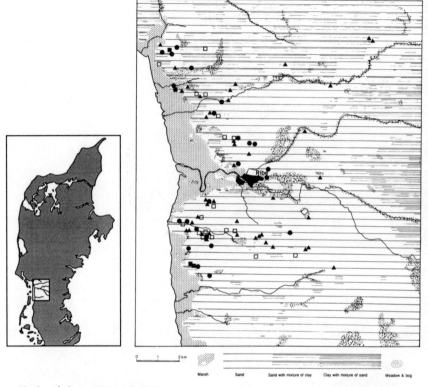

Marsh   Sand   Sand with mixture of clay   Clay with mixture of sand   Meadow & bog

▲ Finds of the pRIA and ERIA
● Finds of the LRIA, EGIA, LGIA and Viking Period
■ Finds of both Early and Late Iron Age
□ Finds which cannot be more precisely dated within the Iron Age

Figure 4.5 The distribution of Iron-Age finds between the rivers Sneum and Rejsby by the North Sea coast of southern Jutland. The map is based upon the soil map of the Ministry of Agriculture supplemented with meadow areas from the survey map of 1860. (Jensen 1980a, figure 7)

of soil – which means, in principle, anywhere in the country – because the form of agriculture was especially flexible and adaptable. When the land was so heavily exploited that new areas could no longer be found, agricultural and technological changes were the only answer to population pressure and soil exhaustion. This is considered further on pp. 209ff. below.

Village Organization and Farming

With the excavations of Grøntoft in west Jutland (Becker 1965, 1968, 1971), Hodde in south-west Jutland (Hvass 1975, 1985b) and Vorbasse in central Jutland (Hvass 1978, 1983) it has become possible for the first time to follow a particular village from its foundation to its abandonment. Since these three villages belong to three different parts of the Iron Age, it has been natural to look upon them as expressive of the development of the Iron-Age village, from the few, smaller farmsteads at Grøntoft in the EpRIA, through Hodde's well-organized village community with a major farmstead as the dominant element in the LpRIA, to conclude with Vorbasse's large, independent farmsteads of the LRIA, EGIA, LGIA and Viking Period (figure 4.6).

But one cannot generalize on the basis of three villages. The many smaller excavations are therefore also of importance: they shed light upon the common features of the village, illustrated by building types, the functional division of the farmstead and the spatial organization of the village.

Building Types

In constructional terms, the buildings of the earlier Iron Age as a whole (fifth century BC to second century AD) belong to one type (figure 4.7).[3] The wall construction, however, can vary from region to region, apparently dependent upon the availability of suitable material. Usually the walls are built of wattle and daub or of turf, but walls built completely of timber are also known. In several places it is possible to find double post rows, which represent one wattle-and-daub wall and an outer row of free-standing posts which carried some of the weight of the roof (Lund and Nielsen 1982). On some sites however, even where the opportunities for observation are good, traces of wall construction cannot be found. The explanation may be that sills and wall plates were already in use. A wall plate is a piece of horizontally laid timber which served as a support for the wall; a sill is a line of stones on which the wall was raised. This wall type has no place for posts sunk into the ground and is therefore difficult to detect archaeologically. But on several sites rows of stones have been found where wall posts might be expected, and these could therefore be sill stones. There is much, then, to suggest

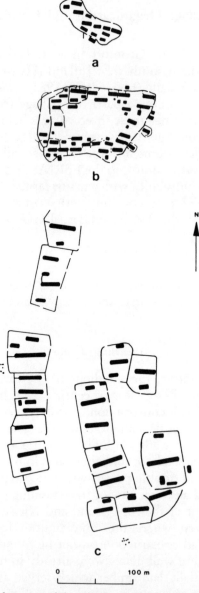

Figure 4.6   The development of the village at a common scale: (a) Grøntoft, village
A of the second century BC; (b) Hodde in the first century BC; (c) Vorbasse in
the fourth and fifth centuries AD. (Hvass 1985b, figure 110)

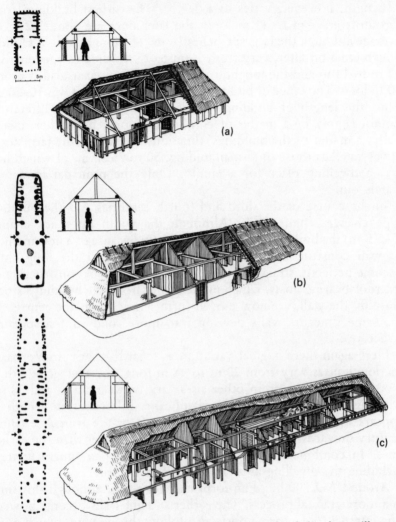

Figure 4.7 The ground plans of longhouses from each of the three villages in figure 4.6: (a) Grøntoft, (b) Hodde and (c) Vorbasse, with their reconstructions. (reconstructions by Flemming Bau, after Hedeager 1988a, p. 191)

that this construction has been used since the earlier Iron Age (Lund and Nielsen 1982).

Building width does not vary greatly. The earliest buildings at Grøntoft seem definitely to be narrower than the later ones: 3.5 m to 4 m, against a later 5 m; in and from the first century BC the width stands unvaried at about 5.5 m.

Length, however, varies to a degree. The earliest buildings from Grøntoft are 7 m to 11 m long; the later ones are about 12 m on average although the largest reaches 16 m. The longhouses at Hodde, which are a bit later, vary from 10 m to 23 m: the average length is 12 m to 14 m and the longhouse of the principal farmstead is nearly 30 m long. The range of building lengths from other sites is 10–20 m. Thus the length of buildings varies so much that the differences cannot simply be a matter of chronology alone, but rather, essentially, a matter of the buildings' functions. Generally the farmsteads are as small as those of a smallholding, 50 to 75 sq m, of which half was a dwelling place for a family. Only the principal farmstead stands out.

In the course of the third and fourth centuries AD the building type changes (figure 4.7). Although the width does not change (5–5.5 m) the building changes form, partly because of a new method of wall construction. The ends are rounded and the long sides become perfectly straight. There are changes in roof construction as the roof-bearing posts, which in the earlier Iron-Age buildings stood close by the wall, are now moved further in towards the centre. At the same time the walls develop into more solid roof-supporting structures.

Here again there is great variation as regards length. In Vorbasse the longhouses vary from 20 m to 48 m long; the average length is 30–35 m. Buildings from other sites vary between 15 m and 38 m. Although there were already significant differences in length it appears that the buildings of the later part of the Iron Age (third century onwards) were on average somewhat longer than the earlier ones. In combination with outhouses, the area in square metres, including the dwelling area, is doubled or tripled.

Around AD 700 building form changes again, although this time in a more gradual process. The earlier straight walls become bowed. The internal roof-bearing posts also follow this bowing, which must mean that the beams that the posts are carrying – the beams that are themselves carrying the roof – no longer now run the length of the building but rather run across it. With this, the buildings can be made a couple of metres or so wider. Large posts at the ends indicate that the buildings were high-gabled.

The longhouses of the Iron-Age farmsteads contain both dwelling areas and stalls under the one roof: the dwelling area in the west end and the stalls in the east. By placing the buildings with one long side facing south and the ends to east and west the greatest benefit was obtained from the warmth of the sun and the greatest protection against the westerly wind.

Longhouses with stalls, longhouses without stalls and minor buildings (usually without stalls or hearths) are known from the earlier Iron Age. The longhouse with stalls is divided into two rooms of almost equal size, separated by a small entrance room. The hearth is located at the western end and the floor may be clay-covered. This part of the building functioned as the dwelling area.

In the eastern half are partition walls for the individual stalls, usually about 70–80 cm apart. When the eastern end functioned as stalls it normally had an earth floor, which was usually lower than the floor of the western end, no doubt to stop the manure seeping the wrong way. The stalls could be paved, in some cases with open, stone-built dung channels, as, for instance, is the case in the farmsteads around Esbjerg in south-west Jutland (Hvass 1982a, with references). In a number of cases, burnt sites have provided a glimpse of the stock kept. From Ginderup in north Jutland four sheep or goats, one pig and one cow (?) were found at the stall end of a burnt-down building (Kjær 1928) and three cows and a horse perished in a fire in a longhouse at Solbjerg, also in north Jutland (Hatt 1928).

The absence of partition walls for stalls may of course mean that they were never there, but it may also be the case that the state of preservation is not good enough. There are however several points that indicate that there were longhouses without stalls, for instance the existence of longhouses with clay flooring in the full length of the building and of longhouses with hearths at both ends (Hatt 1938); at Hodde longhouses were found with a hearth at the western end but no stall divisions in the eastern end, even though the state of preservation in these buildings should have been as good as in the others (Hvass 1982a, p. 132). The largest longhouse without stalls at Hodde is 18 m long. Rather than stalls for larger beasts the area could have been intended for storage, for example, for a work area or perhaps for smaller beasts such as sheep, goats, pigs or hens.

Farmsteads comprising several buildings are first certainly known from the first and second centuries BC. The function of the smaller buildings (4–7 m in length) is not, however, clear. There is definite evidence that some of these were smithies, and the occurrence of hearths and, sometimes, pits likewise indicates a variety of crafts; there is nothing to suggest that they were used as stalls. Some of these well-built minor buildings may have served as storehouses, possibly as barns, henhouses or pigsties. Several of the farmsteads in north Jutland had cellars. One of these is preserved on a burnt site, and proves to have been a storage place, principally used for the keeping of corn (Lund 1979a, b).

In the later Iron Age the farmsteads similarly comprise the long-house and possibly one or two minor buildings. At Vorbasse, where the farmsteads of this period are best documented, there is a difference between larger and smaller longhouses: the larger ones measure 30–48 m, the smaller 20–30 m. As previously, people lived in the western end and had stalls in the eastern half of the building. But rather than being divided into two rooms there can now be up to five. In the western part there may be three rooms: an entrance room, a middle room and the large living room to the west with the hearth. The stalls are to the east, but in some longhouses the eastern end itself contains a larger or smaller room without the foundations of stalls. This room could have been quite open at the end and have functioned as a barn. The smaller longhouses match the larger ones in construction and interior division but the length of stalling is less. Compared with other farmsteads of the later Iron Age the Vorbasse farmsteads are very large, but the longhouses from here are not unique.

The smaller buildings at Vorbasse are between 9 and 16 m long, usually 13–15 m. In terms of construction they are a bit different from the longhouses (Hvass 1979, pp. 74ff.; L. Hvass 1980, p. 137). Forging slag was found in one of these buildings, which must therefore have been a smithy. Another one is shown by a hearth to have been either a workshop or a residential building, and stall foundations along both walls in a third show that it was a byre. Although these minor buildings are of the same size as the earliest farmhouses of the Iron Age they did not function as independent units but were always part of some larger farmstead.

There is another group of minor buildings at Vorbasse. These either have just one row of roofbearing posts along the centre of the building or none at all, and measure between 7 and 14 m in length and are 4 m wide. They can be either free-standing or connected to the great fences of the farmyard in such a way that the fence forms one of the building's long sides. In one corner of such a fenced-in farmyard are often found either four or eight large post holes. These are interpreted as 'stack barns' (Hvass 1979, pp. 79ff.; L. Hvass 1980, p. 137), but could of course have been used for other purposes, such as fuel sheds.

Finally, an entirely new building type can be seen, the sunken hut. These are small, dug-out huts, measuring between 2.4 × 1.8 and 4.7 × 2.8 m at Vorbasse, sunk to a depth of up to 80 cm (Hvass 1979, p. 81). No finds have been made in any of these at Vorbasse; on other sites spindle-whorls, loomweights, whetstones, rubbing stones, pottery and a pair of bronze tweezers have been found (Voss 1976, p. 69). The sunken huts are common on Viking Period farmsteads, where in several cases rows of loomweights have been found at the base of the pit together with traces of posts for the loom. These, then, were work and craft sheds.

Village Organization

The changes in building construction, building types and functional division which took place in the course of the Iron Age were accompanied by changes in the organization of the village. Once again our bases for illustrating the main features of this development are Grøntoft, Hodde and Vorbasse.

The settlement at Grøntoft, however, remains quite unique in representing the earliest Iron-Age farmsteads. It is therefore not possible to say whether the shift from a dispersed collection of buildings in the earliest settlement to an enclosed village (figure 4.8) also took place in other parts of the country.

At Hodde a series of new features can be seen, including an open space in the centre of the village. Each farmstead may now comprise several buildings and the farmsteads are often enclosed by a fence which is connected to the main common fence of the village; the major farmstead, however, is surrounded by its own solid fence. The individual farmsteads each have their own exit through the common fence to the surrounding fields.

Of the many villages of this part of the Iron Age that have been investigated, only a small minority have a plan matching that at Hodde, and none of them is even approximately comparable with Hodde in size. The principal farmstead too is unusual. The village at Hodde cannot therefore be credited as representative of 'the village' in the centuries around the birth of Christ. Settlement could be organized either in villages in which the farmsteads and buildings lie side by side in a row, or in the form of many small units of two or three farmsteads enclosed by a common fence (Becker 1980; Hvass 1982b).

From the third century AD the village changes character. The individual farmsteads are now enclosed within their own fences,

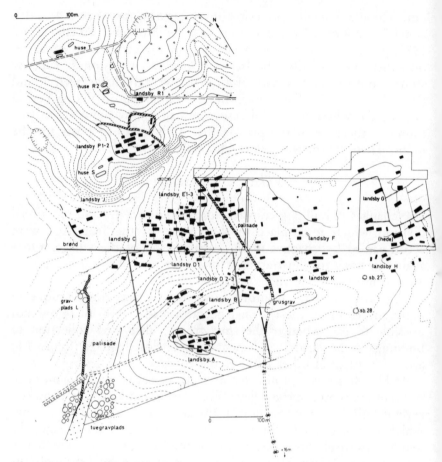

Figure 4.8 Plan of buildings of the EpRIA at Grøntoft in western Jutland. In the early phase (500–300 BC) the farmsteads stood in the open countryside (not all the farmsteads existed at the same time); in the later phase (300–200 BC) the farmsteads of the village (*landsby*) were all surrounded by a common fence (landsby A).

which at Vorbasse enclose an area of about 2,500 sq m. Within the enclosure is the longhouse and, often, one minor building and a stack barn. The fence may be used as a wall for minor buildings, but the main building always stands in the middle of the open area. The earliest sunken huts, which are found in villages of the fourth and fifth centuries, are located immediately outside the farmyard fences.

Unlike Hodde, the major farmstead at Vorbasse is not a feature of the phase of foundation at Vorbasse; it first appears in the third

century AD and continues through the fifth century at least. Like
the other farmsteads, it has its own enclosure, but it is distinguished
by the size of the longhouse and the number of associated buildings.

In comparison with the Bronze Age, the farmsteads of the Iron
Age and later villages represent a radical re-organization both of
work practices and of social life, as we have already seen.[4] But
within the Iron Age, it is in the course of the third and fourth
centuries AD that the major change takes place. The longhouses
become longer, the stalling and storage capacity increases. The
dependent minor buildings also become larger, and both these and
the longhouses have more functional internal divisions; small workshop huts, the sunken huts, appear. Looked at as a whole, the
farmsteads now give the impression that many more people than
before lived and worked under the same roof, people with more
different and more specialized craft roles. The village changes its
character radically, as now it comprises independent, enclosed farmstead units which lie side by side without any surrounding common
fence. The size of the farmstead is relatively uniform within the
individual village and the earlier minor residential buildings, as at
Hodde, disappear. Now each farmstead forms an independent economic unit.

Field Systems and Production

The system of production which is embodied in the field system
forms a critical supplement to our understanding of the organization
of the farmstead and the village.

Fixed field systems surrounded by low boundary banks (Celtic
fields) first appear at the beginning of the Iron Age. The form of
cultivation which was practised in association with boundary banks
began, according to the most recent studies, as early as the middle
of the Bronze Age, around 1200 BC, but the establishment of
permanent fields defined by boundary banks first took place at the
beginning of the Iron Age, around 500 BC (V. Nielsen 1984). Here
they are contemporary with the major shift from the large 'halls' of
the Bronze Age to the smaller longhouses of the Iron Age, in which
for the first time the cattle are installed. The field systems were an
element in a re-creation of productivity of exhausted fields. Through
manuring and regulation of cultivation periods and fallow, combined
with the planting of windbreaks, the farmer sought to re-establish

the quality of the soil. And, relatively slowly, a fertile soil layer was built up (Odgaard 1985).

Dung has to be collected, spread and, ideally, ploughed or dug in. The most valuable and most nutritious dung comes from domesticated animals and this is most easily collected in stalls. Spreading would hardly have been a problem, but effective ploughing-in could only be done when the asymmetric mouldboard plough of the Viking Period was available (Glob 1951a). This turned the furrow, so that the dung was covered and thus the nitrogen sealed in.

The symmetrical ard could not turn the sod (figure 4.9) but by angling it from side to side it was possible to scrape up the soil, to aerate it and to remove weeds. The same principle is used in modern organic farming (L. Hvass 1980, p. 62).

Good fodder plants require a well-watered, rich soil for satisfactory productivity. In high forest and forest pasture good soil conditions were maintained by the growth of the trees and the industry of earthworms. Cultivation means that ground is without vegetation for part of the year. This brings an increased risk of erosion and washing-out, because there is no vegetation to hold the soil in place or to take up the nutrients which are freed. Frequently repeated ground-working therefore encourages erosion and washing-out and

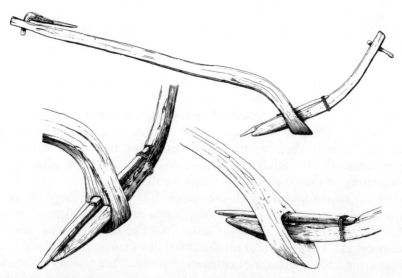

Figure 4.9 The construction of the bow ard from Donneruplund. (drawn by Flemming Bau, after Hedeager 1988b, p. 146)

is a contributory factor in an increased need for dung (Jacobsen 1973, p. 384).

The field systems are laid out around the villages, often on an impressive scale. First, a number of long, straight axes were laid out. The division into fields was taken from these (figure 4.10) (Hatt 1931, 1949; cf. Bradley 1978; Müller-Wille 1965). Surveys have shown that many ancient fields are not formed of randomly laid-out plots but that they were laid out systematically: the basic unit of area is a *tønde land*, a traditional Danish land-measure of about half a hectare (Eir 1980). It seems, then, that this measure has survived all technical agricultural changes from the beginning of the Iron Age to the present day.

The boundary banks in Jutland are primarily formed of blown sand, apparently deposited around hedges. In east Denmark, however, the boundary banks are mostly built from clearance stone; on Bornholm they can also appear as compact stone walls. In other places the boundary banks are simply formed by terrace edges, where access to the fields is protected by earth or stone embankments. The fields must therefore have been enclosed by fences or hedges which have not left visible traces in the terrain (V. Nielsen 1984) – no doubt because drift was very much less on this heavy soil.

The internal division of the field systems also reveals differences between east and west Denmark. In east Denmark, systematic field layouts are found which match the western Jutlandic ones from, for instance, Skørbæk Hede (figure 4.10), but not, however, systems of more advanced character with larger groups of long, narrow fields as at other sites in Jutland. Another fundamental difference is the presence in east Denmark of very small fields (a couple of hundred square metres) which do not appear to be secondary creations. Fields of triangular, ovoid, and other forms which are not paralleled in Jutland are also known from Sjælland (V. Nielsen 1984). The fields of east Denmark are thus less regularly, more spontaneously formed, because they are often laid out in uneven terrain.

The thorough study of the field systems of east Denmark has shown that the productivity of the soil was not determinative in the placement of the fields. The long-term use of very thin soil, however, shows the great importance of manuring, while at the same time it gives evidence of the density of settlement.[5] Other factors, such as water supply, the possibility of drainage and terrain-related features seem, by contrast, to have influenced field placing. Large, integrated cultivation units, both on Sjælland and in Jutland, may be separated

Figure 4.10 Ancient fields and building plots on Skørbæk Hede in Vesthimmer-
land (north-east Jutland). To the west, where the fields run out, the village had
access to good grazing lands along the river.

from one another by topographical features such as very uneven
land, cliffs, gorges, lakes, rivers and so on. At the same time, there
seems to have been uncultivated land at the margins either within
or alongside some of these units. It is a ready inference that this
structure represents the bounds of the resource areas or estate of the
individual villages against one another. The size of one such area
matches that of the known Jutlandic examples as, for example, at
Skørbæk Hede (V. Nielsen 1984).

A characteristic feature of the field systems of east Denmark is
their great variety in extent, which cannot be explained solely by
the smaller areas that have been investigated in this part of the
country. In a number of cases, in which the topographical situation
is discernible, the areas of cultivation clearly did not extend beyond
ten hectares, and some are clearly even smaller (V. Nielsen 1984).
It remains an open question whether these small areas represent a
different pattern of subsistence from the large Jutlandic ones, which
can cover up to 100 hectares, or if, rather, they were associated with
smaller villages or individual farmsteads.

These field systems are abandoned by about AD 200 at the latest. The change in the system of production which this reflects is thus contemporary with the extensive changes in building and village organization which have already been described. Pollen analyses show that the end of these field systems does not necessarily accompany the abandonment of settlements and reforestation but may very well do so (V. Nielsen 1984; S. T. Andersen 1976). Although pollen diagrams have only exceptionally been worked out for areas with preserved field systems, continuity on some of the well-excavated settlement areas shows that settlement did not cease in the relevant area around the second and third centuries AD (e.g. Vorbasse and Hodde).

The abandonment of the field systems must then be linked to the ending of a particular form of production and the establishment of a new one which was based upon permanently cultivated infields immediately adjacent to the farmsteads. The outfields with pasture and open grazing lay further from the village. This shift can be dated to about AD 200/300 in Norway and Sweden; there the new stone boundary markers are still preserved (Sporrong 1971; Widgren 1983, 1984; Windelhed 1984; Myhre 1978).

In all probability the same happened in Denmark, in connection with the major re-organizations in the villages. The excavation of one farmstead with an associated droveway of the later Iron Age, of about AD 400, on Sjælland is evidence for this. Two solid fences led the cattle over a distance of 80 m through the cultivated fields to the lower-lying, wet pasture areas (Kaul 1985).

The difference between this and the old production system is that the land near the village was under permanent cultivation while the pasture areas lay beyond. In the earlier Iron Age it would seem rather that the fields were alternately used for crops, for fallow with useful weeds and for pasture (Helbæk 1958). This is simply a qualified guess, because we do not know exactly what the form of production and the system of rotation were, but we can see that field use in the earlier Iron Age demanded extensive areas and involved long periods of fallow.

The collection of dung can be made by keeping the cattle grazing in the same small fields for longer periods (Liversage 1977) or by separate collection (in stalls) and spreading. Studies of the soil around a settlement of the early Iron Age in the west of the Limfjord area on the North Sea coast have shown clearly that these fields were under cultivation for between forty and one hundred years, in which they were continually manured (Liversage et al. 1985). The manuring of fields in this part of the Iron Age (500–300 BC) has also been shown at Grønbjerg (Odgaard 1985).

Ecology and Production

In the course of the Iron Age the resources of the land were so hard-pressed that the ecological balance became more vulnerable to climatic variation and soil exhaustion (for instance) than it had previously been. It is therefore no coincidence that hunger, war, strife and great migrations were common in the Iron Age; man was in reality more exposed now than before. Changes in the ecological circumstances and in agricultural production are therefore central to an understanding of Iron-Age society.

Climate and Subsistence

Cattle were brought into stalls at the beginning of the Iron Age. This made it easier to collect dung, and milking could be kept going for some of the winter. It demands a great deal more labour, however, especially in the collection of winter fodder. Hay and straw, which were harvested and collected during the summer, need to be stored in barns in order to remain usable, unlike branches which can be gathered in the forest or scrubland throughout the winter. Leaf hay, however, can also be collected and kept like hay and straw, and this improves its quality.

The collection and preparation of winter fodder, be it from trees or harvested, requires effective tools. The iron leaf knife is known, as has been mentioned, from the early Iron Age, and the sickle and scythe from about the time of Christ at the earliest (Steensberg 1943; Myrdal 1982) (figure 4.11), but we must assume that all of these were brought into use at the same time. There is no serious doubt that it was the scythe and the leaf knife that left their clear marks on the development of vegetation at the beginning of the Iron Age, in which the scrub-covered lowlands along the rivers were transformed into harvested meadows with even coverage.

The harvesting of hay, the defoliation and cutting up of branches, could now be done much more effectively than before. Gudmund Hatt was of the opinion that even though it was not impossible to cut hay with a flint or a bronze sickle the effectiveness of these tools was about that of a penknife (Hatt 1937, p. 74). This implies that

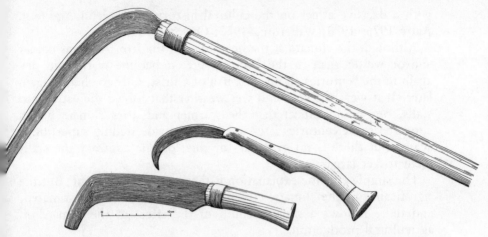

Figure 4.11 Three harvesting tools of the Iron Age: the scythe, the corn sickle and the leaf knife. (drawn by Flemming Bau, after Hedeager 1988b, p. 147)

permanent winter stalling must in previous eras have been virtually impossible.

When the use of stalls is linked with such great demands on labour one may well wonder what urgent needs led the Iron-Age farmer to bring his beasts indoors.

> The cattle, however, essentially had to find their food for themselves by grazing, and were certainly outside the whole year round (in the Bronze Age). The harsher climate of the Iron Age made this form of stock farming less desirable. It became necessary to bring at least the milchcows indoors in the winter and to feed them . . . Thus the Iron Age came to mean an intensification of stock farming. And the most important tool for stock farming was the scythe, which made possible the collection of large quantities of fodder. In the course of the Iron Age the fertile pastures which became one of the most characteristic features of the Danish landscape appeared along the water courses, which previously had been lined with damp strips of woodland. (Hatt 1937, p. 74)

The climatic explanation, which was proposed in 1937, was based upon a long-dominant belief in a single decisive climatic change at the transition to the Iron Age. From the warm and dry weather of the Bronze Age it was supposed to have become colder and wetter in the Iron Age. But we now know, thanks to (among other things) studies in the raised bogs, that the climate was subject to recurrent cyclical change. One can no longer talk about a single climatic change with a decisive effect on the cultural history of the Iron Age (e.g. Aaby 1976, 1978; Willerding 1977; Overbeck 1975 etc.).

Although the climate at the beginning of the Iron Age was colder and/or wetter than in the Bronze Age, it became warm and dry again in the centuries about the birth of Christ, only to change again later. If it were the cold and wet weather that forced the cattle into stalls, one could expect that the warmer and drier climate which appeared some centuries later would have made stalling superfluous again. But there is no evidence for this; on the contrary the stalls seem to get larger.

The simple climatic explanation is therefore not sufficient. But the significance of the climatic conditions must not be underestimated, and there follows a short account of the effect of the climate on agricultural production.

Cool and wet summers are not necessarily synonymous with crisis and slump in agricultural production. It is known that dryness is the greatest threat to the open pasture; a wetter climate thus favours the growth of grass but makes the growing of cereal crops more difficult. Leafage and branches are, however, all but unaffected by varying levels of rainfall in the summers.

Fodder production based on leafage therefore provides greater security in dry periods than grass fodder from open pasture. If the herd is dependent upon the grass fodder of the open pasture, wet, cold summers are no disaster – quite the opposite. The hay harvest too will be richer. But cereal cultivation will be affected by wet summer weather as the ripening of the corn is hindered and the onset of crop diseases is facilitated.

While the stock farming of the Bronze Age was based upon forest pastures and scrublands, in the course of the Iron Age it was increasingly characterized by meadows and open pasture. The drier, warm weather in the Bronze Age thus was of no fundamental relevance to the reliability of fodder supply, and the wet weather at the beginning of the Iron Age permitted increase in stock farming as the over-exploitation and destruction of trees was compensated for by the opportunities for grazing in the ever enlarging open pasturelands. Since, however, larger areas of open pasture are required to compensate for the fodder production of the scrublands, continued deforestation demands ever greater areas of pasture.

When the forest pastures are replaced by open pastures, difficulties in securing an adequate supply of fodder may emerge when drier and warm weather returns, which was the case in the last centuries

BC. The pressure on the scrubland increased, because leaf production, as noted, is not as sensitive to fluctuations in temperature
and wetness. Eventually the forest can no longer regenerate itself,
and alternative sources of fodder have to be found. Hay harvesting
now is of greater importance, and cereal farming becomes more
profitable than before.

When the average rainfall increases again, as it did from about
AD 200 but very markedly from about AD 500, the production of
fodder in the open pasturelands increases. The pressure of grazing
becomes less, and reforestation can obtain sufficient momentum to
enable those kinds of trees which are least attractive to cattle to
grow, while the others are kept down. It is probably one of the
reasons why beech forest appears on good soil in the middle of the
Iron Age. On the lighter soil the forest does not regain a foothold.
Here the heathlands grew larger and provided a supply of winter
fodder, together with hay from the large meadowlands.[6]

The sandiest and least fertile land, which could be cultivated and
exploited under the wetter conditions of the beginning of the Iron
Age, was completely abandoned in the last centuries BC, either
because the climate was drier again or because the wetness of the
previous centuries, together with intensive forest cultivation, meant
a catastrophic extraction of nutrients and the formation of hardpan.

Although cattle do not eat beech, beech forest has something to
offer. It provides fine timber, it is fast-growing (compared to oak)
and it provides a good deal of mast. While the open land, the open
pastures and the extensive meadowlands were the domain of the
cattle, the beech forest was ideal for pig farming. Pigs belong beside
the buildings, where they live on refuse from the farmsteads, and in
the forest where they forage for themselves.

The impact of the climate on the agriculture and landscape of the
Iron Age thus depends upon the production system, which it can,
however, over the longer term, also influence and change. A second
essential factor is soil type.

Production Systems and Soil Types

Different systems of production are the most appropriate in different
parts of the country because of the soil types and resource areas. A
division can be drawn between two types of cultivation system and
field structure, namely arable and pastoral (Frandsen 1983). The
distribution of these follows soil type in that arable is associated

with clays and pastoral with sandy soils (figure 4.12). The farmers of the seventeenth century clearly strove for an ecological balance, both within the individual village between stock farming and arable and externally in the relationship between agriculture and the natural environment, because this gave the best use of the land. But this balance was destroyed when the nobility enclosed forest and open pasture, and this was the true cause of the great agricultural crisis of the seventeenth century.

Although the agriculture of the Iron Age cannot simply be compared with that of the seventeenth century, the point can, however, be used to illustrate how thoughtfully the different soil types were used. The Iron-Age farmers' knowledge of the soil and of its capacities was hardly less than that of their seventeenth-century counterparts. And the density of settlement was – or became from the last centuries BC – so great in many areas that it can be compared with that of the Middle Ages. We can therefore assume that the people strove for the optimal exploitation of the land. In this regard, there cannot have been great differences in agriculture between the two periods.

The ecological balance in the Iron Age must also have rested upon the interplay between pastoral and arable, with further regard to the given soil-type conditions. Iron-Age settlement is found upon nearly every type of soil, from the heavy soils in the east to the sandy heathlands of the west. The optimal subsistence strategy is thus always dependent upon the interplay between soil type, the terrain and agricultural technology, and the definition of marginal lands is consequently dependent upon this factor. The open land, the open pastures and the extensive meadowlands in central and west Jutland became the home of the great herds of cattle in the middle of the Iron Age; the forest-ringed fields and intensive agriculture came to dominate the east.

Although the light soils in central and west Jutland were good for stock raising and easy to cultivate, they were nevertheless more vulnerable to climatic change than the heavier soils. They could more easily be over-exploited, and the many exhausted fields in west and central Jutland, in Himmerland and Vendsyssel, are testimony to this. These areas were abandoned by about the time of Christ at the latest, and they have remained heath ever since.

The cultivation of the sandy soils requires sufficient rainfall on

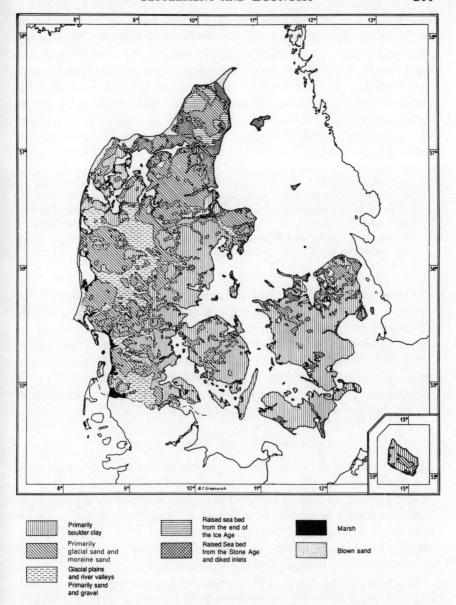

Primarily boulder clay		Raised sea bed from the end of the Ice Age		Marsh
Primarily glacial sand and moraine sand		Raised Sea bed from the Stone Age and diked inlets		Blown sand
Glacial plains and river valleys Primarily sand and gravel				

Figure 4.12 Geological map of Denmark: soil map. (*Danmarks Geologiske Undersøgelser* 1954)

one hand, but on the other hand wetness can also be a cause of catastrophic diminution of the soil through the washing-out of minerals and podzolization, that is, the formation of bleached sand and hardpan. P. V. Glob has drawn attention to the fact that the exhausted Iron-Age fields are found within these podzol areas and he connects these with the cattle disease *vosk*, which is caused by cobalt deficiency (Glob 1951b) and which causes the wasting and death of the beasts. Cobalt deficiency is precisely a consequence of the podzolization of soil.

> From all the evidence, this disease emerged just as far back in time as when the farming of domesticated animals was carried out in the relevant areas, and as far as one knows this wasting disease discussed represents one of the most significant limiting factors for the development of pastoral farming in the heathlands of Jutland in antiquity, where fodder cannot be brought in from other places. This was undoubtedly a factor in making many a farm unprofitable.[7]

The sandy areas of central and west Jutland thus could only be primary agricultural areas at the beginning of the Iron Age. With advancing podzolization these areas were subsequently demoted to agricultural marginals. When such large areas change from being primary to being secondary in the fundamental subsistence economy, new agricultural areas have to be found and production has to be intensified. This was one of the reasons why settlement intensified on the heavier soils in the middle of the Iron Age.

Crisis and New Production Systems

In the course of the earlier Iron Age, the settled and cultivated area was extended over the whole of Denmark. Previously forested areas in east Jutland, in central Fyn and in central Sjælland were ploughed. This is reflected in the pollen diagrams by a steady increase in open-land plants (Berglund 1969; S. T. Andersen 1976; Tauber 1977; Aaby and Odgaard 1987). In many places, however, this was the culmination of a thousand years' development.

In eastern Denmark it appears that the greatest expansion of land use took place in the period between 2000 BC and sometime between AD 200 and 500. After this, many of the open areas became reforested, and evidence for arable fields, such as herbs and grass, disappears from the pollen diagrams (S. T. Andersen 1976; Aaby and Odgaard 1987).

The explanation of natural scientists for this development is that in the course of the earlier Iron Age the soil became exhausted through excessive cultivation and over-intensive cropping. This led to soil impoverishment (possibly in combination with climatic change) and over-exploitation – with famine and depopulation and possible emigration as the result. According to the pollen diagrams, this ecological catastrophe would have made itself felt on the light soil in west Jutland first, but subsequently on the heavier soil to the east as well.

This understanding has been supported over the decades by the pattern of archaeological finds: Jutland's abandoned fields and the striking lack of settlement finds of the later Iron Age. But it has been difficult to accept that soil impoverishment, perhaps combined with a climatic change, would also be the reason for agriculture to be abandoned and for the population to emigrate even from the fertile zones such as, for instance, Als and Angeln in southern Jutland, where the pollen diagrams show the same picture (Iversen 1979, p. 440; Aaby 1986).

The major settlement-site excavations of recent years, such as that at Vorbasse, do not support the notion of agriculture in crisis. There are large stalls and barns here which testify that intensive stock farming and village settlement in central Jutland, as in other areas, was neither abandoned nor moved but stayed put within the same resource area as in the preceding centuries.

There is a pollen diagram for the period of the fourth/fifth to eighth/eleventh centuries AD from Vorbasse (Christensen 1981), precisely the period which is traditionally thought to be that of an agricultural crisis. This diagram shows that the area around Vorbasse was indisputably in use for cereal cultivation throughout this period. Open land was dominant, and the nearest forest area was distant. A careful interpretation of the landscape situation in the later Iron Age and the Viking Period shows: (1) cornfields, which are apparently steadily increasing in extent throughout the whole period; (2) open pasture, which increases, according to the quantity of grass pollen (in the latest periods it appears that stock farming increases at the expense of arable farming); (3) heath, which is of uncertain extent, but which also seems to grow in extent towards the end of the period (Christensen 1981).

The most recent pollen diagram from west Jutland comes from the north-western quarter of Ringkøbing *amt*. It is from Solsø by Herning, a banked outcrop of moraine sand with settlement traces from the Stone Age (Odgaard 1981; Andersen et al. 1984). In contrast with Vorbasse, there are no traces of Iron-Age settlement at this site.

The pollen diagram from here shows that the use of the land from the earliest clearance of the Stone Age down to the Iron Age was quite constant, including heathlands with fields, open, light woodland and bog areas. From about AD 400 there is evidence of great forest clearances; the heath expands and ever-increasing areas are brought into arable use. Towards the end some of the wet areas may have been left as hay meadows because they were too wet for arable or pasture. The pollen diagram also shows that the heather heath was maintained by regular burning.

The pollen diagrams from neither Vorbasse nor Solsø give any evidence of depopulation in the later Iron Age. While the development of vegetation on the heavy soil to the east (i.e. east Jutland, Fyn and Sjælland, Lolland and Falster) shows a great expansion of beechwood at the expense of open land, the two pollen diagrams just described from the light soils of central and west Jutland indicate the maintenance of agriculture.

We can conclude, then, that the theory of a general ecological crisis in the later Iron Age does not seem tenable. The fact remains, however, that vegetation on the heavy soil shows a very low quantity of forest pollen in the period from about 500 BC to between AD 200 and 400/500, but after this, down to about AD 1300, it features a very high quantity of this pollen and a low quantity of grass and herbs (Andersen et al. 1984; Aaby and Odgaard 1987). There can be little serious doubt, then, that through the earlier Iron Age the fertile part of Denmark was dominated by open land, some of which was under the plough. The turf layers in the raised bog Fuglsø on Djursland show clear signs of soil-creep (Bahnson 1972). From the middle of the Iron Age the open land diminishes, and the forest, in particular beechwood, seems to take hold. The open landscape does not return until AD 1300. What was the reason for this?

Many explanations have been proposed and all of them may be partially true. They are: plague, migrations and changes in production systems.

There is no question but that the centuries after the fall of the Roman Empire, the fifth and sixth centuries, saw many group migrations. But was it a surplus of population which emigrated or was it complete population groups, who left everything behind them? The latter is hardly credible. It can be added to this that group migration, which in various degrees has been a feature of all periods, was a symptom rather than a cause, and its causes could very well have been overpopulation and ecological crisis.

It is equally beyond question that the so-called Justinian plague afflicted Europe and Asia in the sixth century and that it cut deeply into the population, especially the urban populations. With the extensive trading connections and movements of this period it is even entirely probable that it reached Scandinavia, where it would have taken its toll. In marginal areas in Norway and Sweden can be found a number of farmsteads that were abandoned in this period (Myhre 1978), but here too the real causes are deeper-seated. The same is true of Gotland and Öland, where recent studies have shown that the numerous deserted farms are attributable to a re-organization of the system of production and settlement (Carlsson 1984). In Denmark too there was apparently a re-organization of villages and of the land as early as in the third century AD. Many smaller villages and estates were undoubtedly grouped into new, larger units, as shown by the results of studies on Fyn (Porsmose 1985). It is only in the Viking Period that the founding of new villages begins again; but although this is a rich and expansive period archaeologically speaking, the pollen diagrams do not reveal any significant change in the landscape (Aaby and Odgaard 1987).

The re-organization and intensification of the production system meant that a number of earlier pasturelands were allowed to return to forest. Conversely, the production of cereals was especially increased on the infields.

In the course of the fifth and sixth centuries plague, frequent wars and raids could all, of course, have caused a degree of decline in settlement, but the fundamental explanation must be that settlement was re-organized because of changes in systems of production with more intensive arable farming, especially in east Denmark, while pastoral farming steadily increased in central and west Jutland where the open lands continued to expand.

In reality, in the course of the earlier Iron Age man had been slowly working towards an ecological crisis. The large, open areas which come to dominate the cultivated landscape in the earlier Iron Age are evidence of an intensive formation of open pasture following the destruction of the forest. The over-exploitation of the fodder capacity of tree growth led to a gradual transformation of forest pasture to open pasture with a consequent decrease in fodder capacity and reliability of winter fodder supply. This could in part be compensated for by harvesting hay and straw. But both of these demand the expenditure of much more effort than does the use of the fodder resources of the forest. The pollen diagrams show that wet areas, which are not suited to grazing, were indeed transformed into hay meadows in the course of the first half millennium of the Iron Age (Iversen 1979, p. 437).

The re-creation of greater fodder production could be achieved by securing the conditions for tree growth and/or by the more intensive cultivation of the land. The pollen diagrams from east Denmark show in fact that cereal production increases quite markedly in the course of the later Iron Age and that the hardy cereals such as rye and oats become ever more predominant. They were types well suited to the cultivation of the impoverished soil of the open pastures.[8] At the same time the areas of forest expand. The Iron-Age farmers thus succeeded both in intensifying arable farming and in re-establishing the forest.

In the cultivated landscape of the less fertile parts of Jutland too, it appears that the sequence of development sketched above agrees with the vegetation picture provided by the pollen diagrams: destruction of the forest and open areas with pasture and heath formation are characteristic of the earlier Iron Age, but this continues in the later Iron Age. The loss of the forest becomes permanent; the heather heath is maintained as an important source of fodder, and the areas which had been cultivated or left open as pasture grow larger (e.g. the pollen analyses from Vorbasse and Solsø). Thus fodder production from the forest was not re-established in the later Iron Age; there is more open land. The possibility of cultivation must disappear completely in the poorest areas because of soil impoverishment, *inter alia* through the formation of acid humus and hardpan. The many field systems in which cultivation ceases at the latest in the early centuries AD are the clearest evidence. With the destruction of the woodland the need for the collection of winter fodder became acute. Heather is important here, but its nutritional value is less than that of hay, straw or branches. Hay meadows and straw production take on greater importance. The open, deforested areas were everywhere either open pasture or cultivated fields.

The re-organization of agricultural production and of the villages from the third century AD was thus also an answer to a developing ecological crisis, which together with economic and political factors made a re-organization essential at just this point.

The Development of Farming

Having surveyed the principal features of settlement, ecology, production systems and village organization, I shall conclude by giving a comprehensive description of agriculture in the Iron Age.[9]

The Earlier Iron Age Thorough-going changes marked the development of agriculture through the one and a half millennia of the Iron Age. At the beginning of the Iron Age cattle were brought into stalls and the cultivated land was divided up into small, well-defined fields which were under permanent cultivation with the aid of manuring. The living places were changed too, as the large buildings (or 'halls') of the Bronze Age were abandoned for the small farmhouses with stalls and dwelling areas under the same roof. This is the 'family holding', which we meet here for the first time.

When the cattle were brought into stalls, the burden of work increased; the beasts had to be fed, watered and milked, the stalls had to be mucked out and winter fodder had to be collected. But the field systems also demanded a greater investment of labour. Although the earliest Iron-Age settlement at Grøntoft moved around so that the well-manured village sites could be cultivated, there was still a need to carry dung to the land even though agriculture was relatively extensive and the fallow periods of the fields relatively long. Dung could be collected most easily in stalls. It was spread on the fields, which were ploughed in two directions in order to get the most out of the manure.

At the beginning of the Iron Age, residence and the system of production are thus joined around the family holding. Commonality survived, however, within the bounds of the village. It is virtually meaningless to speak of private property rights over the land; it is more appropriate to speak of individual use rights. The division into plots which the field systems represent may be rooted in a need to standardize the area of cultivation and thus to ease the distribution/redistribution of use rights (for which the basic units of area have to be equal).

Both the stalls and the fields meant that the earliest Iron-Age farmers had more to do. The production that they achieved thereby was their own, and that was the spur to increased effort. But this also required work from more people. The need for labour thus encouraged a growth of population, and this meant more mouths to feed.

The pollen diagrams show that the farmers of the Iron Age cut into the forest, no doubt because the increasing cattle herds were eating the forest pasture. With the wetter and relatively cool climate at the beginning of the Iron Age leaf fodder could easily be replaced by grass in open pastures. But for how long?

When the climate turned warm and dry again in the last centuries BC, fodder production fell in the open pasture areas; on the other hand cereal cultivation became more productive. Thus a new development was set in train. Larger agricultural areas demanded greater quantities of manure, which in turn required a greater stock of cattle. The need for labour increased and so too did the population. The pressure on the forest pasture was increased and ever greater areas were turned into open pasture. The winter fodder for the beasts was increasingly found by harvesting hay in the meadows.

This hard exploitation of the land could not continue for long. On the light soils of west and north-west Jutland it led to exhaustion and panning. Deserted fields and abandoned villages now make their own clear statements about a system of production which over-exploited and destroyed the ecological foundation in the centuries around the beginning of our era.

In other parts of the country, where the land was better, there was an expansion onto the heavier soils at this time. The effect of the climatic changes was less here and production was therefore more stable. But at the same time there was an explosive increase in the number of new settlements. Many villages were founded in these centuries, one of which was Hodde.

The Iron-Age farmers did not all live in villages. Some individual families found a site, built a farmstead and farmed the land. Frequently they chose to dwell together with one or two other farmsteads. Hodde was one of those settlements founded in this way, but this settlement was intended from the beginning to be much larger than the rest.

The farmsteads steadily became larger in order to accommodate more people and beasts. Now they often comprised several buildings, including barns, storehouses and workshops, and thus seem to have become more specialized production units.

Small farmsteads without stalls were found at the large village at Hodde. The residents in these did not have equal access to the village land with the others. The largest farmsteads, with many beasts and a good supply of dung, thus got the biggest slice of the cake. The profit from the village land must inevitably have varied from farmstead to farmstead, which means that the economic basis was differentiated. The small farmsteads may have been economically linked to the larger farmsteads, with the residents working there.

Thus an economic polarization took place, which was especially evident at Hodde with its large farmsteads, small farmsteads, small buildings and not least the principal farmstead. The principal farmstead was not one among several, although it was located within the major village enclosure; the latter was in fact built on to the fence of the farmstead. It may virtually appear, then, as if the whole village 'belonged' to this farmstead, the leading position of which was maintained through the century and a half in which the history of the village can be followed. It was clearly a function of power also to emphasize the distance between this and the rest of the settlement by means of the great fence which surrounded the principal farmstead throughout three settlement phases.

Other village communities do not, however, show the same economic differentiation; the farmsteads were on the whole of equal size, and thus too the households and the stock.

The Roman author Tacitus described the agriculture of Germania at the end of the first century AD, a form of agriculture that struck the Romans as foreign.

Lands proportioned to their own number are appropriated in turn for tillage by the whole body of tillers. They then divide them among themselves according to rank; the division is made easy by the wide tracts of cultivable ground available. These ploughlands are changed yearly, and still there is enough and to spare. The fact is that although their land is fertile and extensive, they fail to take full advantage of it because they do not work sufficiently hard. They do not plant orchards, fence off meadows, or irrigate gardens; the only demand they make upon the soil is to produce a corn-crop. (*Germania* 26)

The Later Iron Age   At the transition from the earlier Iron Age to the later, the old field systems were abandoned, the farmsteads and villages were re-organized and the cultivated landscape slowly changed character. On the good soil in the east, open land reached its fullest extent in the course of the third and fourth centuries AD; after this many open pasturelands and fields were reforested, most frequently now as beechwood. On the light soil in the west the forest continued to decline and the heath areas grew more extensive. At the same time, the pollen diagrams show that a new cereal appeared, rye, although admittedly it is not certain that this was actually cultivated. If it was, it would, as the most hardy cereal, have been well suited to the impoverished soil of the open pastures.

The farmsteads became distinctly larger; they had both more inhabitants and more functions than before. Each farmstead had, besides the longhouse, one or more minor buildings, of which some certainly were intended for occupation. Others had different craftwork functions, and some were barns or storehouses: more stalls also required more storage capacity. The first small sunken huts also appeared. These were craftwork huts, for weaving for instance. Small buildings without stalls which are known from several of the villages of the earlier Iron Age had disappeared. They had become too small to support an independent population – if they indeed ever did. The landless tillers now belonged completely to the large farmsteads, probably as thralls.

The villages changed correspondingly. The physical bounds around the old village community, the common fence, disappeared, and large, separately enclosed farmsteads appeared instead. Although the number of farmsteads in a village such as Vorbasse was the same as in the earlier village at Hodde, the settlement now covered an area nearly ten times the size.

Larger villages with more people demanded specialization and greater efficiency in craft and production. Iron extraction, smithing, weaving, building and shipbuilding were developed and improved. In daily domestic life the rotary quern replaced the antiquated saddle quern and made it more possible to grind corn for a large household.

The system of production was also made more effective. The extensive and extravagant field system with long periods of fallow was replaced by the more intensive system, requiring less land, with permanent infields and outfields. This yielded a shorter cycle of rotation, but demanded more manure. The exploitation of the soil was closely regulated by a fixed system of well-manured, intensively cultivated and annually sown infields, the common grazing lands, the outfields and, far off, the woodlands. And here we find the explanation, or at least part of it, for the appearance of beechwood upon many old fields and open pasturelands. The intensive production system did not require such great crop and fallow areas.

The infield system represents the first integration of effective arable and pastoral farming, as the stability of the system was directly dependent upon the relationship between the size of the infield and the number of beasts. The winter fodder which was harvested in the meadows was fodder for the cattle but recycled through manure it was also an essential nutrient for the constantly cultivated soil.

This re-organization in the direction of an intensive arable system can be demonstrated in several parts of Scandinavia during the third and fourth centuries, and it is more than probable that it also took place in Denmark. It is difficult to demonstrate here simply because all the structures around the villages were of wood, unlike in Sweden and Norway where they were of stone and have therefore been preserved. The recognition of a large, solid droveway which led the cattle from the farmyard to the pastures in the wet meadowlands does, however, show that here too the permanently cultivated fields were protected, at least between sowing and harvest time.

Certain changes took place in agricultural technology. Knives and scythes became larger, several different types appeared and they became more effective; the harvesting of grass and corn was clearly of great importance. There do not, however, seem to have been any changes to the ard; perhaps there was some improvement in the technique of soil preparation and some more efficient use of the manure. Whatever the case, so far as we can tell, the ard was not changed throughout the Iron Age, although both iron shares and ploughs were known in many parts of Europe. The ard evidently served its purpose just as it was.

A decisive reason for the extensive re-organization must have been that the scope for the expansion of agriculture within the limits as they were had come to an end. The forest pasture was destroyed, the land lay open, the soil was exhausted and the situation must then have been becoming critical.

There were two ways of meeting this crisis, and both were used. One was to re-organize the system of production so that production became more intensive. The second was to obtain a surplus from outside, by robbing neighbouring populations, conquering foreign land and no doubt also by some form of levy or extortion. Great sacrificial hoards of weapons from the third and fourth centuries AD, each with the equipment of hundreds of warriors, are evidence that warfare over territory had reached hitherto unknown proportions.

The re-organization of agriculture may possibly have been even more thorough than we can readily discern. The many small villages of the earlier Iron Age seem to be superseded by fewer but larger units. This means that the resource areas of the individual villages must have grown too, as no land lay unowned and waste. The most distant parts of the village land were allowed to reforest. The intensive arable system for its part meant that the permanently cultivated areas were smaller. Altogether there was more forest, and pollen samples taken at random in this landscape therefore frequently show woodland on earlier open pasture.

From the end of the fifth century the pressure on the grazing lands lightened substantially as the climate became wetter and cooler. Fodder production rose and the forest could reassert its hold. The selective impact of the cattle herds on the tree cover meant that beech was eventually dominant in the woodland; on the other hand the swine could live off the local beechwood. These were the most economical meat animals and thus well suited for the feeding of a large population.

This development in vegetation took place only on the fertile soil of the east, where the productivity of the infields was greatest and where arable agriculture was able to be of greater importance. In the west, by contrast, the open areas grew in size throughout the later Iron Age. The cattle herds (but not necessarily the use of stalls) grew, not least on the extensive meadowlands alongside the rivers of Jutland, alongside the Limfjord and in the marshlands. Heather heath became ever more extensive and important.

A change in tenurial relationships was common to the whole country. When the field systems disappeared, one of the things it signified was that their distributive and standardizing function was no longer required because the land of the village was not annually redistributed after the major re-organization. The right of use/later ownership was now fixed; the farmstead and its land were joined.

Independent leading farmers with a large household comprising kinsfolk, craftsmen and thralls were the social and economic base of later Iron-Age agriculture. The enclosed area was undoubtedly a measure of the farmstead's proper land and also of the size of the household.

NOTES

1 While serious antiquarian recording of grave finds and hoards has been under way since the beginning of the nineteenth century, the settlement sites of the Iron Age remained an unobserved find group for much longer (figure 1.10). The first settlement excavations took place in the 1870s, and in 1906 Sophus

Müller published the results: thirty-five 'settlements' represented by refuse pits and hearths (Müller 1906). The first Iron-Age building was excavated as early as 1977 at Brorup in Ribe *amt*, but it was not recognized as anything other than a chance set of post holes (Hvass 1985a). Traces of two Iron-Age buildings were first noticed in connection with a major excavation at Kraghede in Vendsyssel in 1906 (Klindt-Jensen 1950). Major excavations of Iron-Age buildings and settlements were first properly undertaken at the beginning of the 1920s, with Gudmund Hatt's many excavations. By using machines to uncover single large areas, as was possible for the first time at Grøntoft in west Jutland in the mid-1960s, entirely new perspectives in settlement studies emerged. Not only was it possible with greater reliability and less effort fully to uncover complete villages but it was also economically and practically possible to lay down strip trenches and undertake trial excavations in other systematic ways.

2 Personal communication from Henrik Thrane, Fyns Stiftsmuseum: a find of bracteates in a post hole from Gudme parish and *herred*. Hackgold from settlements is also known on Bornholm.

3 On building construction, see further Hvass 1982a, b; Lund and Nielsen 1982.

4 For a broader perspective on Iron-Age settlement, see, *inter alia*, Jankuhn 1979.

5 This is confirmed by studies undertaken at Lodbjerg and Grøntoft in west Jutland (Liversage et al. 1985; Odgaard 1985).

6 A contributory factor in the strong reforestation of Jutland must certainly lie in the need for fuel for iron extraction.

7 Bendixen and Pedersen; En Utrivelighedsygdom hos Kvæg, der i Aarene 1942-45 har opnået stigende Udbredelse i visse Egne af Jylland, og som syens at helbredes med smaa Doser af Kobolt. ('A wasting sickness of cattle, which spread in certain areas of Jutland in the years 1942–1945, and which seems to be curable with small doses of cobalt.' *Medlemsblad for 'Den danske Dyrlægeforening'*, vol. 28, 1945 (quoted in Glob 1951b).

8 Rye produces so much pollen that it can easily distort the picture in relationship to barley, which has a very low pollen output (e.g. Christensen 1981).

9 A survey of Danish agriculture from the Neolithic to the Middle Ages, with full bibliographical references, is to be found in Hedeager and Kristiansen 1988.

5

Continuity and Discontinuity between the Earlier and Later Iron Age: General Conclusions

Introduction

We have now completed the analyses and separate interpretations of the three basic pillars of society: ideology, social organization and economy. Archaeologically, the first two of these are manifest in rituals in which material symbols are found as part of votive practices and funerary rites; the third, however, is manifest in the diverse evidence for agricultural production, which involves the ecology and settlement of Iron-Age society.

The basic data, of course, of their very nature set certain limitations. The attempt has been made to compensate for these limitations by interpreting the data within the framework of a general theory which allows the diverse and apparently chaotic variations in the material culture to be understood and explained in a general social perspective. The relevant methods are simply a means to bring the data into an empirical formula. The basic data are no direct testimony about antiquity, and never have been. The context in which the archaeologist finds the material culture is just one of many contexts – the most recent – in which it has functioned at some time. Theory building which rests on knowledge of pre-industrial societies is therefore our only tool for probing into the static material remains to reach an interpretation and explanation of the dynamic connections and processes in which that material once functioned.

In order to avoid pressing both the material and the interpretations too hard, each of the major chapters (chapters 2, 3 and 4) has been constructed as an independent entity. This has been done under the direction of the general theoretical and analytical framework, but in the cases of chapters 2 and 3 some further development and sharpening of both the theorizing and the analytical methods was undertaken. The purpose of this procedure has been to create self-standing and (at least partially) independent sectional results that respect the specific archaeological and cultural contexts which in their different ways characterize religious, social and economic life. It is only at the end, then, that it is possible to assess how far the results support and strengthen one another, and only after that will it be possible to offer a satisfactory explanation of the interplay between the different 'sectors' of Iron-Age society.

Like the individual chapters, then, the concluding interpretations and explanations have independent status in interpretative terms. As a result, there will be no traditional type of summary of the results obtained. In the next section I summarize and discuss some of the central changes in the process which typifies the transition from the Earlier Roman Iron Age to the Later in order to weigh them against one another. The result is summarized in a model. After that the significance of regional variations in this interpretation is discussed. Only in the final chapter (chapter 6) are the long lines of development in Iron-Age society from 500 BC to AD 700 followed through.

Processes of Change

In the preceding chapters a number of ruptures affecting both settlement and rituals in the course of the Iron Age have been demonstrated, most noticeably at the transition from the Earlier to the Later Iron Age. The principal thesis of this study is that here an archaic state was under development. It is a natural consequence, therefore, to focus upon this period, and to try to construct an integrated interpretation of the changes observed. It must be emphasized that it is an historical process that is under scrutiny, beginning in the ERIA and culminating in the EGIA – a series of continuities and discontinuities which do not, apparently, run parallel. In the historical view, the determinative changes can probably be located in a relatively short phase in the LRIA, but this was preceded by a phase of foundation which was followed by a phase of consolidation. The way in which this is reflected in the archaeological material can be hoped to provide new insight into historical processes of change and their material correlates (Kristiansen 1991, figures 3 and 5).

Let us then keep the sectional results of the study together in what follows, that is, consider the process of social reproduction, as it was interpreted on the basis of the ritual investments, together with the economic basis of Iron-Age society (agricultural production) and place especial stress upon the clear ruptures which both of these display.

Re-organization of settlement and increase in production   One thing is striking: that the ruptures visible in funerary rituals and in the use of Roman imports at the transition from the ERIA to the LRIA are contemporary with one of the most substantial re-organizations in Iron-Age agriculture. At this point settlement seems to have been completely re-organized. The farmsteads were changed both in terms of construction and in respect of their size and functional structure, and the villages also changed character (figures 5.1, 5.2). To some extent they became larger – at least in those areas of Jutland where villages of the later Iron Age (i.e. from the LRIA onwards) have been excavated – and the individual farmsteads became separately enclosed. Altogether, this presents a picture of villages composed of

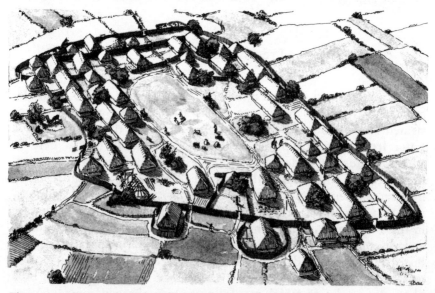

Figure 5.1   Reconstruction of the village at Hodde, *c*.75 BC. (drawn by Flemming Bau, after Hedeager 1988a, p. 31)

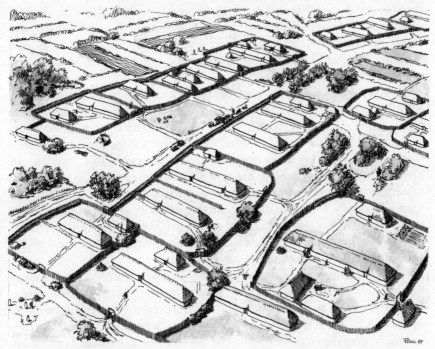

Figure 5.2 Reconstruction of the village at Vorbasse, c.AD 400. (drawn by Flemming Bau, after Hedeager 1988a, p. 187)

large, independent economic units of approximately equal size within individual villages.

On the strength of regional settlement studies, in north-east Fyn (Porsmose 1985) and in south-west Jutland (S. Jensen 1980a, personal communication 1989), it has been possible to corroborate a comprehensive re-organization at just this point. Many small villages of the earlier Iron Age are deserted, and farmsteads and villages are apparently collected into fewer but larger units. This is inconceivable without some accompanying redistribution of land; presumably no land was allowed to remain waste and unowned.

The productive capacity of the system which was found in the earlier Iron Age, that is extensive arable farming on small plots surrounded by hedges, set certain clear limits to the size of the village, which as yet only at Hodde seems to exceed a maximum limit of ten farmsteads. Generally the picture of Iron-Age settlement which emerges is so fine-meshed that villages lay at distances of just a few kilometres from one another. This applies as well to south-west Jutland (S. Jensen 1980a) as to north-west Jutland (S. Jensen 1979), east Jutland between Horsens and Vejle (Steen Hvass, personal communication), north-east Fyn (Porsmose 1985) and east Sjælland (Svend Åge Tornbjerg, personal communication), that is, on all types of soil.

The re-organization into larger settlement units therefore could only be logical if agricultural production could be increased, encouraging a more intensive system of production, apparently based upon a well-defined system of intensively cultivated infields and extensively used outfields as is documented in Norway and Sweden. In Denmark we have to be content with confirming that the old field systems were generally abandoned; generally settlement now seemed to prefer heavy soil. Greater productive capacity is reflected in larger farmsteads with more specialized functions from the LRIA onwards.

Many of the huge cemeteries which were established in the LpRIA and which are typical of the picture in many regions of Jutland in the ERIA went out of use at the same time. Perhaps the old cemeteries of the villages had to be given up when the settlement moved. New cemeteries were founded, but not as extensively or conspicuously as in the ERIA. It appears that the deceased were increasingly buried in family burial places linked to the land of the individual farmsteads (e.g. Vorbasse). As far as we can judge this was a development which had already begun in the ERIA where the well-furnished graves were always sited on their own or in quite small cemeteries; only very rarely (and primarily on Fyn, where Møllegårdsmarken is the clearest example) were they incorporated with the common graves in a large cemetery.

If we accept that a redistribution of land and a re-organization of settlement took place in between the ERIA and the LRIA, it implies that the real social changes were exceptionally thorough-going: it is the whole social structure that was altered. It is difficult to conceive of these re-organizations being the simple result of the local farming populations' own initiative when one considers their range and their extensive consequences. Where, then, are we to look for the other actors and dynamic reasons?

Army and retinue   In the ERIA, indeed as early as the LpRIA, the retinue was found in its simple form. This was hardly a standing army, which had to be kept supplied. The leader may have had some small bodyguard around him which could be increased for war or raiding campaigns. The grave finds express a well-established geographical and political structure in which mobilization took place through several links and in which local leaders could certainly establish their own small bands: thus corresponding most closely to the intermediary phase in the development of a military retinue as described by Steuer (1982, p. 55). But a development had been set in train which could not be stopped. Young men could now make a career and secure for themselves not only respect and hero status but also gold and perhaps other goods by serving a military leader. Conversely, a successful military leader could succeed in keeping a larger and more permanent retinue in order to consolidate and extend his personal and political power.

The question of the Germanic *comitatus*, as described by Tacitus, has been the subject of many interpretations, most recently by Anne K. G. Kristensen (1983). I find these results so crucial in relation to the archaeological interpretations that a brief account of them is given here.

Tacitus speaks of two Germanic institutions, the popular assembly (*consilium*) and the *comitatus*. The *consilium* was the central organ of the tribe and had the final say in common tribal matters, including the election of a chieftain to lead the army. The *comitatus* was responsible for local law in the *herreds* and villages, it protected the leader, the chief, and formed the military unit. The *comitatus* comprised a hundred fighting men from the nobility and the free farmer class, and they were selected by the *consilium*. A chief with a *comitatus* was found in each administrative unit (*pagus*, probably the *herred*). The *comitatus* comprised cavalry and foot, and ranks were distributed by the leader according to prowess. In this way the institution of the *comitatus* was the opening that allowed social mobility in an otherwise structurally static kinship society. The leading chieftain and *comitatus* thus formed an institution whose origin lay in the moots and whose function was 'public', which is to be understood in the sense that they were responsible for communal tribal affairs such as jurisdiction and war. The *comitatus* was thus not private in the sense of belonging to the leader – and this is the essential difference from a feudal retinue which was the baron's private army. And it was finally no insignificant fact, that no eminent German could become leader of an army unless he was accepted – elected – by the *consilium*. But the precondition for being chosen was membership of the nobility (Kristensen 1983).

For the Romans it was a quite incomprehensible (and therefore remarkable) situation, that the Germanic leadership was an authority elected at a popular assembly, and, according to Anne K. G. Kristensen, united three functions, the military, the political and the juridical, in one institution – the *comitatus*. This interpretation must imply that the military, the political and the legal functions were woven together into a network which in principle was well protected against abuse and despotism. The axis around which the whole system seems to have turned was more than anything else the election to the governing institutions of the community. But both election and selection are variable entities. How large, for instance, was the group of nobles from whom the leader of the *comitatus* was taken, and how often did an election take place: was leadership, for instance, for life? And how many could aspire to the highest authority, to that which Tacitus describes as regal status? The size of these groups must undeniably have set limits to the system's ability to withstand abuse of power: the smaller the enfranchised group and the less frequently elections took place, the greater would be the opportunities for the military, political and legal institutions gradually to come to serve sectarian interests. And this is probably what happens in the LRIA at the latest, and perhaps from as early as the end of the ERIA.

The surplus required to maintain a retinue, in order to have a supply of war gear, smiths, ships, well-trained horses and so on, could either have been obtained from outside by raiding or by making a territory tributary. Only the latter strategy could secure the continuous existence of the system of military king and retinue (*comitatus*).

This expansive system inevitably caused greater conflict. And precisely from the end of the ERIA and throughout the LRIA there is evidence for war and conflict of extensive dimensions, not only in the many defensive structures which shot up all over the country, like walls (the best known, but far from unique, is Olmerdiget in southern Jutland) and stake barriers across important sea entrance routes. The location of settlement also shows that the coasts had now become too dangerous to live close to. Not only raiding, but also territorial subordination was the goal from the end of the ERIA. With this, the foundation was laid for a new politico-economic structure. Steuer (1982, pp. 55ff.) speaks of an historically rule-bound process, in which the development of a retinue leads to raiding wars, territorial conquest and the consolidation of a new elite, the members of which are paid with estates in the conquered territories – processes we find repeated in the ERIA and LRIA. The last phase, payment in the form of lands or possibly right to exact tribute, may be reflected in some of the place names of the LRIA.

Inheritance and property   When the archaeological and the scientific results concerning agriculture and settlement are put together, they show that Iron-Age society from the LRIA onwards was highly expansive, both economically and militarily. And it is perhaps in the light of this that we should also see the strong expansion in place names, which may be at its most interesting where the -*lev* names are concerned (see above, p. 187). Characteristic of these names is precisely the fact that the ending -*lev* has a meaning which refers to inheritance, and the first element in the name (e.g. Landar in the name Landerslev) is a personal name. These names probably spread across southern Sweden and Denmark in the third and fourth centuries, and are also found in one other place, Thuringia (-*leben*, as in Hassleben) (figure 5.3). The practice of naming land and property after oneself was followed by the Romans in Italy; Germanic colonists in Gaul did the same; it was clearly common in Thuringia; and the practice found its way to Scandinavia (Mildenberger 1959/60).

We have seen that there is reason to note that more than 50 per cent of examples of this name type are now found as parish names. The old name types clearly had differing significance in the social context, and thus had unequal likelihood of becoming central places in the Christian administrative division of the country. There may then also be reason to suggest that the -*lev* names had a special significance already in the Iron Age, possibly in respect of religious and/or legal-administrative functions. Their distribution in east Denmark shows a statistically significant correlation with the grave finds of the LRIA, but not with the grave finds of the ERIA (H. Nielsen 1978, 1979). In the case of Thuringia, a correlation between the -*leben* names and finds of the Roman Iron Age has been shown (with no differentiation made between ERIA and LRIA), but not with finds of the Migration Period (Mildenberger 1959/60, p. 28).

Although, of course, it can never be proved, it is still a reasonable proposition that the -*lev* names are to be interpreted in the light of the great village re-organization which took place in the LRIA, and that at the same time they are to be seen in relation to the incipient social and political re-organization which the rich grave finds of the prestige goods system reflect. If their interpretation and dating is correct, these names indicate straightforwardly that the right of

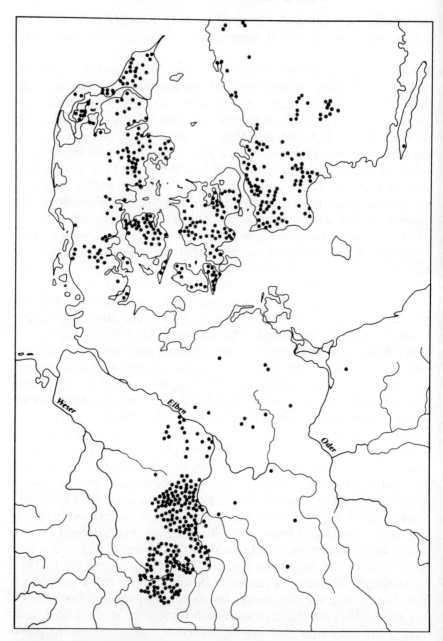

Figure 5.3 The distribution of place names with the ending *-lev* (in Germany *-leben*). (after G. Mildenberger 1959/60)

disposal of land was of such a character that it could be passed on as inheritance. Thus it was the kindred's land, which remained in the possession of the kindred through generations.

One does not have to take a large step from here to postulate that it was the newly established kindreds which founded the *-lev* settlements in the LRIA (e.g. Varpelev), possibly with certain administrative powers in connection, for instance, with the collection of tribute, with which the retinue was also associated, and which thus formed a power base which was grounded in control of the land. By control, I have in mind that the land belonged to the kindred or the family, which had the right of use of, or access to, it, and that it could possibly also be handed over to others for cultivation for a suitable fee, but that it could not be sold to suit one's means or pleasure.

The handing-over of land would have remained within quite fixed limits which would have been social rather than economic in character, and which in all probability would have been rooted in inheritance rules and marriage. With each new generation, land changed hands; it may have been divided between several heirs, as may be reflected by 'twin farmsteads' (i.e. two farmsteads of equal size built within the same enclosure) at Vorbasse, for example. If women could inherit land, even if it were not on an equal basis with men, marriage would be one way to obtain land or increase the amount owned, which the rules of inheritance were intrinsically designed to divide.

Of course, we do not know the rules of inheritance in this period, either for goods or for land, but in the early Middle Ages, from when the earliest Danish inheritance rules are known, women could inherit land and goods, even if there were brothers (Kromann and Juul 1968, pp. XXIff.). There is reason to believe that this was the case too in the later Iron Age; the east Danish graves of the LRIA characteristically have women's graves which are as fully furnished as any men's graves, as at Himlingøje in eastern Sjælland and Årslev on Fyn. A second striking feature of the graves of this period is that there are very few gender-specific grave goods, and it is worth noting that neither the Roman imports nor (what can justifiably be regarded as the elite's new status symbol) the armrings and finger rings of gold with the snake's-head motif are associated with men's graves alone.

The funerary rituals indicate, then, that there was a desire to mark the women's full membership of the elite on an equal basis with the men in their burial rites. If this is correct, it must also mean that women were members of these kindreds and groups of rightful inheritors (which we have interpreted as land-owning) with regard to land, property and gold. In other words we see that from the LRIA onwards there emerges a land-owning or land-controlling group, and since this is economically based as well, I would label it as an emerging economic class.

Means of payment and new economic functions   As I have already shown, territorial domination and tribute through a land-owning/ land-controlling class are inseparable phenomena. When an enemy army was defeated, access to taxation or tribute was concurrently won, the very foundation for the maintenance of the new political infrastructure. A professional army, which possessed ships, weapons, horses trained for battle and so on, and trade and production sites, harbours, routeways – all these depended upon the demand for tribute in produce, and perhaps too in currency form.

Besides food and weapons, the members of the retinue would also have exacted tribute, and in all probability this would originally have been in the form of Roman coinage, later primarily in the form of the Germans' own payment, gold. Payment for war service was something the Germanic soldiers learnt in the Roman army, and thus from the very earliest war booty offerings, from the end of the second century, Roman coins belong among the personal accoutrements of the Germanic soldier (Ilkjær and Lønstrup 1983; Hedeager 1988b).

Although many other payments within the community were made in the form of produce such as corn, butter and cattle, these could hardly be used for payment to members of the retinue; here coins and payment gold took their place. It is quite plausible that gold was used in other forms of transaction, for instance in payment of fines and certain forms of goods exchange (Hedeager 1988b). As a means of payment, coins and the coarsely worked payment gold are distinct from the Roman prestige goods which were used in the LRIA in the construction of a new political and social system. Gold was practical to handle; it was also negotiable outside the sphere of social payments. Monopoly, control and prestige were not linked to gold in the EGIA in the same way as they were to Roman prestige goods in the LRIA; on the other hand the working of the gold was probably an expression of the control the elite had over the finest craftsmen. It was they who invested the gold with the extra dimension by which it became a status symbol for the select – and also valuable gifts to the gods.

In the EGIA, then, gold serves several different functions; beyond its use in connection with different social payments and sacrifices it must also have functioned in an incipient economic system, freed from the alliance and tribute relations of personal contacts. Compared with the Roman prestige goods the gold thus had an extra dimension, by being able to serve as payment gold. We must, however, pay due regard to the fact that Roman coins may have been used in certain commercial transactions as early as the LRIA without our necessarily being able to detect it (Hedeager 1988b); the current excavations at the 'trading site' of Lundeborg in southeastern Fyn may be able to throw light on goods exchange in the LRIA. In any case the coins, just as seems to be the case with payment gold in the EGIA, must be exchanged outside the prestige goods sphere (figure 5.4).

Payment gold, be it in the form of coin or ring gold, fulfilled, as has been stated, a function which was impersonal. Its presence in the archaeological data thus is evidence that a new economic force had come in, a force whose function cut across alliances, kindreds and tribute relations. The economy and social ties have now taken a decisive step on the road towards a conclusive separation.

Summary I have tried to summarize and to interpret the massive changes which the archaeological evidence shows between the ERIA and LRIA. Everything indicates that there was a thorough social change in the course of the third and fourth centuries AD, with its foundations laid in previous centuries and consolidation in the EGIA.

In the form of figure 5.5 I have tried to summarize this interplay between factors. It must be emphasized that this is a case of interplay, as I find it impossible to isolate determinative individual factors. Were there any, the emergence of the retinue in the LpRIA/ERIA could well be attributed with markedly determinative significance as a motivating force, not least as experience of service in the Roman army must have directly influenced Germanic society. While both demographic and ecological factors were essential preconditions because they forced development up to the limits of the old system, demographic pressure also spurred young men to seek glory and wealth in war bands. The Roman imports and the legitimizing function of the rituals played a certain part, but especially in prepar-

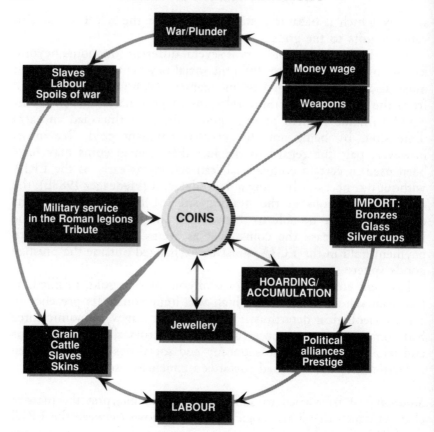

Figure 5.4 Diagram of the theoretical functioning of coins of standard value as the medium of exchange between the Roman market economy and the Germanic prestige goods economy, for example as money wages or as a stable investment. Bronze had been the means by which political and dynastic alliances were formed and maintained, and was used to uphold special status. (after Hedeager 1988b, p. 151)

ing the ground in the ERIA. They likewise contributed to the increase of social and economic differentiation, as by means of these it was possible to create relationships of dependency and debt. In this way, leading farmers, as at Hodde, appeared on a local basis, farmers who at the end of the Earlier Roman Iron Age must have played a decisive role in the re-organization. But war and territorial conquest still remained an apparently essential supplementary factor for the tearing apart of the old kinship and loyalty ties before the new structure was consolidated in the EGIA.

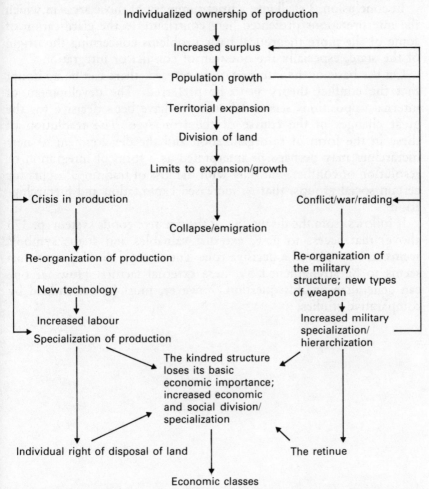

Figure 5.5 Model of the major interacting factors in the transformation of Iron-Age society.

Although, therefore, there is a complex interplay of factors, they had different significance at different stages in the sequence. In the ERIA the most important factor was undoubtedly the use of Roman imports to establish new positions of status and corresponding dependency. The importance of the retinue really asserts itself at the end of the ERIA when the territorial battles and conquests gather speed, and the consequences of these clashes can be seen in the re-organization and new places names of the LRIA.

In conclusion, I shall give a brief summary of those areas in which the interpretations presented here contribute to the clarification of some of the more theoretical basic problems concerning the origin of the state, especially the question of conflict or integration.

On the basis of the interpretations offered, there can be no doubt that the conflict theory is to be preferred. The development of internal oppositions seems definitely to have been decisive for the great changes in the course of the Iron Age. The resolution of these in the form of re-organization and the development of new hierarchies may perhaps be interpreted as a form of integration or resolution of conflict, but only with the loss of traditional rights for certain social groups, that is, increased exploitation and hierarchization.

It follows from the discussion of the prestige goods system (p. 173 above) that access to new, external valuables and status symbols seems to have played a decisive role. The internal development thus seems to be strengthened by these external factors. How far one can generalize on this question, however, must be determined by comparative studies.

6

Social Transformations – Between Tribe and State

Introduction

There seems to have been deep and comprehensive social change over the whole of Denmark in the Roman Iron Age. It is in this change that the seed of the early state structure, as defined in this book, is to be found. Here we can discern those politically and economically irreversible changes which led on to the expansive royal powers of the Viking Age.

Although the great watershed lies in the LRIA, this must be seen as the result of a development which was already in train. I shall now therefore look at the interplay between different variables in the process of change within each of the archaeological periods used here, and in the course of this I shall attempt to identify the seed of change and the source of motivation for development.

In the course of the Iron Age there were fundamental changes in the organization of society. Despite the autonomy of the individual chapters, the interpretations and explanations of these join together in the preceding text into a progressive process, in which the interpretation of the ritual changes implies certain hypotheses concerning social change, which lead on to hypotheses concerning changes in economic organization and in agricultural production. It has transpired that on decisive points there is congruency and agreement between the religious, the social and the economic changes, so that the interpretations and explanations proposed have been corroborated. It remains to discuss the interplay between the different variables in the process of change in order to produce, finally, a general model of change.

The Earlier pre-Roman Iron Age

The first centuries of the Iron Age were a period of separation between two ages, between two ways of life. We see tradition surviving in the rituals, in votive deposits and in burials: the bronze rings of the bogs, unfurnished cremations, graves in or by ancient barrows. To a considerable degree, the rituals are the same, but the artefacts change their form.

When the rituals remain the same, we are immediately inclined to suppose that much else in the society was unchanged, but this need not have been the case. On the contrary, the rituals could be used to distort the real world: people behaved as if everything was as it used to be. But at the beginning of the Iron Age things were not, of course, what they used to be. Quite the opposite. Real life, as we can see it on the settlement sites, presents a very different appearance.

The large longhouses of the Bronze Age are no longer found; they are superseded by the smaller buildings of the earlier Iron Age. The large houses are replaced by a number of smaller ones, the clan by families. The cattle are brought into stalls in the individual farmsteads instead of remaining outside as part of the great herd of the clan. The farmsteads are clustered into small village communities, whose land is cultivated in a sensible system of small fields, divided by low, broad ditches and banks of earth.

We see the seed of a new and much more labour-intensive way of life presenting itself here at the beginning of the Iron Age. Life in the earliest villages was distinguished by everyone having to take part in production. Although some farmsteads were a bit bigger than others and had space for a few more cattle, this did not mean that the kindred or the family sought to show their special status through funerary rituals; the grave forms were the same, the grave goods few and exclusively simple, being functional dress pins and belt buckles.

The village society of the earlier Iron Age was something new, and it was an innovation to bury the dead in large cemeteries. Community and unity must have been of vital importance for those generations which lived in the watershed between the clan-based society of the Bronze Age and the family- and village-based society of the Iron Age. The rituals and traditions of the late Bronze Age played their part as a spiritual sheet anchor which prevented the world from going entirely off course in a phase in which thorough-going change and reformation in daily life were taking place. We can observe, consequently, that the new social organization of production apparently contained an intrinsic contradiction in its religious universe. On the one hand man attempted to maintain some of the rituals of the Bronze Age while on the other he demonstrated a marked egalitarianism for all in the funerary rituals, an equality which corresponded to the changed relations of production.

It is, however, necessary to distinguish at this point between collective and individual rituals. Sacrifices with their sources in the Bronze Age have the character of collective offerings to the gods, while funerary rituals are grounded in the kindred and the village. The use of scarce bronze in communal rituals also reveals the ancient traditions; the bronze represented contact with the outside world in a time when these lines of contact had largely ceased to function. The Earlier pre-Roman Iron Age is characterized instead by strong regional groupings in material culture, especially clearly so in Jutland but also in north Germany. In spite of this, a living ritual tradition concerning distant contacts and exotic metals carried on.

What capacity for change was there in this early Iron-Age society?

Although social organization in the EpRIA must be regarded in its origins as a re-organization of society in a crisis, the new, individualized form of production nevertheless had essential potential. In the longer view, it formed the basis both for an increase in production and for individual families eventually to appropriate for themselves the right of use of substantial tracts of land, as the right of disposal belonged to the clan.

Thus early Iron-Age agriculture, like contemporary religion, contained contradictory tendencies. On the one hand, the division of rights of use in inheritance resulted in a general tendency towards more and smaller units. On the other hand, ownership of domesticated animals and the right of use of land within the community of the village provided the first opportunities for individual kindreds to expand their productive base through strategic marriages.

Thus, early Iron-Age society contained the ingredients for a development of more hierarchic forms. For a time these were kept in check by a strong collective tradition which was strengthened by the absence of foreign trading connections and influence. They were also held in check by the innate contradictions of constant division in inheritance. These must have created a tendency for younger families to be sent off to colonize new land, and this indeed is what characterizes the pre-Roman Iron Age. Only when settlement finally was stabilized and the new system of production had developed its productive potential can we expect this process to make serious progress.

The Later pre-Roman and Earlier Roman Iron Age

The LpRIA and ERIA represent the culmination of the system of production of the earlier Iron Age – and of the processes which were set in train in the EpRIA. The new settlement pattern on the heavier soil was fully established and the independent character of the farmsteads was emphasized by fences, albeit within the community of the village. But solitary farmsteads too appeared. A degree of separation or special position in relation to the old village community seems to have developed, particularly as far as the larger farmsteads were concerned.

In Hodde, we find the leading farmer, who constructed and, presumably, controlled a whole village, and whose kindred managed to preserve this leading position throughout the lifetime of the village. Such a leading farmer, however, was not found in every village. We must believe, rather, that Hodde was the home of the kindred of the chieftains of a larger area, and that the differentiation in size of its farmsteads indicates that minor farmers and landless men must have stood in a servant relationship to the leading farmer or other farmers.

Productivity had clearly increased; the farmsteads were both larger, and functionally more complex than before; the warmer climate and the leafy open forest or scrub formed the basis for a greater stock of cattle and for greater cereal production. But agriculture was still extensive.

A new class of warriors and chieftains appeared in the grave finds. In the LpRIA prestige goods were Celtic above all, and in several cases antiquities centuries old were deposited. With contact with the continent now re-established, it was possible to exchange these. Subsequently, Roman imports took over in the graves. The collective offerings of foreign valuables ceased, except for the war booty offerings at the end of the ERIA. The ideal of collective equality in burials was ousted over most of the country, although the village cemeteries did continue.

An elite had separated itself off, and defined itself by contrast with the rest of the population. Both rituals (especially cemeteries and funerary practices) and foreign prestige goods were used for this. These had previously been elements in the rituals of the community and treated as gifts to the gods. In the LpRIA individual families also used them, to raise themselves up above the commonality, a development which is completed in the ERIA. The prestige goods became an exclusive symbol of pre-eminence in relation to the community and the gods. They were monopolized by the few, select kindreds who were in a position to organize and mobilize alliances with other chieftains in a system extending as far as the Roman Empire.

This development coincides with the distinction of a special warrior class in the graves; a triple rank system can be observed, most clearly in Jutland. Each chieftain stood at the head of an area of the size of a *herred* and had by him a retinue of young warriors. Especially rich graves such as Dollerup indicate that there were leaders within this group of chieftains who stood at the head of the chieftains of larger areas – some sort of petty kingdoms. They could mobilize the resources of the area for war or trading parties, but they did not have a private power base.

The picture drawn here raises two questions: what was the background to this development, and how did such a system operate?

It has already been noted that the system of production in the EpRIA contained an intrinsic potential for individual families to be able to gain control over production or over other producers. At the same time there were long-standing traditions concerning the significance of foreign prestige goods. In as far as these could be monopolized, they too had potential for establishing control over others. We are back at the classic problem: was it the internal development in the social organization of production which provided the basis for individual families with the power of greater productivity being able to re-establish long-distance trade and thus to develop and support their own position, or was it the other way round, so that the prestige goods were used to establish and develop special status positions which could also be exploited in order to obtain control over greater shares of production?

In the first place it has to be made clear that although a continued development and continued differentiation can be observed from the LpRIA to the end of the ERIA, the explanation does not lie here. The new social order was fully established in the LpRIA: the leading farmer, who founded Hodde, was already there, and so too were prestige goods and weapons. The changes must have taken place in the previous period, or at the latest around the beginning of the LpRIA.

It is a general historical rule, rarely used in practice, that the explanation of the period under investigation is always to be sought in the preceding period. But here we face a problem in that well-documented finds are few. There is only one fully excavated village from the preceding period, namely the village at Grøntoft. Here a development towards greater differentiation can arguably be observed, as there appear fewer larger farmsteads and more small ones. But a single village is a weak foundation.

We can provisionally propose the hypothesis that the development towards the socially and economically more differentiated society that we confront in the LpRIA must of necessity have taken place in the previous centuries. With this we have also answered our original question: this means, in fact, that the internal motivating forces were the decisive ones. It was increased control of production in the hands of the leading families which formed the basis for the re-establishment of trade in prestige goods. When this got going again it gave a further push to the development by opening the way for new social, military and economic influences, first from the Celts and subsequently from the Roman Empire. Thus the prestige goods were a decisive instrument in the legitimization of the new elites.

In order to explain the further development in the Iron Age, however, it is essential to understand how the social and political organization of production functioned. It is not sufficient to observe that society was socially and economically differentiated. We need to know how surplus production was distributed and devoted to trading and military expeditions. The system in fact required the leaders to have a surplus at their disposal, for the establishment of trading connections, for gathering an army, and, at least periodically, to keep that army in supplies and payment. This involves warhorses, ships, weapons and other gear. Raiding parties could, of course, of themselves have provided a proportion of the payment. But organized armies do not appear and stay in being just like that: they require a pre-existing leadership which has the necessary means, and a military tradition. This leads us into the question of control of agricultural production.

It is no coincidence that principal farmsteads appear in this period, contemporary with the differentiation of this group from the other farmers increasing in certain villages such as Hodde. The principal farmer at Hodde must have been a local chieftain, who not only ruled over the greatest share of land and beasts but who also had some form of control over the other farmsteads in the village who contributed to his household, that is, a form of tribute. We can presuppose, then, that the new chieftains and leading farmers were able to levy some form of (semi-)voluntary tribute from those farmers whom they led, possibly not only from their own village but also from surrounding villages, in which we therefore would not expect to find principal farmsteads.

In Thompson's historical interpretation of the Germanic tribes along the Roman frontier in Caesar's time, the land was regarded as common property which was also cultivated communally. A council of free men undertook an annual redistribution of the right of use and the surplus went to the individual kindreds. There was a right of private ownership of cattle but not of land, and thus the scope for individual accumulation was severely limited. All free men could bear weapons and formed an assembly which chose the council, which undertook the redistribution of the land, had authority to judge and so on. In time of war a central leadership was chosen from this group. The military leadership was no fixed position but existed only in periods of war or threat of war.

In this historical interpretation, then, stress is laid upon the lack of scope for accumulation in basic reproduction. This is contradicted by the archaeological evidence, which I have chosen to interpret as reflecting expansive and individualized opportunities for accumulation, which are regarded as an essential motive force in the historical development.[1]

In this case, it is also to be expected that severe internal conflict would appear within the society, and this is precisely what can be seen. Some areas display a clear resistance to the establishment of the new status groups, especially north Jutland. But in those areas where the development did take place we can also expect it to have caused internal conflicts and battles. The early weapon deposits, Hjortspring and Krogsbølle, and perhaps also the bog corpses, can be regarded as elements in this. But the emigration of the Cimbri and the Teutons also ought to be capable of interpretation in this light, although ecological and demographical factors were also of significance here. It is, however, worth noting that the emigration took place just at the point of culmination of the processes of differentiation, at the beginning of the LpRIA.

Archaeologists of earlier times have indicated that it was just these

migrations that opened the way for new connections to the south
with the Celts. If, however, we treat the emigration and military
expedition as the result of internal conflict in Germanic society, in
other words as an effect rather than a cause, such limited folk
displacements can also be seen as an element in the competition for
control over producers and trading alliances, competition which
continued in the following centuries.

The Later Roman Iron Age

In the LRIA the find picture changes character completely: this holds
equally for the villages, the graves and the system of production.
The changes reflect a comprehensive restructuring of society, the
character of which we shall now attempt to outline.

Village society was re-organized. The movement towards division
into individual farmsteads was completed. The common enclosure
disappeared. The same holds for the smaller farmsteads and buildings
without stalls, which were subsumed by the new farmsteads. The
system of production was re-organized too: the field systems were
abandoned and replaced by an infield/outfield system, which means
that there was an intensification of production. Productivity
developed too through technological innovations: the rotary quern,
the shaft furnace for iron extraction, new work huts and more.
Increased productivity is also clearly reflected by the farmsteads,
whose internal layouts now became functionally more divided; the
stalls grew larger and barns and working huts appeared.

The re-organization of the village and of the system of production
were concomitant with a redistribution of land, and now at last these
were unified. The farmstead became a productive and legal unity. The
minor farmers and landless workers entered the leading farmsteads'
households as clients and thralls.

Politically, there now emerged a central power which had a professional army at its disposal. A kingship with a network of vassals
around it can be observed on Sjælland, where Roman prestige goods,
gold and silver were used as elements in the gift exchange of the
central power. The use of prestige goods in graves disappeared
almost entirely in Jutland. Here, evidently, they were no longer
necessary. The many local groups vanish, and so too do the old
tribal names in the Germanic area. The last ancient tribal traditions
have gone.

The great weapon finds confirm that war was now waged for

political control of strategic resources: trading places, raw materials (Jutlandic bog iron), land and producers (tax/tribute). These battles presuppose a system of tribute or taxation, both as a motive and to support the existence of the armies. The armies were composed of local chieftains and their retinues. Both weapons and the establishment of armies are evidence for professional armies with fixed command structures and specialization – and to a large extent equipped with Roman weapons.

The system described here developed further in the Germanic Iron Age. But first we should discuss the prerequisites for and the character of the changes in the LRIA. Here, indeed, was founded the social system which continued through the Viking Age down to the re-organization of the state and the villages of the Middle Ages.

One of the most important factors in the establishment of a central political power is the re-organization of the village and agricultural production. Two explanations can be put forward: that there was a gradual re-organization as the result of adaptation to the demographic and ecological crisis, or that there was an imposed re-organization and equalization of the producers from the central power as an element in a new rights and taxation system.

In favour of the first explanation could be the case that the development of the ERIA had reached the ecological and economic limits to continued expansion and intensification. An incipient fall in average temperature may have sharpened the crisis. On top of this, the smallest farmsteads and the landless tillers could no longer manage for themselves. They were eventually swallowed up into the larger farmsteads, which subsequently could co-operate in re-organization. According to this hypothesis the course of events would have been gradual and not necessarily contemporary.

In favour of the second explanation is that the redistribution of the land and the right to dispose of it is so fundamental an attack on the ancient traditions – even though, in actuality, these were no longer realistic – that it could not be pushed through without the strength of a strong central power. It demanded a comprehensive re-organization and assessment of the land, and with this also some decision on many contentious matters. The process also involved the destruction of the smallest villages, to be replaced by fewer but larger estates. In the same way, the re-organization comprised a re-organization of the legal system, the proprietorial foundations of which now became individual productive units rather than the earlier mixture of collective and individual systems of production governed by the traditions and custom of the village community. According to this explanation the change should have taken place rapidly and without intermediary stages.

Because of the still relatively uncertain dating of settlements of the LRIA it is difficult on chronological grounds to prefer one explanation to the other. If, however, we compare the organization of villages and farmsteads of the ERIA and the LRIA the rupture looks very abrupt, without intermediary stages.

For this reason, and not least because of the intrinsic logic of the second explanation, that is the one that has to be preferred. It does not, however, exclude demographic and production-related problems from being contributory factors. But the most important reason was that under the old system the limit for continued political centralization had been reached. The village community was too inconvenient and ineffective an economic unit.

In favour of the second explanation, there is also the fact that the leading farmers and the central power shared a common interest in re-organization. And since many, perhaps the majority, of the smaller farmsteads and homes were in a relationship of dependency or debt to the leading farmers, reform could be effected. Besides the changed legal and revenue-related conditions, this provided the individual farmsteads with much better opportunities for sorting out production effectively, and the results were not long in coming. The price of course was the creation of a large class of landless men, who entered into the households of the farmsteads.

The explanation proposed here implies that as early as the ERIA there existed, if not a fully-fledged central political power, at least a central power factor which was able to assert itself politically and administratively at the beginning of the LRIA.

As was noted before, there must already have been political and military leadership at the *herred* level with an associated retinue of warriors. What was critically new with the retinue was that it represented a power factor which was free of the ties of tribe and kindred and could therefore fight for the leader's interests. This process was probably not completed in the ERIA, although I believe that it was well advanced, on the grounds, for instance, of the incipient employment of Germanic troops in Roman military service. A primitive system of tribute was also in existence. That by this time there was already battle over territories and the capacity to undertake major central works is evidenced by the construction of the Olgerdiget and the submarine stake barriers, which date precisely to the end of the ERIA/beginning of the LRIA, when the processes described really gathered speed. Naturally other factors also played some part: soldiers returning from Roman service would have brought new military traditions with them, as well as familiarity with a money economy, tribute and taxation. All this no doubt fermented and put the old traditions not simply under pressure but certainly in some cases quite out of the picture even before the re-organization took place.

The ability to carry through so demanding a task as that sketched here must then be presumed to have been there. The re-organization of the villages and the farms was an element in the establishment of a central power. It therefore had wide-ranging consequences in all parts of social life, although undoubtedly much was already in place during the LpRIA and the ERIA.

A taxation and legal system presupposes that the central power had vassals centrally placed in its territory: local and regional leaders who could oversee the exaction of tribute, the enforcement of fines, the assembling of the army and so on. This further encouraged a system of writing so that important reports, agreements, decisions and the like could be written down and circulated. Finally it also brought in its train the monopolization of trade. We can expect, as a result, trading places to be established.

All of the elements mentioned here are to be seen in the LRIA. The earliest runic alphabet is found as early as the ERIA. That we have only a few, quite unrepresentative traces of the use of runic script can be attributed to the fact that it was inscribed onto wood, bark, leather and other perishable material: reports and memoranda would hardly have been set down on stone or metal. The written language too was monopolized and mastered by the elite, something that can, for instance, be seen in that the craftsmen who often inscribed names or brief messages on weapons, jewels and tools clearly did not always understand what they were writing nor indeed were always familiar with the runic graphs.

The preconditions for a system of vassalage, under which a leading man had responsibility for a particular area, were already there in the ERIA but were consolidated in the LRIA. This appears not only in the grave finds from Sjælland, but also, clearly, in the group of place names ending in -lev, which were functionally associated with inheritance (the new system of production) and perhaps also with taxation.

Finally, the first trading sites were founded; for the present we know Gudme/Lundeborg and Dankirke of the LRIA, although both of these, like Helgö, first really flourish in the Germanic Period.

On the basis of a series of arguments I have chosen to link the emergence of the earliest central power in the form of kingship in Denmark to the transition from the ERIA to the LRIA. I shall now give a brief account of its future course in the Germanic Period, before it reaches its zenith and its limits in the Viking Period.

The Germanic Iron Age

In the course of the Germanic Iron Age royal power was consolidated as a social institution. It makes itself manifest in increased specialization and growth in craftwork, trade and agricultural production. Proper trading sites emerge, as can be seen at Ribe and Lindholm Høje/Bejsebakken, no doubt under the full control and protection of the king.

Taking the archaeological perspective, this consolidation emerges in a continually diminishing need to use prestige goods in graves. The weapon offerings likewise carry the marks of symbolic votive practice – a far cry from the complete destruction of an army's equipment which was the case in the LRIA. Now it is rather the symbols of the leaders of the army which are made over to the gods; these did not only represent the defeated army but also the conquered territory. We have to assume that now armies were more subordinated to a fixed central leadership and that the king himself had at his command a larger personal retinue. The absence of weapon offerings may be associable with good weapons becoming a rare commodity after the fall of the Roman Empire.

The kings and the leading men appear increasingly as military leaders, symbolically, as well as in fact. Display weapons and outstanding horse gear can virtually be regarded as royal regalia, perhaps better suited to wearing for show than to use when armies clashed. Since the LRIA the golden rings had been the symbols of the elite. The decoration of weapons and jewellery also shows that difference in rank and position was qualitatively marked, not quantitatively, with imports, as it was particularly in the ERIA and LRIA. This no doubt was also due to the fact that the supply of gold could no longer be centrally controlled as imports could in the Roman Period. But the best craftsmen could be controlled.

Germanic craftwork bloomed. Magnificent gold jewels are evidence of the importance of gift giving among the elite. Boons and services were a central element in the unwritten laws of gift giving: if the recipient were more powerful than the giver he reciprocated with boons; were the recipient of lower rank than the giver the gift conferred a duty of service.

The strength of royal power in the course of the Germanic Period further required the organization of trading and war parties on a scale hitherto unknown. The written sources are few, but the archaeological sources show that at least in the LGIA the connections were established for the great expansions of the Viking Age to both east and west.

Through trading and raiding expeditions in the EGIA, the great quantities of gold which were accumulated after the division of the Roman Empire, together with glass and other luxury goods which could not be locally manufactured, were brought home. The gold was remoulded, not only into magnificent jewels but also into simple rings which could be used in connection with certain commercial transactions and for the payment of the army. This must have been an elite-orientated cash function with only limited disposability.

The consolidation of the new social order also finds expression through the re-organization of ritual investments, from graves to sacrifices. The elite did not need to demonstrate a special position through their ancestors; there was however a continued need for the gods' favour. The personal accumulation and burial of valuables is another new feature which agrees well with the individualized property and legal rights which undoubtedly also permeated the social economy. In the LGIA this find group disappears almost completely. Here, however, one must take into consideration the fact that the greater the centralization the less, statistically, are the chances of recovering representative archaeological data on the elite, because the finds become fewer.

What were the driving forces behind the consolidation of the central power in the Germanic Iron Age, and what potential did the system have?

The EGIA represents a continuation of the processes of centralization which had begun in the LRIA, that is, territorial battles between the different minor kingdoms. Such battles were a continuing element in the internal dynamic of the system as long as the limits to the scope for territorial control by royal power had not been reached.

With the disappearance of the sacrificial deposits of weapons in the LGIA and the very few princely graves from the whole of north-

west Europe, we must suppose that the earliest central power and
kingship had by this time reached the limits of its territorial growth,
which means that Scandinavia and northern Europe were divided
into a fixed number of kingdoms. In the LGIA the powers could
therefore be used in trading and war expeditions outside of the
domestic territories, that is into eastern and north-west Europe.

It was undoubtedly an important precondition for all of this
development that there was a surplus of sons, who could not take
over the paternal farm. We do not know the rules of inheritance,
but in the case of individual, well-studied villages like Vorbasse we
can observe that both the number of farmsteads and their size
remains absolutely stable through several generations. There were
apparently rules which prevented a division of the farmsteads into
smaller units. New villages could of course always be founded,
although no land is likely to have been lying waste and unoccupied.
But neither archaeological evidence nor pollen analyses suggest that
this was the case – quite the opposite.

There were, instead, opportunities in the army, where through
trading and war expeditions it was possible for a man to win honour
and wealth. A constant supply was thus ensured for the army, which
was an important consideration for the many expeditions.

If we suppose that both kings and leading men controlled large
blocks of land in the form of several farms worked by 'clients'
(people who owed them service) this would also provide the means
for paying off time-served retainers. Land and farmsteads were not
free to be disposed of.

Trading and raiding expeditions thus brought wealth to the king,
to the leading men and to their retainers. This wealth, in the form
of ring gold and coins, could be used for certain commercial transactions, for instance for the purchase of luxury goods, or be worked
into jewels and rings with which, as gifts, one could tie clients to
oneself. What could be obtained within this system by trade or
plunder could thus within the second system be disposed of through
gift giving, and in this lay a significant dynamic.

This system too had its limits, but they seem not to have been
reached before the Viking Age, when the pressure of population
became so great that neither the founding of new emigrant villages
nor the army could cope with the influx. Trading and raiding
expeditions escalated and now were often followed by colonization.
The Viking Age thus is to be understood against the background of
the development which took place in the Germanic Period, especially

in its later half. But in the deepest perspective it represents the culmination of a social structure which was founded in the LRIA.

General Processes of Change

On several occasions in the foregoing chapters it has been indicated that the marking of cultural identity and the use of prestige goods in rituals were apparently subordinate to certain social factors of more general character. Since such variations are often well plotted in archaeological literature, an increased knowledge of their meaning can be an aid in picking out those places and times in which change takes place, at the same time as providing some indication of the character of this change.

The use of material culture as an element in social and economic strategies is indeed an area of research in growth. What follows can be regarded as a provisional contribution to the understanding of this use.

The Rise of Elites

On the basis of the changes in ritual investment through the course of the Iron Age, a pattern can be demonstrated. The establishment of new elites is particularly manifested through graves in the form of large barrows or rich grave goods (usually of foreign origin) or both, as a manifestation of power and honour. It is the special position of the new kindreds which is asserted.

In the phase of consolidation the investment of prestige goods in graves gradually ceases. It is superseded by official sacrifices, deposited in sacred bogs and consecrated places, in order in this way to emphasize the divine character of the leading kindreds and their significance as intermediaries between the community and the gods. In the later Iron Age personal valuables too are hidden in the ground.

The general validity of this sequence is confirmed by its being closely paralleled in the Bronze Age (Kristiansen 1984a), but some irregularities in the general pattern require further exploration.

In the LRIA, when investment in graves had ceased in Jutland and in extensive tracts of northern Europe, great investment took place in graves on Sjælland with a point of origin at Stevns, where large barrows were also raised. We can see the same picture in Thuringia in south-eastern Germany. This abnormality could be explained under the model proposed by a new, foreign dynasty establishing itself and replaying the sequence. We can understand the barrows at Gamla Uppsala and Jelling in the same way.

Resistance and Cultural Barriers

North Jutland and east Jutland each display very clear cultural identity for themselves in the ERIA and difference from the rest of the country. The purpose was to show that people had their own traditions and were united around these (including the stone cists and pottery forms). But since the population at the same time maintained a reserved posture in relation to Roman imports and the establishment of new classes which followed these, it is reasonable to see the marking of cultural identity as a sort of barrier and opposition to the surrounding world. It could indeed also be observed that the funerary rituals were strongly democratic and egalitarian, and that the villages appear to be without principal farmsteads. The traditions of the village community were held in honour.

Such a hypothesis concerning cultural barriers is in agreement with the provisional results from certain ethnographic studies (e.g. Hodder 1982a). These results, however, need many more examples before they can be attributed general validity.

A variant of the hypothesis concerning cultural barriers is the view that the many local groups which emerge in the pre-Roman Iron Age are the result of the collapse of the systems of international alliances. Such a situation creates conflict and stress, and beyond this an increased need to develop stronger local and regional identity. This example shows that different causes can lead to a particular result, and it emphasizes how in each case one must study the historical context in which the changes occur.

Contradictions and Cultural Diversity

One of the difficulties in interpreting the archaeological data of the Iron Age is that they are so heterogeneous. Different burial rites and regional characteristics apparently emerge in a complete jumble, quite unlike the Bronze Age. This is however a reflection of society going through certain very violent changes, marked by strong influence from outside. These processes of change mean that powerful conflicts arise both between the social traditions of different regions and between different groups in the society.

I have shown how the variations can be explained as elements in the establishment of new classes who define themselves by contrast with 'the others' in the community. It is in the Iron Age that we see for the first time in Danish archaeological data the establishment of different classes, each with its material culture and symbolic language. Such processes of change can of course proceed differently. Undoubtedly examples can be found of them proceeding gradually and without regional or social conflicts of any importance. But in the Iron Age the process was full of conflict. And this is reflected in the material culture.

We can therefore propose the provisional hypothesis, that increased diversity in material culture, both horizontally (geographically) and vertically (hierarchically), is a symptom of social change and internal contradictions.

Conclusion

The explanations put forward above go beyond the individual chapters on a number of points. With a comprehensive review of the results of those chapters, it seems to me that such clear connections appear that they justify the more wide-ranging interpretations, not least concerning the foundation of state power.

If one looks at the whole sequence from before the Roman Iron Age to the Viking Period, certain further general characteristics present themselves which I have tried to summarize in a model of those processes which I believe were the driving forces in the development from tribe to state.

It must finally be emphasized that primary importance has been attached to providing an explanation of the internal processes of change in Iron-Age society. There is certainly no doubt that the establishment and consolidation of central power are aspects of a general northern European course of development, and the important points in the local understanding become visible only in a larger, structural perspective of that kind. For the time being, this study has at least provided a foundation for further progress along this path.

NOTE

1 The interpretation which Thompson (1965) constructs on the basis of Tacitus and which, therefore, covers the first century AD does however agree well with the scope for expression in the archaeological material.

Bibliography

Aaby, B. (1976): Cyclic climatic variations in climate over the past 5.500 yrs. reflected in the raised bogs, *Nature*, 263, 5575.

——(1978): Cyclic changes in climate during 5.500 yrs. reflected in Danish raised bogs, in *The Danish Natural History Society and the Danish Meteorological Institute. Proceedings of the Nordic Symposium on Climatic Changes and Related Problems*, K. Frydendahl (ed.), Copenhagen.

——(1986): Mennesket og naturen på Abkær-egnen gennem 6000 år, *Sønderjysk Månedsskrift*, 9.

Aaby, B. and B. V. Odgaard (1987): Mennesket og miljøet siden istiden, *Danmarks geologiske Undersøgelser. Jubilæumsbog 1987*.

Albrectsen, E. (1954): *Fynske Jernaldergrave I. Førromersk Jernalder*, Copenhagen.

——(1956): *Fynske Jernaldergrave II. Ældre Romersk Jernalder*, Copenhagen.

——(1968): *Fynske Jernaldergrave III. Yngre Romersk Jernalder*, Odense.

——(1970): Den ældre jernalders bebyggelse på Fyn, *Kuml*.

——(1971): *Fynske Jernaldergrave IV. Gravpladsen på Møllegårdsmarken ved Broholm*, Odense.

——(1973): *Fynske Jernaldergrave V. Nye fund*, Odense.

——(1974): *Fyn i Oldtiden*, Odense.

Almgren, B. (1955): *Bronsnycklar och Djurornamentik*, 2 vols, Uppsala.

Almgren, O. (1897): *Studien über Nordeuropäische Fibelformen der ersten nachchristlichen Jahrhunderte*, Stockholm.

Ambrosiani, B. (1964): *Fornlämninger och Bebyggelse*, Uppsala.

——(1982): Hundare, skeppslag och fornlämningar, *Bebyggelsehistorisk Tidskrift*, 4.

Andersen, H. Hellmuth (1985a): Kongegrave, *Skalk*, 1985:4.

——(1985b): Hedenske danske kongegrave og deres historiske beggrund – et forsøg på en syntese, *Kuml*.

Andersen, N. H. (1976): Arkæologi langs den østjyske motorvej, Skanderborg-Århus, *Kuml*.

Andersen, S. T. (1976): Local and regional vegetational development in eastern Denmark in the Holocene, *Danmarks Geologiske Undersøgelser. Årbog*.

Andersen, S. T., B. Aaby and B. V. Odgaard (1984): Environment and man. Current studies in vegetational history at the geological survey of Denmark, *Journal of Danish Archaeology*, 2.

Bahnson, H. (1972): Spor af muldflugt i keltisk jernalder påvist i højmoseprofiler, *Danmarks Geologiske Undersøgelser. Årbog.*

Bakka, E. (1968): Methodological problems in the study of gold bracteates, *Norwegian Archaeological Review*, 1.

Barker, G. (1985): *Prehistoric Farming in Europe*, Cambridge.

Becker, C. J. (1948): Die zeitliche Stelling des Hjortspring-Findes, *Acta Archaeologica*, 19.

——(1956): Fra Jyllands ældste jernalder, *Kuml.*

——(1957): Førromersk jernalder fra Try Skole i Vendsyssel, *Kuml.*

——(1961): *Førromersk Jernalder i Syd- og Midtjylland*, Copenhagen.

——(1965): Ein früheisenzeitliches Dorf bei Grøntoft, West Jütland, *Acta Archaeologica*, 36.

——(1968): Das zweite früheiszeitliche Dorf bei Gröntoft. West Jütland, *Acta Archaeologica*, 39.

——(1971): Früheisenzeitliche Dörfer bei Gröntoft. West Jütland, *Acta Archaeologica*, 42.

——(1976): Problemer omkring de tidlige jernalderlandsbyer i Jylland, belyst af udgravningerne ved Grøntoft, *Iskos*, 1.

——(1980): Ein Einzelhof aus der jüngere vorrömischen Eisenzeit in Westjütland, *Offa*, 37.

Beckmann, B. (1966): Studien über die Metallnadeln der Römischen Kaiserzeit im Freien Germanien, *Saalburger Jahrbuch*, 23.

Beckmann, C. (1969): Metallfingerringe der Römischen Kaiserzeit im Freien Germanien, *Saalburger Jahrbuch*, 26.

Berglund, B. E. (1969): Vegetation and human influence in South Scandinavia during prehistoric time, *Oikos Supp.*, 12.

Binford, L. R. (1972): Mortuary practices; their study and their potential, *An Archaeological Perspective*, New York.

——(1987): Data, relativism and archaeological science, *Man*, 22.

Blackmore, C., M. Braithwaite and I. R. Hodder (1979): Social and cultural patterning of the late Iron Age of Southern Britain, in *Space, Hierarchy and Society*, B. C. Burnham and J. Kingsbury (eds), British Archaeological Report, International Series 59, Oxford.

Bloch, Marc (1961): *Feudal Society* I-II (English translation, London, 1961).

Bloch, Maurice (1977): The disconnection between power and rank as a process: an outline of the development of kingdoms in Central Madagascar, in *The Evolution of Social Systems*, J. Friedman and M. J. Rowlands (eds), London.

Bolin, S. (1926): *Fynden av romerska mynt i det fria Germanien*, Lund.

——(1929): Die Funde römischer und byzantinischer Münzen im freien Germanien, *19. Bericht Römisch Germanischen Kommission.*

Borg, K., U. Näsman and E. Wegraeus (1976): *Eketorp. Fortification and Settlement on Öland/Sweden. The monument*, Stockholm.

Bradley, R. (1978): Prehistoric field systems in Britain and North-West Europe – a review of some recent work, *World Archaeology*, 9:3.

——(1981): Economic growth and social change: two examples from prehistoric

Europe, in *Economic Archaeology*, A. Sheridan and G. Baily (eds), British Archaeological Report, International Series 96, Oxford.

——(1982): The destruction of wealth in late prehistory, *Man*, 17.

——(1987a): A comparative study of the hoarding in the late Bronze Age and the Viking economies, in *Theoretical Approaches to Artefacts, Settlement and Society*, G. Burenhult, A. Carlsson, Å. Hyenstrand and T. Sjøvold (eds), British Archaeological Report, International Series 366, Oxford.

——(1987b): Stages in the chronological development of hoards and votive deposits, *Proceedings of the Prehistoric Society*, 53.

Brink, S. (1988): Folkvandringstids namn? Ortsnamn som källmaterial för att belysa bosättningen i Norden vid mitten av det första årtusendet, in *Folkevandringstiden i Norden. En krisetid mellem ældre og yngre jernalder*, U. Näsman and J. Lund (eds), Århus.

Brøndsted, J. (1966): *Danmarks Oldtid III. Jernalderen*, Copenhagen.

Carlsson, D. (1979): *Kulturlandskapets Utveckling på Gotland*, Visby.

——(1984): Change and continuity in the Iron Age settlement of Gotland, in Kristiansen (ed.) 1984b.

Carniero, R. L. (1970): A theory of the origin of the state, *Science*, 169.

Chapman, R. W. (1977): Burial practices – an area of mutual interest, in *Archaeology and Anthropology. Areas of Mutual Interest*, M. Spriggs (ed.), British Archaeological Report, British Series, Oxford.

Chapman, R., I. Kinnes and K. Randsborg (eds) (1981): *The Archaeology of Death*, Cambridge.

Chisholm, M. (1962): *Rural Settlement and Land Use*, London.

Christensen, A. E. (1938): Danmarks befolkning og bebyggelse i middelalderen, *Nordisk Kultur* II (30 vols), Oslo.

Christensen, B. Brorson (1981): Landskabet ved Vorbasse, in *Det Skabende Menneske. Festskrift til P. V. Glob*, Copenhagen.

Christensen, V. and J. Kousgård Sørensen (1972): *Stednavneforskning I*, 2 vols, Copenhagen.

Claessen, H. J. M. (1978): The early state: A structural approach, in H. J. M. Claessen and P. Skalnik (eds) 1978.

Claessen, H. J. M. and P. Skalnik (eds) (1978): *The Early State*, The Hague.

Clarke, D. L. (ed.) (1977): *Spatial Archaeology*, London.

Clastres, P. (1977): *Society Against the State*, English translation, Oxford (1st edn in French, 1974).

Clausen, H. V. (1916): Studier over Danmarks Oldtidsbebyggelse, *Årbøger for nordisk Oldkyndighed og Historie*.

Cohen, R. (1978): State origins: A reappraisal, in H. J. M. Claessen and P. Skalnik (eds) 1978.

Cohen, R. and E. Service (eds) (1978): *Origins of the State. The Anthropology of Political Evolution*, Philadelphia.

Cour, V. La (1927): *Sjællands ældste Bygder*, Copenhagen.

Eggers, H. J. (1949/50): Lübsow, ein germanischer Fürstensitz der älteren Kaiserzeit, *Praehistorische Zeitschrift*, 34/35.

——(1951): *Der römischen Import im freien Germanien*, Hamburg.

——(1955): Zur absoluten Chronologie der römischen Kaiserzeit im freien Germanien, *Jahrbuch des Röhisch-Germanischen Zentralmuseums Mainz*, 2.

Eir, B. (1980): Måleenheder i oldtidsagre, *Årbøger for nordisk Oldkyndighed og Historie*.

Ekholm, K. (1972): *Power and Prestige: The Rise and Fall of the Kongo Kingdom*, Uppsala.

——(1977): External exchanges and the transformation of Central African social systems, in *The Evolution of Social Systems*, J. Friedman and M. Rowlands (eds), London.

——(1981): On the structure and dynamics of global systems, in *The Anthropology of Pre-Capitalist Societies*, J. S. Kahn and J. R. Llobera (eds), London.

Ellison, A. and J. Harris (1972): Settlement and land use in the prehistory and early history of southern England: a study based on locational models, in *Models in Archaeology*, D. Clarke (ed.), London.

Engelhardt, C. (1867): *Kragehul Mosefund. Fynske Mosefund I*, Copenhagen.

——(1877): Skeletgrave på Sjælland og i det østlige Danmark, *Årbøger for nordisk Oldkyndighed og Historie*.

Engels, F. (1891): *Familiens, privatejendommens og statens oprindelse* (Origin of the Family, Private Property, and the State), with postscript by A. Christensen and P. Aaby, Copenhagen 1977.

Engström, J. (1984): *Torsburgen. Tolkning av en gotländisk fornborg*, Uppsala.

Fonnesbech-Sandberg, E. (1985): Hoard finds from the Early Germanic Iron Age – a study of their general representativity, in *Archaeological Formation Processes*, K. Kristiansen (ed.), Copenhagen.

Frandsen, K.-E. (1983): *Vang og Tægt*, Copenhagen.

Frankenstein, S. and M. Rowlands (1978): The internal structure and regional context of Early Iron Age society in southwestern Germany, *University of London. Institute of Archaeology, Bulletin 15*.

Fried, M. H. (1960): On the evolution of social stratification and the state, in *Culture and History, essays in honor of Paul Radin*, D. Diamond (ed.), New York.

——(1967): *The Evolution of Political Society*, New York.

Friedman, J. (1975a): Tribes, states and transformations, in *Marxist Analyses and Social Anthropology*, M. Bloch (ed.), London.

——(1975b): Religion as economy and economy as religion, *Ethnos 1:4* (reprinted in Friedman 1979).

——(1976): Marxist theory and systems of total reproduction, *Critique of Anthropology, 7*.

——(1979): *System, Structure and Contradiction in the Evolution of 'Asiatic' Social Formations*, Copenhagen.

——(1982): Catastrophe and continuity in social evolution, in *Theory and Explanation in Archaeology*, C. Renfrew, M. Rowlands and B. Segraves (eds), London.

——(1983): Evolutionary Models in Anthropology, unpublished lectures delivered at the University of Copenhagen.

——(1989): Culture, identity and world process, in *Domination and Resistance*, D. Miller, M. Rowlands and C. Tilley (eds), London.

Friedman, J. and M. Rowlands (1977): Notes towards an epigenetic model of the evolution of 'civilization', in *The Evolution of Social Systems*, J. Friedman and M. Rowlands (eds), London.

Friis, P. (1963): Iron Age graves at Gjurup with tent-shaped grave-houses, *Kuml*.

Friis, P. and P. Lysdahl Jensen (1966): En jernalderhustomt med kælder på Grønhedens Mark, *Kuml.*

Gebühr, M. (1970): Beigabenvergellschaftungen in mecklenburgischen Gräberfeldern det Älteren Römischen Kaiserzeit, *Neue Ausgrabungen und Forschungen in Niedersachsen,* 6.

——(1974): Zur Definition älterkaiserzeitlicher Fürstengräber vom Lübsow-Typ, *Præhistorische Zeitschrift,* 49.

——(1977): Kampfspuren aus Schwerter des Nydam-Fundes, *Die Heimat,* 84.

——(1980): Kampfspuren an Waffen des Nydam-Fundes, *Materialheft zur Ur- und Frühgeschichte Niedersachsen,* 16.

Gebühr, M. and J. Kunow (1976): Der Urnenfriedhof von Kemnitz, Kr. Potsdam-Land, *Zeitschrift für Archäologie,* 10.

Geisslinger, H. (1967): *Horte als Geschichtsquelle,* Neumünster.

Glob, P. V. (1951a): *Ard og Plov i Nordens Oldtid,* Århus.

——(1951b): Jyllands øde agre, *Kuml.*

Godelier, M. (1971): *Ekonomisk Antropologi. Analysen av Förkapitalistiska Samhällen,* Stockholm.

——(1973): *Bas och Överbyggnad,* Stockholm 1975.

——(1978): Infrastructures, societies and history, *Current Anthropology,* 19:4.

Goody, J. (1973): Bridewealth and dowry in Africa and Eurasia, in *Bridewealth and Dowry,* J. Goody and S. J. Tambiah (eds), Cambridge.

Grant, E. (ed.) (1986): *Central Places, Archaeology and History,* Sheffield.

Gräslund, B. (1974): *Relativ datering. Om kronologisk metod i Nordisk arkeologi,* Uppsala (= *Tor* 26).

Gurevitj, A. J. (1970): *Feodalismens Uppkomst i Västeuropa,* Swedish translation 1979, Borås.

——(1978): The early state in Norway, in H. J. M. Claessen and P. Skalnik (eds) 1978.

Haarnagel, W. (1979): Das eisenzeitliche Dorf 'Feddersen Wierde', seine siedlungsgeschichtliche Entwicklung, seine wirtschaftliche Funktion und Wandlung seiner Socialstruktur, in *Geschichtswissenschaft und Archäologie,* H. Jankuhn and R. Wenskus (eds), Sigmaringen.

Haas, J. (1982): *The Evolution of the Prehistoric State,* New York.

Hagberg, U. E. (1967): *The Archaeology of Skedemosse,* 2 vols, Stockholm.

Haggett, P. (1965): *Locational Analysis in Human Geography,* London.

Hald, K. (1950): *Vore Stednavne,* Copenhagen.

——(1966): *Stednavne og Kulturhistorie,* Copenhagen.

Hansen, U. Lund (1969): Kvarmløsefundet. En analyse af Sösdalastilen og dens forudsætninger, *Årbøger for nordisk Oldkyndighed og Historie.*

——(1971): Blik- og glasornamenterede fibler af Mackeprangs typ IX, *Årbøger for nordisk Oldkyndighed og Historie.*

——(1977): Das Gräberfeld bei Harpelev, Seeland, *Acta Archaeologica,* 47.

——(1987): *Römischer Import im Norden,* Copenhagen.

Härke, H. (1987): Angelsächische Waffengräber des 5. bis 7. Jahrhunderts, dissertation for Georg-August University at Göttingen, forthcoming.

Hatt, G. (1928): To bopladsfund fra ældre jernalder fra Mors og Himmerland, *Årbøger for nordisk Oldkyndighed og Historie.*

——(1931): Prehistoric Fields in Jylland, *Acta Archaeologica,* 2.

——(1937): *Landbrug i Danmarks Oldtid*, Copenhagen.

——(1938): Jernalderens Bopladser: Himmerland. *Arbøger for nordisk Oldkyndighed og Historie.*

——(1949): *Oldtidsagre*, Copenhagen.

Hauck, K. (1987): Gudme in der Sicht der Brakteaten-Forschung, *Frühmittelalterliche Studien*, 21.

Hedeager, L. (1978a): Bebyggelse, social struktur og politisk organisation i Østdanmarks ældre og yngre romertid, *Fortid og Nutid*, 27:3.

——(1978b): A quantitative analysis of Roman imports in Europe north of the Limes and the question of Roman-Germanic exchange, in *New Directions in Scandinavian Archaeology*, K. Kristiansen and C. Paludan-Müller (eds), Copenhagen.

——(1978c): Processes towards state formation in Early Iron Age Denmark, in *New Directions in Scandinavian Archaeology*, K. Kristiansen and C. Paludan-Müller (eds), Copenhagen.

——(1980): Besiedlung, sociale Struktur und politische Organisation in der älteren und jüngeren römischen Kaiserzeit Ostdänemarks, *Praehistorische Zeitschrift*, 55:1.

——(1982): Settlement continuity in the villages of Stevns – an archaeological investigation, *Journal of Danish Archaeology*, 1.

——(1984): Review of I. Särlvik: Paths towards a Stratified Society, *Journal of Danish Archaeology*, 3.

——(1985): Grave finds from the Roman Iron Age, in *Archaeological Formation Processes*, K. Kristiansen (ed.), Copenhagen.

——(1987): Empire, frontier and the barbarian hinterland. Rome and Northern Europe from AD 1-400, in M. Rowlands, M. T. Larsen and K. Kristiansen (eds), 1987.

——(1988a): *Gyldendal & Politikens Danmarkshistorie 2, Danernes land*, O. Olsen (ed.), Copenhagen.

——(1988b): Money economy and prestige economy, in *Trade and Exchange in Prehistory, Studies in Honour of Berta Stjernquist*, B. Hårdh et al. (eds) Lund.

——(1990): *Danmarks Jernalder – Mellem stamme og stat*, Århus.

Hedeager, L. and K. Kristiansen (1981): Bendstrup – a princely grave from the Early Roman Iron Age: Its social and historical context, *Kuml.*

——(1985): Nørre Broby – en fyrstegrav fra ældre romertid med vogn og hesteudstyr, in *Hikuin, Ole Klindt-Jensens Mindeskrift*, Århus.

——(1988): Oldtidens landbrug, in *Det Danske Landbrugs Historie I*, (4 vols) C. Bjørn et al. (eds), Odense.

Hedeager, L., B. Poulsen and S. Å. Tornbjerg (1982): Land og By: En undersøgelse af østersøkeramikkens datering og spredning på Stevns, *Hikuin*, 8.

Helbæk, H. (1958): Grauballemandens sidste måltid, *Kuml.*

Herbst, C. F. (1866): Brangstrup Fundet, *Årbøger for nordisk Oldkyndighed og Historie.*

Herrmann, J. (1982): Militärische Demokratie und die Übergangsperiode zur Klassengesellschaft, *Ethnographisch-Archäologische Zeitschrift*, 23.

Hines, J. (1989a): Ritual hoarding in Migration-Period Scandinavia: A review of recent interpretations, *Proceedings of the Prehistoric Society*, 55.

——(1989b): *Weapons and warfare in Anglo-Saxon England*, Oxford.

Hodder, I. (1978): Social organization and human interaction: the development of some tentative hypotheses in terms of material culture, in *The Spatial Organization of Culture*, I. Hodder (ed.), London.

——(1982a): *Symbols in Action*, Cambridge.

——(ed.) (1982b): *Symbolic and Structural Archaeology*, Cambridge.

——(1986a) *Reading the Past*, Cambridge.

——(1986b): *The Present Past*, London.

Hodder, I. and C. Orton (1976): *Spatial Analysis in Archaeology*, Cambridge.

Hodson, F. R. (1979): Inferring status from burials in Iron Age Europe; some recent attempts, in *Space, Hierarchy and Society*, B. C. Burnham and J. Kingsbury (eds), British Archaeological Report International Series 59, Oxford.

Hvass, L. (1980): *Jernalderen 1. Landsbyen og Samfundet*, Copenhagen.

Hvass, S. (1975): Das eisenzeitliche Dorf bei Hodde, Westjütland, *Acta Archaeologica*, 46.

——(1978): Die volkerwanderungszeitliche Siedlung Vorbasse, Mitteljütland, *Acta Archaeologica*, 49.

——(1979): Fra Hodde til Vorbasse; linier i jernalderens bebyggelsesbillede, in H. Thrane (ed.) 1979.

——(1982a): Huse fra romersk og germansk jernalder i Danmark, in *Vestnordisk byggeskikk gjenom to tusen år*, B. Myhre, B. Stoklund and P. Gjarder (eds), Stavanger.

——(1982b): Ländliche Siedlungen der Kaiser- und Völkerwanderungszeit in Dänemark, *Offa*, 39.

——(1983): Vorbasse. The development of a settlement through the first millennium AD, *Journal of Danish Archaeology*, 2.

——(1985a): Iron age settlements in *Archaeological Formation Processes*, K. Kristiansen (ed.), Copenhagen.

——(1985b): *Hodde*, Copenhagen.

Hyenstrand, Å. (1974): *Centralbygd – Randbygd. Strukturella, ekonomiska och administrativa huvudlinjer i mellensvensk yngre järnålder*, Stockholm.

Højlund, F. (ed.) (1979): Symboler og Materiel Kultur, *Hikuin*, 5.

Ilkjær, J. and J. Lønstrup (1975): Nye udgravninger i Illerup Ådal, *Kuml*.

——(1983): Der Moorfund im Tal der Illerup Å bei Skanderborg in Ostjütland, *Germania*, 61.

Ingold, T. (1980): *Hunters, Pastoralists and Ranchers*, Cambridge.

Iversen, J. (1960): Problems of the early post-glacial forest development in Denmark, *Danmarks Geologiske Undersøgelser*, 4:4.

——(1979): Naturens udvikling siden istiden, revised by S. T. Andersen, in *Danmarks Natur I*, 12 vols, Copenhagen.

Jacobsen, B. (1973): Skovens betydning for landbrugets udvikling i Danmark indtil ca. 1300, *Det Forstlige Forsøgsvæsen i Danmark*, 33:4.

Jacobsen, J. A. (1977): De fysiske omgivelsers betydning ved placering af den ældre jernalders bopladser i to geografisk forskellige områder af Jylland, unpublished Ph.D. thesis, University of Århus.

Jankuhn, H. (1976): Siedlung, Wirtschaft und Gesellschaftsordnung der germanischen Stämme in der Zeit der römischen Angriffskriege, *Aufstig und Niedergang der römischen Welt*, H. Temporini and W. Haase (eds), 2 vols, Berlin.

BIBLIOGRAPHY 263

—— (1979): Siedlungsarchäologie als Forschungsmethode, in *Geschichtswissenschaft und Archäologie*, H. Jankuhn and R. Wenskus (eds), Sigmaringen.

Jensen, J. (1982): *The Prehistory of Denmark*, London and New York.

Jensen, S. (1976): Byhøjene i Thy, Museerne i Viborg Amt.

—— (1978): Overgangen fra romersk til germansk jernalder, *Hikuin*, 4.

—— (1979): Byhøjenes rolle i jernalderens bebyggelsesbillede, in H. Thrane (ed.) 1979.

—— (1980a): To sydvestjyske bopladser fra ældre germansk jernalder. Jernalderbebyggelsen i Ribeområdet, *Mark og Montre*.

—— (1980b): Fredbjergfundet. En bronzebeslået pragtvogn på en vesthimmerlandsk jernalderboplads, *Kuml*.

—— (1982): Stengården, an east Jutland occupation site from the Early Germanic Iron Age. The problem of settlement continuity in Late Iron Age Denmark, *Journal of Danish Archaeology*, 1.

Jeppesen, T. Grøngaard (1979): Bebyggelsesflytninger på overgangen mellem vikingetid og middelalder, in H. Thrane (ed.) 1979.

—— (1981): *Middelalderlandsbyens Opståen*, Odense.

Johansen, A. B. (1979): *Nordisk Dyrestil – Bakgrunn og Opphav*, Stavanger.

Jørgensen, B. (1979): *Stednavne og samfærdselshistorie*, Copenhagen.

Kaul, F. (1985): A settlement site of the Later Iron Age at Vallensbæk, near Copenhagen, *Journal of Danish Archaeology*, 4.

Kjær, H. (1928): Oldtidshuse ved Ginderup i Thy, Nationalmuseets Arbejdsmark.

Klindt-Jensen, O. (1950): *Foreign Influences in Denmark's Early Iron Age*, Copenhagen (= Acta Archaeologica 20, 1949).

—— (1953): *Bronzekedlen fra Brå*, Århus.

Knudsen, A. (1982): En front i Sahara – politisk organisation og politisk magt hos Kel Ahaggar, *Stofskifte*, 8.

Knudsen, G. (1939): De danske stednavne, *Nordisk Kultur V*, 30 vols, Copenhagen.

Kossack, G., K.-E. Behre and P. Schmid (eds) (1984): *Archäologische und naturwissenschaftliche Untersuchungen an Siedlungen im deutschen Küstgebiet*, Weinheim.

Kristensen, A. K. G. (1983): *Tacitus' germanische Gefolgschaft*, Copenhagen.

Kristiansen, K. (1974a): En kildekritisk analyse af depotfund fra Danmarks yngre bronzealder, *Årbøger for nordisk Oldkyndighed og Historie*.

—— (1974b): Glerupfundet, *Hikuin*, 1.

—— (1978a): Periodeovergange i bronzealderen, *Hikuin*, 4.

—— (1978b): The consumption of wealth in Bronze Age Denmark. A study in the dynamics of economic processes in tribal societies, in *New Directions in Scandinavian Archaeology*, K. Kristiansen and C. Paludan-Müller (eds), Copenhagen.

—— (1978c): Bebyggelse, erhvervsstrategi og arealudnyttelse i Danmarks bronzealder, *Fortid og Nutid*, 27:3.

—— (1980): Besiedlung, Wirtschaftsstrategie und Bodennutzungen in der Bronzezeit Dänemarks, *Praehistorische Zeitschrift*, 55.

—— (1982): Formation of tribal systems in European history, in *Theory and Explanation in Archaeology*, C. Renfrew, M. Rowlands and B. Segraves (eds), London.

—— (1984a): Ideology and material culture: an archaeological perspective, in *Marxist Perspectives in Archaeology*, M. Spriggs (ed.), Cambridge.

——(ed.) (1984b): *Settlement and Economy in Later Scandinavian Prehistory*, British Archaeological Report, International Series 211, Oxford.

——(1985): Bronze hoards from the Late Neolithic and Early Bronze Age, in *Archaeological Formation Processes*, K. Kristiansen (ed.), Copenhagen.

——(1991): Chiefdoms, states and systems of social evolution, in *Chiefdoms: Power, Economy and Ideology*, T. Earle (ed.), Cambridge.

Kromann Balling, A. and P. Vang Petersen (1985): Romerske mønter, skattefund og jernalderhuse, Nationalmuseets Arbejdsmark.

Kromann, E. and S. Juul (1968): *Skånske Lov og Jyske Lov*, Copenhagen.

Kunow, J. (1983): *Der römische Import in der Germania libera bis zu den Marcomannerkriegen*, Neumünster.

Kunst, M. (1978): Arm und Reich – Jung und Alt, *Offa*, 35.

Levy, J. (1982): *Social and Religious Organization in Bronze Age Denmark. An Analysis of Ritual Hoard Finds*, British Archaeological Report, International Series 124, Oxford.

Lindqvist, S.-O. (1968): *Det Förhistoriska Kulturlandskapet i Östra Ostergötland*, Stockholm.

——(1974): The development of agrarian landscape on Gotland during the early Iron Age, *Norwegian Archaeological Review*, 7:1.

Liversage, D. (1977): Landbrugsrevolutionen i det 1. årtusinde e. Kr, in H. Thrane (ed.) 1977.

——(1980): *Material and Interpretation*, Copenhagen.

Liversage, D., M. A. R. Munro, M.-A. Courty and P. Nørnberg (1985): Studies of a buried Early Iron Age field, *Acta Archaeologica*, 56.

Lund, J. (1979a): Ældre jernalders landsbyer med neddybede huse, in H. Thrane (ed.) 1979.

——(1979b): Three Pre-Roman Iron Age cellars from Overbygaard, *Kuml*.

——(1988): Jernalderens bebyggelse i Jylland, in *Folkevandringstiden i Norden. En krisetid mellem ældre og yngre jernalder*, U. Näsman and J. Lund (eds), Århus.

Lund, J. and J. N. Nielsen (1982): Nordjyske jernalderbygninger med fodremskonstruktion, *Årbøger for nordisk Oldkyndighed og Historie*.

Lundström, A. (ed.) (1988): *Thirteen Studies on Helgö*, Stockholm.

Lysdahl, P. (1971): Vendsyssel som lokalgruppe i ældre romersk jernalder, in *Brudstykker. Holger Friis tilegnet*, Hjørring.

Mackeprang, M. B. (1952): *De Nordiske Guldbrakteater*, Århus.

Malmer, M. P. (1963): *Metodproblem inom Järnalderens Konsthistoria*, Lund.

——(1968–9): Comments on: Bakka: Methodological problems in the study of gold bracteates, *Norwegian Archaeological Review*, 1 and 2.

Mathiassen, T. (1948): *Studier over Vestjyllands Oldtidsbebyggelse*, Copenhagen.

Mikkelsen, D. Kaldal: House-Typology for the III-X Century AD, *Acta Archaeologica* 61 (forthcoming).

Mildenberger, G. (1959/60): Archäologische Betrachtungen zu den Ortsnamen auf -leben, *Archäologica Geographica*, 8/9.

Miller, D. and C. Tilley (eds) (1984): *Ideology, Power and Prehistory*, Cambridge.

Montelius, O. (1895–7): Den nordiska jernålderns kronologi 1-3, *Svenska Fornhinnesförenings Tidskrift*, 9 and 10.

Morgan, L. H. (1877): *Ancient Society*, Chicago.

Müller, S. (1874): *En Tidsadskillelse mellem Fundene fra den ældre Jernalder i Danmark*, Årbøger for nordisk Oldkyndighed og Historie.

——(1888–95): *Ordning af Danske Oldsager III. Jernalderen*, 3 vols, Copenhagen.

——(1897): *Vor Oldtid*, Copenhagen.

——(1900a): Bronzebælter fra førromersk tid, *Årbøger for nordisk Oldkyndighed og Historie*.

——(1900b): En fremmed halsring af guld fra førromersk tid. *Årbøger for nordisk Oldkyndighed og Historie*.

——(1906): Bopladsfund. Den romerske tid, *Årbøger for nordisk Oldkyndighed og Historie*.

——(1933): *Oldtidens Kunst i Danmark, III: Jernalderens Kunst*, Copenhagen.

Müller-Wille, M. (1965): *Eisenzeitliche Fluren in dem festländischen Nordseegebiet*, Münster.

Munksgaard, E. (1955): Late-Antique scrap silver found in Denmark. The Hardenberg, Høstentorp and Simmersted hoards, *Acta Archaeologica*, 26.

Myhre, B. (1973): The Iron Age farm in Southwest Norway, *Norwegian Archaeological Review*, 6.

——(1978): Agrarian development, settlement history and social organization in Southwest Norway in the Iron Age, in *New Directions in Scandinavian Archaeology*, K. Kristiansen and C. Paludan-Müller (eds), Copenhagen.

——(1987a): Chieftains' graves and chiefdom territories, *Studien zur Sachsenforschung*, 7.

——(1987b): Fra smårike til stat, in *Hafrsfjord*, Stavanger.

——(1987c): Naust, skep og leidang, in *Kystliv*, I. Øye (ed.), Bergen.

Myrdal, J. (1982): Jordbruksredskap av järn före år 1000, *Fornvännen*.

Nash, D. (1977): Foreign trade and the development of state in the Pre-Roman Gaul, unpublished.

——(1987): Imperial expansion under the Roman Republic, in M. Rowlands, M. Larsen and K. Kristiansen (eds) 1987.

Näsman, U. (1979): En arkeologs syn på kulturgeografisk grävningsmetod, med eksempel särskilt från Mellansverige, in H. Thrane (ed.) 1979.

——(1984): *Glas och Handel i Senromersk Tid och Folkvandringstid*, Uppsala.

——(1988): Analogislutning i nordisk jernalderarkæologi. Et bidrag til udviklingen af en nordisk historisk etnografi, in *Fra Stamme til Stat i Danmark*, I. B. Rasmussen and P. Mortensen (eds), Århus.

Nielsen, H. (1978): Det tilfældige fundstofs anvendelse i bebyggelsesarkæologien med Østsjælland som eksempel, in H. Thrane (ed.) 1978.

——(1979): Jernalderfund og stednavnetyper – en sammenligning af fynske og sjællandske forhold, in H. Thrane (ed.) 1979.

Nielsen, J. N. (1980): En jernalderboplads – en gravplads ved Sejlflod i Østhimmerland, *Antikvariske Studier*, 4.

Nielsen, V. (1984): Prehistoric field boundaries in Eastern Denmark, *Journal of Danish Archaeology*, 3.

Norling-Christensen, H. (1942): Une trouvaille de parures de l'ancien âge du fer romain faite a Vester Mellerup, Vendsyssel, *Acta Archaeologica*, 13.

——(1943): Une trouvaille de parures de l'ancien age du fer romain faite a Gjølstrup, Vendsyssel, *Acta Archaeologica*, 14.

——(1954): *Katalog over Ældre Romersk Jernalders Grave i Århus Amt*, Copenhagen.
——(1956): Haraldstedgravpladsen og ældre germansk jernalder i Danmark, *Årbøger for nordisk Oldkyndighed og Historie*.
Odgaard, B. V. (1981): Hedebønder, *Skalk*, 1981:2.
——(1985): A pollen analytical investigation of a Bronze Age and Pre-Roman Iron Age soil profile from Grøntoft, Western Jutland, *Journal of Danish Archaeology*, 4.
Odner, K. (1973): *Økonomiske Strukturer på Vestlandet i Eldre Jernalder*, Bergen.
Ortner, S. B. (1981): Gender and sexuality in hierarchical societies, in *Sexual Meanings. The Cultural Construction of Gender and Sexuality*, S. B. Ortner and H. Whitehead (eds), Cambridge.
Overbeck, F. (1975): *Botanisch-geologische Moorkunde unter besonderer Berücksichtigung der Moor Nordwestdeutschlands als Quellen zur Vegetations-, Klima- und Siedlungsgeschichte*, Neumünster.
Pearson, M. Parker (1982): Mortuary practices, society and ideology: an ethno-archaeological study, in I. Hodder (ed.) 1982b.
——(1984): Economic and ideological change: cyclical growth in the pre-state society of Jutland, in D. Miller and C. Tilley (eds) 1984.
Petersen, H. (1888): *Vognfundene i Dejbjerg Præstegaardsmose ved Ringkjøbing 1881 og 1883*, Copenhagen.
——(1890): Hypotheser om religiøse offer- og votivfund fra Danmarks forhistoriske tid, *Årbøger for nordisk Oldkyndighed og Historie*.
Polanyi, K. (1957): *Trade and Market in the Early Empires*, Glencoe.
——(1968): The semantic of money use, in *Primitive, Archaic and Modern Economies, Essays of Karl Polanyi*, G. Dalton (ed.), Boston.
Porsmose, E. (1985): *De Fynske Landsbyers Historie i Fællesskabets Tid*, Odense.
Raddatz, K. (1966): *Die germanische Bewaffnung der vorrömischen Eisenzeit*, Göttingen.
——(1967a): *Das Wagengrab der jüngeren vorrömischen Eisenzeit von Husby, Kreis Flensburg*, Neumünster.
——(1967b): *Die Bevaffnung der germanen in der jüngeren römischen Kaiserzeit*, Göttingen.
Ramskou, T. (1976): *Lindholm Høje. Gravpladsen*, Copenhagen.
Randsborg, K. (1974): Social stratification in Early Bronze Age Denmark: a study in the regulation of cultural systems, *Praehistorische Zeitschrift*, 49.
——(1980): *The Viking Age in Denmark*, London.
Reichstein, J. (1975): *Die kruzformige Fibel*, Neumünster.
Resi, H. Gøstein (1986): *Gravplassen Hunn i Østfold*, Oslo.
Ringtved, J. (1986): Jyske gravfund fra yngre rohertid og ældre germanertid, *Kuml*.
Rowlands, M. J. (1982): Processual archaeology as historical social science, Theory and Explanation in Archaeology. The Southampton Conference, C. Renfrew, M. J. Rowlands, B. A. Segraves (eds.), London.
Rowlands, M. J. and J. Gledhill (1977): The relation between archaeology and anthropology, in *Archaeology and Anthropology*, M. Spriggs (ed.), British Archaeological Report, Suppl. Series 19, Oxford.
Rowlands, M. J., M. T. Larsen and K. Kristiansen (eds) (1987): *Centre and Periphery in the Ancient World*, Cambridge.

Runciman, W. G. (1982): Origins of state: the case of Archaic Greece, *Comparative Studies in Society and History*, 24:3.

Salin, B. (1904): *Die altgermanische Tierornamentik*, Stockholm.

Särlvik, I. (1982): *Paths Towards a Stratified Society. A Study of Economic, Cultural and Social Formations in South-West Sweden during the Roman Iron Age and the Migration Period*, Stockholm.

Schetelig, H. (1906): *The Cruciform Brooches of Norway*, Bergen.

Schiffer, M. B. (1976): *Behavioral Archaeology*, New York and London.

Service, E. R. (1975): *Origins of the State and Civilization. The Process of Cultural Evolution*, New York.

——(1978): Classical and modern theories of the origins of governments, in R. Cohen and E. Service (eds) 1978.

Shennan, S. (1975): The social organization at Bran'c, *Antiquity*, 49.

Skaarup, J. (1976): *Stengade II*, Rudkøbing.

Skovmand, R. (1942): De danske skattefund fra vikingetiden og den ældste middelalder indtil omkring 1150, *Årbøger for nordisk Oldkyndighed og Historie*.

Spencer, H. (1897): *Principles of Sociology*, New York.

Sporrong, U. (1971): *Kolonisation, Bebyggelsesutveckling och Administration*, Lund.

Spriggs, M. (ed.) (1984): *Marxist Perspectives in Archaeology*, Cambridge.

Steensberg, A. (1943): *Ancient Harvesting Implements*, Copenhagen.

Steenstrup, J. (1894): Nogle Bidrag til vore Landsbyers og Bebyggelsens Historie, *Historisk Tidsskrift*, 6th series, 5.

Steuer, H. (1982): *Frühgeschichtliche Sozialstrukturen in Mitteleuropa*, Göttingen.

Stjernquist, B. (1962–3): Präliminarien zu einer Untersuchung von Opferfunden. Begriffsbestimmung und Theoriebildung, *Meddelande Lunds Universitets Historiska Museet*.

Søndergaard, B. (1972): *Indledende Studier over den Nordiske Stednavnetype lev (löv)*, Copenhagen.

Sørensen, P. Harder (1982): The use of air photographs in Celtic field studies, *Journal of Danish Archaeology*, 1.

Tacitus: *Germania*, tr. Mattingly and Handford, Harmondsworth, 1970.

Tauber, H. (1977): *Investigations of Aereal Pollen Transport in a Forested Area*, Copenhagen.

Terray, E. (1975): Classes and class consciousness in the Abron kingdom of Gyaman, in *Marxist Analyses and Social Anthropology*, M. Bloch (ed.), London.

——(1977): Event, structure and history: the formation of the Abron kingdom of Gyaman (1700–1780), in *The Evolution of Social Systems*, J. Friedman and M. Rowlands (eds), London.

Thompson, E. A. (1965): *The Early Germans*, Oxford.

——(1966): *The Visigoths in the Time of Ulfila*, Oxford.

Thrane, H. (1967): Fornemme fund fra en jernaldergrav i Uggeløse, *Nationalmuseets Arbejdsmark*.

——(1975): *Europæiske Forbindelser*, Copenhagen.

——(ed.) (1976): *Bebyggelsesarkæologi*, Odense.

——(ed.) (1977): *Kontinuitet og Bebyggelse*, Odense.

——(ed.) (1978): *Bebyggelseshistorisk Metode og Teknik*, Odense.

——(ed.) (1979): *Fra Jernalder til Middelalder*, Odense.

Thrane, H. and T. Grøngaard Jeppesen (eds) (1983): *Gårdens Udvikling fra Jernald-eren til Nyere Tid*, Odense.

Turney-High, H. (1971): *Primitive War. Its Practice and Concepts*, 2nd edn, Columbia, S.C. (1st edn 1949).

Ucko, P. J. (1969): Ethnography and archaeological interpretation of funerary remains, *World Archaeology*, 1.

Vebæk, C. L. (1944): En østjysk offermose fra keltisk jernalder, *Nationalmuseets Arbejdsmark*.

Voss, O. (1954): The Høstentorp silver hoard and its period, *Acta Archaeologica*, 25.

——(1976): Drengsted. Et bopladsområde fra 5. Årh. e. Kr. ved Sønderjyllands vestkyst, *Iskos*, 1.

Webster, G. (1975): Warfare and the evolution of the state: A reconsideration, *American Antiquity*, 40:4.

Wenskus, R. (1961): *Stammesbildung und Verfassung*, Cologne.

Werner, J. (1952): Nørrejyske bronzebælter fra jernalderen, *Kuml*.

Widgren, M. (1983): *Settlement and Farming Systems in Early Iron Age*, Stockholm.

——(1984): The settlement and farming system in Östergötland Sweden, 1 to AD 500, in K. Kristiansen (ed.), 1984b.

Wijkander, K. (1983): *Kungshögar och Sockenbildning*, Stockholm.

Willerding, U. (1977): Über Klima-Entwicklung und Vegetationserhältnisse im Zeitraum Eisenzeit bis Mittelalter, in *Das Dorf der Eisenzeit und des frühen Mittelalter*, H. Jankuhn et al. (eds), Göttingen.

Windelhed, B. (1984): 'Celtic fields' and prehistoric agrarian landscapes, in K. Kristiansen (ed.) 1984b.

Wittfogel, K. A. (1957): *Oriental Despotism: A Comparative Study of Total Power*, New Haven.

Worsaae, J. J. A. (1866): Om nogle Mosefund fra Bronzealderen, *Årbøger for nordisk Oldkyndighed og Historie*.

Yellen, J. E. (1977): *Archaeological Approaches to the Present*, London.

Ørsnes, M. (1966): *Form og Stil i Sydskandinaviens Yngre Germanske Jernalder*, Copenhagen.

——(1967): Et billedfragment fra Bejsebakken. Nogle bemærkninger og stiludvi-klingen i Norden i 7.–8. årh, *Årbøger for nordisk Oldkyndighed og Historie*.

——(1968): Der Moorfund von Ejsbøl bei Hadersleben, in *Vorgeschichtliche Heilig-tümer und Opferplätze in Mittel- und Nordeuropa*, H. Jankuhn et al. (eds), Göttingen.

——(1969a): *Forord til Sønderjyske og Fynske Mosefund*, Copenhagen.

——(1969b): Südskandinavische Ornamentik in der jüngeren germanischen Eisen-zeit, *Acta Archaeologica*, 40.

——(1984): *Sejrens Pris*, Haderslev.

——(1988): *Ejsbøl I*, Copenhagen.

Åberg, N. (1924): *Den Nordiska Folkevandringstidens Kronologi*, Stockholm.

Index

Italicized numerals refer to figures.

agriculture 161, 192, 201–6, 208, 209, 210–22, 226
  arable land 192, 209–10, 214, 215, 216
  and climatic change 207–9, 247
  crisis 212–16, 218, 221
  development 217–22, 242
  field systems 201, 203–5, 216, 217, 220–1, 246
  fodder 192, 202, 206, 207, 215–16, 218
  implements 202, 206, 207, 221, *4.11*, see also ard
  livestock 197, 206–7, 209, 212, 217, 222
  manuring 201–2, 203, 205–6, 217
  meadows and pasture 190, 205, 206, 207, 214, 215, 216
  and social organization 244–5, 246, 247
amts 169, *3.6*
archaeology
  and anthropology 22, 24, 27, 83, 87
  chronological framework 6–14, 25 n. 2, *1.5*
  and history 2–3, 3–4, 8, 21, 22, 73, 245
  methodological problems 3–5, 6, 8, 14–21, 25 n. 1
  'new' 21, 22

and ritual 31–2, 33–7, 78–81, 95–6, 224, 240, 240–1
  and social structures 152–4, 155, 224–5, 253–5
  theoretical frameworks 21–2, 24–5, 27–8, 93–5
  typology 6–8, 25 n. 1
ard 202, 221, *4.9*
armour 162
armrings 40, 71, *1.4*, *2.1*, *2.3*
  gold 46, 48–9, 60–4, 68, 70, *2.16*, *2.18*
  in graves 40, 46, 70
  in hoards 40, 48–9, 67, 68
army 162, 169–71, 228–9, 234, 246, 247, 252
  see also warfare
arrowheads 121, 162
artefact sets 8, 34, 35, 36, 37, 53, 55–6, 75, 76, 77, 82 n. 1, *1.11*
  and NAT analysis 104, 105
  see also under individual artefact types
awls 117
axe 121

barrows 14
beads 60, 68
belts 43–5, 67
Bloch, M. 28, 30–1, 81

looped 40–2, 67, 71
valued by weight *1.4*
see also armrings; finger rings;
    neckrings
Roman Empire 161
    contacts with 156, 157, 160, 174,
        243, 248–9
runic script 249

scissors 128, 133, 161, *3.25–6*
settlement 242
    patterns 185, 190
    research 4, 180–1, 185, 187–8
settlement sites 5, 14
    and agricultural land 190
    analysis of finds 5, 15, 16, 21, 182,
        1.10
    dating 183
    distribution 16, 182–3, 185–7, 190,
        4.1
    excavations 2, 4, 222 n. 1
    and grave finds 185–7, *4.3*
    and hoards 185–7
shields 43
    bosses for 68
    as component of weapon set see
        weapons, sets
silver 49–52, 72, 73
    hacksilver 50, 66, 68
Skalla-Grimsson, Egill 73
Skedemose 162
Skørbæk Hede 203, *4.10*
slaves 88, 89
Smederup bog 70
society
    centralization of power 84, 86, 91,
        93, 176, 246, 247, 248, 249, 250,
        251–2, 255
    and change 24, 78, 81, 174–5,
        225–6, 228, 235–8, 239, 240–1,
        243–4, 246, 253–5, *5.5*
    class formation, 83, 85, 87, 255
    conflict in 85, 230, 245, 246
    individuals and 28, 29, 30, 79, 80–1
    power in 30–1, 84, 85, 86, 87, 88,
        91, 93, 176–7, 246
    primitive/tribal 23, 28, 29, 87, 91,
        170

relationships within 84, 153–8,
    170–1
and ritual 77–81, 224, 240–1, 251
theoretical frameworks 22–5, 27–31,
    152–3, 224–5
soil 203
    impoverishment 210, 212, 216, 218
    and settlement patterns 190–2, 210
    types 190, 192, 209–10, 210–12, *4.5,
        4.12*
Solsø 213–14
spindle-whorls 117
spurs 128, 132, 159–60, *3.25–8*
state formation
    origins 1–2, 87–90, 96, 173–5,
        176–7, 255
    theories 1–3, 83–7
statuettes 68, *1.3*
Stevns 46, 253
Strabo 72
swords 45, 179 n. 12
    La Tène 45, 67
    as component of weapon set see
        weapons, sets

tableware *1.3*
Tacitus 219, 229
tankards *1.3*
taxation 84, 156, 171, 247
terra sigillata 148
Teutons 245
torques 43
Torsbjerg 162
trade 86, 121, 161, 243, 244, 249, 250

Uggeløse 148, 160

Varpelev 148
vessels (drinking) 34, 70
Vikings
    origins of state 2
    treasure hoards 73
villages 240, 242, 254
    development 4, 184, 199–201,
        218–19, 220, 221–2, *4.6*
    excavations 181, 193
    re-organization 4, 184, 219, 222,
        226–7, 228, 231, 246, 247–8, 249
    see also buildings

Index by Jennifer Speake